Literary Visions
of
Homosexuality

The *Research on Homosexuality* series:

Series Editor: John P. De Cecco, PhD, Director, Center for Research and Education in Sexuality, San Francisco State University, and Editor, *Journal of Homosexuality*.

Number 1

Homosexuality and the Law, edited by Donald C. Knutson, JD

Number 2

Historical Perspectives on Homosexuality, edited by Sal Licata, PhD, and Robert P. Petersen, PhD candidate

Number 3

Nature and Causes of Homosexuality: A Philosophic and Scientific Inquiry, edited by Noretta Koertge, PhD

Number 4

Homosexuality & Psychotherapy: A Practitioner's Handbook of Affirmative Models, edited by John C. Gonsiorek, PhD

Number 5

Alcoholism & Homosexuality, edited by Thomas O. Ziebold, PhD, and John Mongeon

Number 6

Literary Visions of Homosexuality, edited by Stuart Kellogg

This series is published by The Haworth Press, Inc., under the editorial auspices of the Center for Research and Education in Sexuality, San Francisco State University, and the *Journal of Homosexuality*.

Literary Visions
of
Homosexuality

Stuart Kellogg
Editor

The Haworth Press
New York

2O7298

Literary Visions of Homosexuality has also been published as *Journal of Homosexuality*, Volume 8, Numbers 3/4, Spring/Summer 1983.

The Haworth Press, Inc., 28 East 22 Street, New York, NY 10010

Library of Congress Cataloging in Publication Data
Main entry under title:

Literary visions of homosexuality.

(Research on homosexuality ; no. 6)
"Also . . . published as Journal of homosexuality, volume 8, numbers 3/4, Spring/Summer, 1983"—Verso t.p.
Includes bibliographical references.
1. Homosexuality in literature—Addresses, essays, lectures. I. Kellogg, Stuart. II. Series: Research on homosexuality ; v. 6.
PN56.H57L57   1983   809'.93353   83-4300
ISBN 0-86656-183-8

Literary Visions of Homosexuality

Journal of Homosexuality
Volume 8, Numbers 3/4

CONTENTS

The *Journal of Homosexuality* is devoted to theoretical, empirical, and historical research on homosexuality, heterosexuality, sexual identity, social sex roles, and the sexual relationships of both men and women. It was created to serve the allied disciplinary and professional groups represented by psychology, sociology, history, anthropology, biology, medicine, the humanities, and law. Its purposes are:

   a) to bring together, within one contemporary scholarly journal, theoretical, empirical, and historical research on human sexuality, particularly sexual identity;

   b) to serve as a forum for scholarly research of heuristic value for the understanding of human sexuality, based not only in the more traditional social or biological sciences, but also in literature, history, and philosophy;

   c) to explore the political, social, and moral implications of research on human sexuality for professionals, clinicians, social scientists, and scholars in a wide variety of disciplines and settings.

EDITOR

JOHN P. De CECCO, PhD, *Professor of Psychology and Director, Center for Research and Education in Sexuality (CERES), San Francisco State University*

MANUSCRIPT EDITOR

WENDELL RICKETTS, *Center for Research and Education in Sexuality*

ASSOCIATE EDITORS

STUART KELLOGG, PETRA LILJESTRAND, and MICHAEL G. SHIVELY, *Center for Research and Education in Sexuality*

FOUNDING EDITOR

CHARLES SILVERSTEIN, *Institute for Human Identity, New York City*

EDITORIAL BOARD

ROGER AUSTEN, *Teaching Fellow, University of Southern California, Los Angeles*
ALAN BELL, PhD, *Department of Counseling, Indiana University*
PHILIP W. BLUMSTEIN, PhD, *Associate Professor of Sociology, University of Washington*
VERN L. BULLOUGH, PhD, *Dean, Faculty of Natural and Social Sciences, State University of New York College, Buffalo*
ELI COLEMAN, PhD, *Assistant Professor and Coordinator of Clinical Services, Program in Human Sexuality, University of Minnesota*
LOUIE CREW, PhD, *Associate Professor of English, University of Wisconsin, Stevens Point*
LOUIS CROMPTON, PhD, *Professor of English, University of Nebraska, Lincoln*
MARTIN DANNECKER, PhD, *Abteilung für Sexualwissenschaft, Klinikum der Johann Wolfgang Goethe Universität, Frankfurt am Main, West Germany*
JOSHUA DRESSLER, JD, *Professor of Law, Wayne State University Law School*
LILLIAN FADERMAN, PhD, *Professor of English, California State University, Fresno*
BYRNE R. S. FONE, PhD, *Associate Professor of English, The City College, City University of New York*
JOHN GAGNON, PhD, *Professor of Sociology, State University of New York at Stony Brook*
JOHN GONSIOREK, PhD, *Clinical Psychologist, Twin Cities Therapy Clinic, Minneapolis, Minnesota; Clinical Assistant Professor, Department of Psychology, University of Minnesota*
ERWIN HAEBERLE, PhD, *Director of Historical Research, Institute for the Advanced Study of Human Sexuality, San Francisco*

RICHARD HALL, MA, *Writer, New York City*

JOEL D. HENCKEN, MA, *Private Practice, Boston; PhD Candidate in Clinical Psychology, University of Michigan*

EVELYN HOOKER, PhD, *Retired Research Professor, Psychology Department, University of California, Los Angeles*

RICHARD J. HOFFMAN, PhD, *Associate Professor, Department of History, San Francisco State University*

FRED KLEIN, MD, *Clinical Institute for Human Relationships, San Diego*

MARY RIEGE LANER, PhD, *Associate Professor of Sociology, Arizona State University, Tempe*

ELLEN LEWIN, PhD, *Medical Anthropology Program, University of San Francisco*

DON LILES, MA, *Instructor in English, City College of San Francisco*

A. P. MACDONALD, JR., PhD, *Acting Director and Associate Professor, Center for the Family, University of Massachusetts, Amherst*

WILLIAM F. OWEN, MD, *Private Practice, San Francisco*

L. ANNE PEPLAU, PhD, *Associate Professor of Psychology, University of California, Los Angeles*

KENNETH PLUMMER, PhD, *Department of Sociology, University of Essex, England*

SHARON RAPHAEL, PhD, *Associate Professor of Sociology, California State University, Dominguez Hills*

KENNETH READ, PhD, *Professor of Anthropology, University of Washington, Seattle*

MICHAEL ROSS, PhD, *Senior Demonstrator in Psychiatry, The Flinders Institute of Australia, Bedford Park*

DOROTHY SEIDEN, PhD, *Professor, Department of Home Economics, San Francisco State University*

G. WILLIAM SKINNER, PhD, *Professor of Anthropology, Stanford University*

RICHARD W. SMITH, PhD, *Professor of Psychology, California State University, Northridge*

JOHN P. SPIEGEL, MD, *Director, Training Program in Ethnicity and Mental Health, Brandeis University; Current President, American Academy of Psychoanalysis*

FREDERICK SUPPE, PhD, *Chair, Committee on the History and Philosophy of Science, University of Maryland, College Park*

JOHN UNGARETTI, MA, *Classics; MA, Literature; San Francisco*

JAMES WEINRICH, PhD, *Psychiatry and Behavioral Sciences, Johns Hopkins University*

JACK WIENER, MSW, *Retired, National Institute of Mental Health, Bethesda, Maryland*

DEBORAH WOLF, PhD, *Institute for the Study of Social Change, University of California, Berkeley*

WAYNE S. WOODEN, PhD, *Assistant Professor, Behavioral Science, California State Polytechnic University, Pomona*

Foreword

The *Journal of Homosexuality* has been devoted to the publication of scholarly research that would advance the understanding of homosexuality as threads in the fabric of human sexuality. Although the articles published thus far in the *Journal* have been largely in the social sciences, there have also been several studious inquiries and disquisitions by historians, lawyers, philosophers, and classical scholars. By combining contributions from both the social sciences and the humanities the editors have hoped to illuminate the complexity of attitudes about homosexuality and their relationship to both the past and present.

Over the centuries, even before the construction of the social sciences, literature enjoyed a pre-eminence in contemplating and revealing the skeins of emotion and desire that inhabit sexual relationships. This literary tradition, however, has been largely ignored by the social scientists in their vain efforts to emulate the biological and physical sciences. Literary knowledge was dismissed by them as being ephemeral and idiosyncratic. Yet a well-drawn literary portrait of a sexual relationship can reveal basic divisions of motivations and attitudes that could be of inestimable theoretical and empirical value in the research of social scientists.

In his discussion of uses of homosexuality in literature, Stuart Kellogg, the guest editor of this double issue of the *Journal,* has lucidly demonstrated that there is no inevitable antinomy between literature and the social sciences. According to Kellogg literary approaches to homosexuality can be placed in the social science categories of the utopian, political, sociological, or psychological. His conceptual distinctions, I believe, make this collection of essays useful for students who wish to pursue the study of homosexual themes in literature and for social scientists who would like to locate their theories of sexual orientation and sexuality within the framework of literature.

Whereas social science leans heavily on analysis, literature combines the detail of observation and imagination with the synthesis of the finished portrait. Not in literature but in the social and socio-medical sciences is human sexuality dissolved into disconnected "conditions," "identities," "behaviors," and "statuses." The view of homosexuality which emerges from several of the articles does not oppose it to heterosexuality. Rather it strongly implies that one form of sexuality is inevitably defined by the other and indeed requires the other for any reified presence in human experience.

I wish to express my deepest appreciation to Stuart Kellogg for assembling a most distinguished panel of contributors and for his editorial wisdom and solicitousness in bringing this project to a most successful conclusion. I also wish to thank the contributors for their generosity of time and spirit.

John P. De Cecco, PhD
Editor

Introduction:
The Uses of Homosexuality
in Literature

Stuart Kellogg

Abram and Sarai were sorrowful, yet their seed became as the sand of the sea. . . . But a few verses of poetry is all that survives of David and Jonathan.
"I wish we were labelled," said Rickie.

E.M. Forster, *The Longest Journey*[1]

Secrecy has this disadvantage: we lose the sense of proportion; we cannot tell whether our secret is important or not.

E.M. Forster, *A Room with a View*[2]

I

Before considering why some authors of literature write about homosexuality, we must lean back and wonder why other poets, playwrights, and novelists contrive to ignore the subject. And before tackling that question, we must first determine what is meant by *literature* and by *homosexuality*, for both these words are used daily to preen and to damn, but with little agreement as to their meaning.

By literature is here meant works of verbal imagination. It is not required that a book or poem be High Art, only that it be fanciful. But fiction is much more than a plot. It is often an unwitting account of appetite, dress, weaponry, etc.; it is always a record of the author's intentions and prejudices, as well as the prejudices of his or her first audience. And just as it is fair, even wise, to study an "Annunciation" to learn about lilies, it is helpful to read stories in order to understand the history of humanity's self-portrait. One aspect of human nature is homosexuality, defined here as sexual appreciation of, desire for, or sexual behavior with a member of the same sex.

Stuart Kellogg is an Associate Editor of the *Journal of Homosexuality* and Managing Editor of *The Advocate*.

1

This definition depends in turn on the meaning of *sexual*. In literature, as in everyday life, sexuality is larger, more general, than intercourse and steaming dreams. It is virtually omnipresent in individuals' responses to each other. Not all sexual appreciation leads to a desire to reproduce, not even to a wish to "have sex." Nevertheless, almost any appraisal of another person's body will contain a sexual element. This response will be homosexual or heterosexual depending on the sexes of the people involved.

For example, consider Jane Eyre's first clear view of Miss Temple, the superintendent of Lowood:

> I suppose I have a considerable organ of veneration, for I retain yet the sense of admiring awe with which my eyes traced her steps. Seen now, in broad daylight, she looked tall, fair, and shapely; brown eyes with a benignant light in their irids, and a fine pencilling of long lashes round, relieved the whiteness of her large front. . . .[3]

Or Howard Pyle's description of Myles Falworth, the hero of *Men of Iron*, written for an audience of boys:

> To Lord Mackworth, perhaps, it seemed even more strange that six short months should have wrought so great a change in the young man. The rugged exposure in camp and field during the hard winter that had passed had roughened the smooth bloom of his boyish complexion and bronzed his fair skin almost as much as a midsummer's sun could have done. His beard and mustache had grown again (now heavier and more mannish from having been shaved), and the white seam of a scar over the right temple gave, if not a stern, at least a determined look to the strong, square-jawed young face.[4]

Although we can almost smell Miss Temple's breath or trace Myles's jaw before kissing him, so close do we stand, neither Brontë nor Pyle set out to inflame lust. They meant simply to introduce a character and arouse the reader's admiration. This was done in a lifelike, economical fashion by allowing the reader to know the character's body — its physical assets and weaknesses — and to experience an undeniably sexual attraction, perhaps a homosexual attraction.

If, therefore, sexuality permeates our relations with everyone, whether of the same or the opposite sex; and if literature is indeed a record of social relations; then it would seem to be impossible for an author *not* to address homosexuality. In fact, however, few do write about it. Homosexuality may occasionally be referred to in the pages of a book devoted to other topics — gay readers are especially quick to discover allusions to homosexuality and to crack coded references to it, sometimes so quick that they hear a thump where no apple fell — but the roster of authors who deliberately set out to describe and evaluate homosexual relations is tiny when compared to the number of authors who have looked the other way as they wrote. The reason for this avoidance is all too well known: Western cultures have usually regarded homosexual behavior as a sin, a crime, or a disease. But whereas crime, sin, and even disease (Little Nell, Camille, Ben Hur's mother) are the foundation of best-selling popularity, homosexuality is different. For rather than being comfortably remote like most sins and crimes, no matter how sympathetic, and rather than being avoidable, like most diseases, no matter how infectious, homosexual attraction is something everyone "suffers" from. To the many people who fear this aspect of themselves, the idea of a dormant homosexuality, which can be wakened at any moment by beauty or a low voice, is as frightening as the idea of their own aging. In an effort to ignore their homosexuality, they try to deny all references to it. They won't read about it, and they would sooner walk naked to church than be seen buying a book about homosexuality — perhaps the most powerful reason why authors turn to other themes.

Nevertheless, there have always been men and women who wrote boldly about homosexuality. Why? What did the idea of homosexuality offer these artists that was so valuable, so concise, it outweighed the risks of their being misunderstood or censored?

II

Four reasons why an author might treat the phenomenon of homosexuality can be categorized as Arcadian, political, sociological, and psychological. Inevitably, some authors write of homosexuality for more than one purpose.

> On the bank there was an equally gigantic man lying at his ease, with a dog beside him. . . . He stood or lay seven feet without his shoes, and he was dressed in nothing but a kind of kilt made of Lincoln green worsted. He had a leather bracer on his left forearm. His enormous brown chest supported the dog's head . . . which the muscles gently lifted as they rose and fell. . . . The curled hairs on his chest made a golden haze where the sun caught them. . . . "Mostly folks call us Little John," [said the giant].
>
> T. H. White, *The Once and Future King*[5]

The universal desire to be free but safe, to be far from all critics and creditors and yet not utterly lonely, has given birth to a literature of *Arcadia*, that almost mythical land of sweet airs and contentment. City dwellers, impatient with crowds and tired of the soot on their collars and sills, place Arcadia in the country; everybody, wherever they live, is convinced that in Arcadia all nymphs are lovely, all youths have firm round arms, and love is for the taking. What is more, the countryside is kind. It is never bitingly cold, and you can sit down anywhere without getting your seat wet. The Arcadian who guards his sheep has no serious fears that wolves will harry his flock, nor that death will come for the shepherd himself. Still, a gentle sadness attends these musings (e.g., "Ode on a Grecian Urn," *Peter Pan*, Watteau's "A Pilgrimage to Cythera") because right at the heart of the myth is a conflict between the desire for a not quite impossible improbability, and the knowledge that Arcadia is, after all, a dream.

Many homosexuals, especially as children, were convinced that they were the only ones in the world to have homoerotic feelings. Until they discovered other homosexuals, all they could do was dream of comrades and lovers. Other children, somewhat more sophisticated, knew there were many people who felt the way they did. But they also understood that homosexuality must be kept secret, lest it be punished by dishonor or worse; so they, too, resorted to fantasy. The desires of both the naive and the fearful have survived in literary daydreams of the freedom to express homosexual feelings, in fantasies of a homosexual Arcadia where people can love others of the same sex with no danger of being arrested or dying of shame. This Arcadia can exist at a distance, as in the travel books of Charles Stoddard, or in another time, as in the Greek novels of Mary Renault. It can even be a universe parallel to the everyday — nearby, but seeming scarcely to intersect ordinary life — as in the several Parises of Proust, the Alexandrias of Cavafy.

The wistfulness characteristic of all Arcadias may even be greater in the case of the homosexual Arcadia, which is based not only on familiar yearnings for an easy life and many young lovers, but also on a desire to be pardoned for being homosexual, to be kissed on the eyelids and included among the innocent. It is sad when the burden of shame and personal guilt can only be put aside in fantasy; it is a brief forgiveness that is only as strong as the dreamer's ability to keep on dreaming.

Many poets and novelists, reminded daily that society regards them as inferior because of their sexual orientation, respond by fantasizing for all they are worth and imagining a world in which homosexuals are honored above all others. Not content with tolerance for homosexuality, they argue that it is a loftier ideal than exclusive heterosexuality. But then a sleeve of doubt passes over the page, and the authors begin to negotiate with reality: granted that the idea of homosexual superiority is unlikely to catch on, might not society at least condone homosexuality if homosexuals were careful to remain strictly spiritual and nonphysical? Of course, this suggestion violates the very nature of wish fulfillment, as well as the essence of homosexuality, but it is often to be found hovering about the literature of homosexual Arcadia.

> There is another angle; seen from that
> he appears attractive, appears
> a simple, genuine child of love,
> without hesitation putting
> the pure sensuality of his pure flesh
> above his honor and reputation.
>
> Above his reputation? But society,
> totally narrow-minded, had all its values wrong.
>
> C. P. Cavafy, from "Days of 1896"[6]

Some authors write to demonstrate support for the conventions of society, others to question them. Specifically, there are authors who write to bolster the general prejudice against homosexuality, and there are those who plead for acceptance of homosexual men and women. These partisan works, because they are intended to influence social behavior, can be called *political*.

A popular gambit of antihomosexual authors is to attribute homosexuality to a character the writer wishes to blacken; another is to add the stain of homosexuality to a character already shown to be execrable. An example of the latter occurs, of all places, in Oscar Wilde's *The Picture of Dorian Gray*. Basil Hallward confronts Dorian with rumors that he has ruined young men by leading them into sodomitical practices:

> Why is your friendship so fatal to young men? There was that wretched boy in the Guards who committed suicide. You were his great friend. There was Sir Henry Ashton, who had to leave England with a tarnished name. You and he were inseparable.[7]

This is a form of narrative shorthand and no worse a literary sin than to have the heroine be an orphan with large gray eyes in order to make her immediately sympathetic. But to denigrate a character by having him or her be homosexual is also something more than a storyteller's device. To the extent that it depends on homosexuality being regarded as weak or criminal, it rehearses that assumption.

Gilbert and Sullivan's *Patience* illustrates an outright battle between sexual deviance and conformity and celebrates the "proper" subjugation of deviance. Reginald Bunthorne, in love with the milkmaid Patience, is, strictly speaking, heterosexual — but just barely. Modeled on the twenty-five-year-old Wilde of the velvet knee breeches and the blue-and-white china, Bunthorne prances about in ultra-Aesthetical artiness and triumphant effeminacy until the very end of the operetta, when he is shouted down by his rival and a chorus of stolid dragoons, who sing the healthier delights of being "commonplace." At the final curtain, everyone is paired off to be married — except for Bunthorne, who is described by Gilbert as "out of the way," "miminy-piminy," and "foot-in-the-grave," i.e., deviant, effeminate, and morbid, the timeless slanders against homosexual males.[8] Bunthorne is punished by being left alone, a fate tantamount to death in the world of operetta. He is not much sillier, and no more self-absorbed, than anyone else in the play; his mortal sin is to be a recidivist Aesthete (read "nelly queen"). In other words, Bunthorne is banished for posing as a sodomite.[9]

The other tribe, authors who write in order to free homosexual men and women from censure, e.g., E. M. Forster in *Maurice* and Radclyffe Hall in *The Well of Loneliness*, often appeal to the reader's sympathy by describing the trials that face an honorable character for no other reason than because he or she is homosexual. It comes as no surprise that many of these "political" prohomosexual works refer at some point to the Theban band of warriors, to Sappho, to Michelangelo, etc., as if to exonerate homosexuality by calling on its saints. In turn, these books are gobbled up by readers who seek, even in fiction, permission to be gay.

> The transaction between a writer and the spirit of the age is one of infinite delicacy, and upon a nice arrangement between the two the whole fortune of his work depends. Orlando . . . need neither fight her age, nor submit to it; she was of it, yet remained herself. Now, therefore, she could write, and write she did. She wrote, she wrote, she wrote.
>
> Virginia Woolf, *Orlando*[10]

If you hold your eye smack up against a pear, you cannot see the pear, because light must intercede between the eye and an object for the object to be seen, and that requires distance. This law of distance can serve a *sociological* purpose in literature.

Homosexuals have usually been removed from the rest of society: whether literally, as in mental hospitals, in prison, at the gallows; or figuratively, by being forced to keep their homosexuality secret and by being excluded from many of society's important rites and privileges.

The condition of being a stranger makes homosexuals keen observers of the world around them, indeed doubly keen, for a false step can be literally fatal in an antihomosexual environment. Consequently, homosexual characters make marvelous agents for the author of fiction who wishes to record the structure and manners of a civilization. Once again, *Maurice* and *The Well of Loneliness* supply ready illustrations. In addition to being apologies for homosexuality, both novels are savage portraits of English county society. By looking over the shoulders of Maurice Hall and Stephen Gordon, who are familiars of that society but also strangers to it by virtue of their sexual orientation, we are in a much better position to observe. Homosexual men and women are not the only deviants who can serve this sociological function — Hester Prynne of *The Scarlet Letter* (a heterosexual adultress) and Lucy Snowe of *Villette* (a heterosexual dependent, foreigner, and Protestant in a Catholic city) are unblinking windows into Salem and Brussels — but homosexuals, having spent their whole lives as deviants, make especially wary, sharp-eyed observers.

> What am I suffering from? From knowledge — is it going to destroy me? What am I suffering from? From sexuality — is it going to destroy me?
>
> Thomas Mann, letter to Otto Grautoff[11]

> It was not the prince's fault that he was so clever. The cruel fairy had made him so. . . . The other people were just as much in fault for being born so stupid; but the world, my dear children, can never be induced to remember this. If you are clever, you will find it best not to let people know it — if you want them to like you.
>
> Andrew Lang, *Prince Prigio*[12]

Being different from the norm can force observation of the self as well as of society. An author of a *psychological* bent, eager to study the formation and management of individual identity, has a perfect subject in the man or woman who, staring down the fear that knowledge of the forbidden may lead to forbidden acts and thence to madness or death, dares to scrutinize his or her own homosexual feelings. Not every hero of a *Bildungsroman* need be homosexual, but a homosexual can be the fervently self-aware subject of such a novel, forever asking: What is this I feel? How does it differ from what others seem to be feeling? Why me? Shall I kill myself? How shall I live, cautiously or openly, decorously or with abandon? Must I be superior to everyone else, or must I be worse? In short, how am I to live with the knowledge of what I am, this forbidden knowledge?

The issue of forbidden knowledge is hardly unique to homosexual coming out. All of Western literature is shot through with the idea that it is blasphemous to know certain things. Information or experience too keen for mortals brings its own undeflectable punishment. Adam and Eve eat the apple and gain wisdom, but almost at once they are caught by the Lord and banished from Eden. Phaeton, too puny to master the horses of his father, the sun, brings ruin to the whole world before being executed by Jupiter. In "Our Lady's Child" of the Brothers Grimm, a girl unlocks the thirteenth door of heaven against the express command of the Virgin Mary. For denying that she has disobeyed, that is, for thinking she is cannier than the Virgin, the girl is punished by being struck dumb.

The corollary to these cautionary tales is the body of stories in which knowledge is acquired at the price of great suffering. Odin sacrifices one of his eyes for a single drink from the spring of Mimir, whose waters give understanding. (Somewhere in the middle between the *frisson* elicited by blasphemy and our awe at Odin's willing barter for wisdom stands our reaction to Degas going blind, Beethoven going deaf — horror and grief, yes, but also a sense that justice has been fed.)

It is especially dangerous to know too much about sex. When the proper bounds are overstepped, the punishment may be perpetual slavery, as befalls Ham after he spies on the nakedness of his father, Noah; or blindness, as with Oedipus, who sleeps with his mother; or even death, the fate of Semele, who is loved by Jupiter not in a diminished, human guise but in his full, towering deity:

> "Show yourself to me," [Semele] said, "as you appear to Juno, when you share love's embrace with her!" The god tried to stop her lips as she spoke, but already her hasty utterance had escaped into the air. . . . Semele's mortal frame could not endure the exaltation caused by the heavenly visitant, and she was burned to ashes by her wedding gift.[13]

In particular, self-knowledge must be kept in check: peep, but don't fall in. The epitome of this danger is Narcissus, who, in punishment for having scorned all suitors, is killed by a surfeit of self-understanding:

> When her time was come, that nymph most fair [Liriope] brought forth a child with whom one could have fallen in love even in his cradle, and she called him Narcissus. When the prophetic seer [Tiresias] was asked whether the boy would live to ripe old age, he replied: "Yes, if he does not come to know himself."[14]

Narcissus does not starve or drown: what kills him is the awareness that he loves himself and can never possess that self. He would not have pined away had he been less perceptive:

> Alas! I am myself the boy I see. I know it: my own reflection does not deceive me. . . . But what then shall I seek by my wooing? What I desire, I have. My very plenty makes me poor. How I wish I could separate myself from my body! . . . . Now grief is sapping my strength. . . .[15]

The myth of Narcissus owes its popularity to society's own self-absorption. Human beings cannot bear to be disregarded, and in the story of the selfish boy who dies, we welcome the downfall of one who presumed not to require us. (Not all tales of revenge against the independent are as silvery as Ovid's Narcissus. Dickens' Miss Havisham, a macabre parody of youth as she sits alone before her gilded looking-glass, is the dark side of the same moon. When she catches fire and dies of her burns, she is punished not only for having toyed with other people's lives, but also for having dared to be powerful in isolation.)

Implicit in these central myths of Western literature are the beliefs that any new knowledge is a reminder of alternatives to the familiar; that this realization offers freedom, which is power; and that the powerful individual will inevitably challenge God and Man — or in other words, will inevitably sin. Adam defied God directly; Semele mocked the laws against "unnatural" sex partners; Narcissus rejected society altogether. But if Adam, Semele, and Narcissus were sinners, then the man or woman who persists in homosexuality is triply "sinful" — and triply useful to an author interested in examining the psychology of people who know that they are sinning.

Nothing could be more blasphemous than to scoff at mortality. After all, to disregard your own death shows a lack of proper awe for the signature immortality of the gods. This is the blasphemy of men and women who are exclusively homosexual and content to be so. Given that their sexual relations cannot produce offspring, they appear to have reached an accord with the fact of their own dying, to have decided that this one life is sufficient. Worse still, unrepentant homosexuality mocks the sodomy laws and shows up society's willful ignorances (for example, its ignorance of homosexuality). Bold as Semele, a young woman defies all the loathsome warnings she has heard in church and the locker room and has her first lesbian experience; arrogant as Narcissus, a gay man risks being exiled and comes out publicly. Their future lives may be freer or narrower as a result, but at least, like Odin, they will have learned something new.

The possession of forbidden knowledge, even the knowledge that you are innocent, is never easy. It is painful to learn that what once appeared to be divine proscriptions are in fact the stained records of human fear, for with this understanding comes the requirement that you do your own thinking. It is disorienting to discover that, after all, you *can* live outside the city gates — to realize there are no wolves there, or that you can live happily among wolves. Just when you had adapted to the cobbled everyday, it is vexing to hear of Arcadia. This dilemma, though not uniquely homosexual, is richly illustrated by stories of homosexual men and women.

III

The eleven essays that make up this special issue of the *Journal of Homosexuality* investigate the ways in which homosexuality has been viewed by a variety of authors writing in various Western languages from the Middle Ages to the present. Scarcely anyone writes with only one purpose, and the authors discussed here are no exception. Time and again the Arcadian, political, sociological, and psychological themes can all be found nestled together in a single work, and often with a hearty dose of lubricity or sentiment thrown in for good measure. Readers intrigued by a particular idea, or interested in comparing several treatments of one theme, may appreciate a few pointers at the outset.

The first article in this collection, Byrne Fone's "This Other Eden: Arcadia and the Homosexual Imagination," identifies the characteristics of classical Arcadian poetry and shows how these are shared by many homosexual poems and novels, from the verse of Richard Barnfield to novels by Gore Vidal. Robert Martin's "Edward Carpenter and the Double Structure of *Maurice*" is almost as encyclopedic. Martin discusses Forster's response to two very Arcadian questions — Is spiritual homosexuality superior to the physical variety? and Must homosexuality be superior to heterosexuality if it is to be allowed at all? — and examines the theme of the greenwood as a haven for homosexuals. This notion of going far from the madding crowd, or at least abroad, to find the permission to be homosexual is elaborated by Louis Crompton in "*Don Leon*, Byron, and Homosexual Law Reform," Roger Austen in "Stoddard's Little Tricks in *South Sea Idyls*," and Inez Martinez in "The Lesbian Hero Bound: Radclyffe Hall's Portrait of Sapphic Daughters and Their Mothers." Byron went all the way to Constantinople, Stoddard sailed again and again to the South Seas, and Hall's Stephen Gordon exiled herself to Paris, simply to be able to make love as they wished. Edmund White's "The Inverted Type: Homosexuality as a Theme in James Merrill's Prophetic Books" illustrates another sort of Arcadian wish fulfillment, the fantasy of a cosmos in which all the very nicest, and most powerful, people are just as gay as can be.

Private dreams of Arcadia are often the antechamber to political action in the real world, so it comes as no surprise that many of the essays that treat Arcadian themes also investigate an author's plea for tolerance of homosexuality. Xavier Mayne's *Imre*, cited by Fone, is as much a tract as a novel; *Don Leon*, the subject of Crompton's article, is an out-and-out political satire aimed at the sodomy laws and specifically at the death penalty for convicted homosexuals. E. M. Forster's *Maurice* and Radclyffe Hall's *The Well of Loneliness* (discussed here by Martin and Martinez respectively) have already been mentioned as examples of novels written in part to illustrate the plight of gay men and lesbians in an antihomosexual society. The *sine qua non* of antihomosexual prejudice, of course, is the rather debatable notion that heterosexuality and homosexuality are vastly different, warring states, each one threatened by the existence of the other. This rivalry between heterosexuality and homosexuality is examined in detail by Seymour Kleinberg in "*The Merchant of Venice*: The Homosexual as Anti-Semite in Nascent Capitalism" and by Richard Dellamora in "An Essay in Sexual Liberation, Victorian Style: Walter Pater's 'Two Early French Stories.'" But perhaps the most effective argument for homosexuality is the least political of all: a hymn to a lovely boy written by a man who understands the manifold beauties of both sexes. Thomas Stehling offers translations and criticisms of several such poems in his essay "To Love a Medieval Boy."

If the signal characteristic of the homosexual experience in Western cultures has been its deviant status, there can be no more accurate metaphor for homosexuality than the painful one of an excluded person looking in though a window at the warmth and play of normalcy. This metaphor is the subject of Richard Hall's article "Henry James: Interpreting an Obsessive Memory." The sociological and psychological truth that homosexuality is but one deviance among a welter of outlawed states is brought home to us by Don Liles's "William Faulkner's *Absalom, Absalom!*: An Exegesis of the Homoerotic Configurations in the Novel," and by Kleinberg's essay on *The Merchant of Venice*, which leads us through that tangle of anti-Semitic and antihomosexual beliefs, all well drenched in ambiguous feelings toward money. Martin's essay on *Maurice*, Martinez' study of two novels by Radclyffe Hall, and White's article on Merrill's trilogy offer many examples of the way in which homosexuals, precisely because they are deviant, may be gifted with extraordinary insight into the constitution of society and their own selves.

Taken as a whole, the eleven essays teach a final valuable lesson: homosexuality may be stigmatized, but in this it is not alone; it can offer its adherents vision or unusual strength, but here, too, homosexuality is far from unique. This is reflected in the quality of the books discussed by the essayists and in the personalities of the homosexual characters. Some of the books are masterpieces, others are strong offerings from authors capable of better. A few of the works cited as examples are thin soup by anyone's definition. So, too, with the homosexual heroes, both men and women, of these novels, poems, and plays: some are keenly gifted, many others doughlike in their ordinariness. If a moral may be drawn, it is that homosexuality is a human condition, a human behavior, no more and no less. This may be disappointing to some, but in fact it offers a reprieve from the prodigies of compensation, and the attendant sense of failure, that have characterized homosexuals who did not understand that they were innocent. If only they had known — what might they have done, what stories might they have written?

IV

I would like to thank Dr. John De Cecco, editor of the *Journal of Homosexuality*, for honoring me with his invitation to edit this special issue; the eleven authors who contributed articles, for their diligence and resilience, and for their lively correspondence; the many, many colleagues who reviewed manuscripts and read drafts of accepted articles; Ron Ranum and Wendell Ricketts for their editorial assistance. In particular, I thank Michael Shively for his support throughout this project.

NOTES

[1]E. M. Forster, *The Longest Journey* (1922; rpt. New York: Vintage Books, 1962), p. 69.

[2]E. M. Forster, *A Room with a View* (n.d.; rpt. New York: Vintage Books, n.d.), p. 139.

[3]Charlotte Brontë, *Jane Eyre*, ed. Q. D. Leavis (Harmondsworth: Penguin, 1966), p. 79.

[4]Howard Pyle, *Men of Iron* (New York: Harper & Brothers,n.d.), pp. 270-71.

[5]T. H. White, *The Once and Future King* (New York: G. P. Putnam's Sons, 1958), pp. 92-93.

[6]C. P. Cavafy, "Days of 1896," in *C. P. Cavafy: Collected Poems*, trans. Edmund Keeley and Philip Sherrard, ed. George Savidis (Princeton: Princeton Univ. Press, 1975), p. 279.

[7]Oscar Wilde, *The Picture of Dorian Gray* (Leipzig: Tauchnitz, 1908), p. 194.

[8]W. S. Gilbert, "When I Go Out of Door," from *Patience: Or Bunthorne's Bride*, by Arthur S. Sullivan and W. S. Gilbert, in *A Treasury of Gilbert and Sullivan*, ed. Deems Taylor (New York: Simon and Schuster, 1941), pp. 166-68.

[9]On 18 Feb. 1895, Lord Queensberry left his card, on which he had written, "To Oscar Wilde posing as a somdomite[sic]," at Wilde's club. The story is told in countless biographies. Wilde's own immediate response is recorded in *The Letters of Oscar Wilde*, ed. Rupert Hart-Davis (New York: Harcourt, 1962), p. 384.

[10]Virginia Woolf, *Orlando: A Biography* (London: The Hogarth Press, 1928), pp. 239-40.

[11]"To Otto Grautoff," 8 Nov. 1896, quoted in Richard Winston, *Thomas Mann: The Making of an Artist 1875-1911* (New York: Knopf, 1981), p. 96.

[12]Andrew Lang, *Prince Prigio and Prince Ricardo* (London: J. M. Dent, 1961), p. 19.

[13]Ovid, *Metamorphoses*, trans. and introd. Mary M. Innes (Harmondsworth: Penguin, 1955), pp. 81-82.

[14]Ovid, p. 83.

[15]Ovid. p. 86.

This Other Eden:
Arcadia and the Homosexual Imagination

Byrne R. S. Fone, Ph.D.

Those who would dwell in Arcadia seek out that secret Eden because of its isolation from the troubled world and its safety from the arrogant demands of those who would deny freedom, curtail human action, and destroy innocence and love. Arcadia can be a happy valley, a blessed isle, a pastoral retreat, or a green forest fastness. Those who search for that hidden paradise are often lovers, or the truly wise, trying, as one questing pilgrim put it, to escape from "the clank of the world."[1]

I would like to suggest that the Arcadian ideal has been used in the homosexual literary tradition in a fashion that speaks directly to the gay sensibility. The homosexual imagination finds a special value and a particular use for this ideal, employing it in three major ways: 1) to suggest a place where it is safe to be gay: where gay men can be free from the outlaw status society confers upon us, where homosexuality can be revealed and spoken of without reprisal, and where homosexual love can be consummated without concern for the punishment or scorn of the world; 2) to imply the presence of gay love and sensibility in a text that otherwise makes no explicit statement about homosexuality;[2] and 3) to establish a metaphor for certain spiritual values and myths prevalent in homosexual literature and life, namely, that homosexuality is superior to heterosexuality and is a divinely sanctioned means to an understanding of the good and the beautiful, and that the search for the Ideal Friend is one of the major undertakings of the homosexual life. Only in this metaphoric land can certain rituals take place, rituals that celebrate this mythology. These rites are transformational and involve the union of lovers, the loving and sexual fraternity of men, and the washing away of societal guilt. The symbolic events of the rituals include the offering of gifts, usually from nature, and the purification by water to prepare for an eternity of blissful habitation in the garden.

Byrne R. S. Fone, Ph.D., is Associate Professor of English at the City College of the City University of New York. He is at work on a book tentatively titled *Travelers to Arcadia: The Homosexual Imagination and Literary Tradition* and has edited an anthology, *Hidden Heritage: History and the Gay Imagination*.

I

Virgil's *Second Eclogue* is one of the great poems in the homosexual tradition and embodies a theme familiar to poets before him and after, the green forest as a place where love can flourish and where suitable wedding gifts can be offered, in short, a secret Arcadia. Virgil sends Corydon "among the thick beeches with their shady summits" to lament his unhappy situation with the faithless Alexis. There, "alone in fruitless passion," free to "fling these artless strains to hills and woods," Corydon feels safe to declare his love. He urges Alexis, far out of hearing, alas, to "but live with me in our rude fields and lowly cots, shooting deer and driving flocks of kids to green mallows. With me in the woods you shall rival Pan in song."[3] Pan usually sang songs of seduction.

To lure Alexis to the woods, Corydon offers gifts: his "thousand lambs," his "pipe formed of seven uneven hemlock-stalks," and "two roes . . . their hides still sprinkled with white," not to mention offerings of fruit and flowers: quinces, chestnuts, plums, and laurel and sweet myrtle.

Richard Barnfield, in his pastoral "The Affectionate Shepherd: The Teares of an Affectionate Shepherd Sicke for Love, or the Complaint of Daphnis for the Love of Ganimede,"[4] provides Daphnis with a lover who is quite as troublesome as Corydon's Alexis. By the Renaissance, Ganymede had come to be as much a code word for a homosexual as Arcadia had come to be indicative of homosexuality. Barnfield has his shepherd, in love with "a sweet-fac'd boy," invite his true love to share his shepherd's cot. Together, Daphnis hopes, they will

> . . . walke abroad,
> Abroad into the fields to take fresh ayre,
> The meades with Floras treasure . . . strowde,
> The mantled meaddowes, and the fields so fayre.

These fair fields, of course, are the same as those where Corydon sang. Barnfield as Daphnis, invites his Ganimede to share his sheepcote:

> If thou wilt come and dwell with me at home
> My sheepcote shall be strowed with new green rushes;
> Weele haunt the trembling pickets as they rome
> Aboutt the fields, along the hauthorne bushes;
> I have a pie-bald curre to hunt the hare,
> So we shall live with daintie forest fare.

Daphnis is far richer than Corydon, for not only does he have sheep, he has a garden plot full of herbs and "Sweet smelling beds of lillies, and of roses,/ Which rosemary banks of lavender encloses." Multitudes of flowers will be Ganimede's, as well as gifts: "sweet smelling arbours made of eglantine/ Should be thy shrine, and I would be thy dove./ Cool cabinets of fresh greene laurell boughs," and "apples, cherries, peares, plumbs,/ Nuts, walnuts, fil-reads, chestnuts." Indeed, Daphnis will do anything for Ganimede if he will "pittie my complaint . . . All these and more Ile give thee for thy love,/ If these and more may tyce thy love away." He even promises that if Ganimede wants to "bathe thy naked limbs/ Within the cristall of a pearle bright brooke," that they will "go to Ladon, whose still trickling noyse/ Will lull thee fast asleepe amids thy joyes." No doubt Barnfield knew that Ladon is a river in Arcadia. All the elements of the Virgilian tradition are in Barnfield's poem, elaborated, embellished.

Barnfield wrote his poem in 1594. Christopher Marlowe had written "The Passionate Shepherd" sometime before 1588.[5] It was one of the most influential poems of its time, and Barnfield and many others were indebted to it. Certainly Barnfield's "If thou wilt come and dwell with me at home" is a reference to Marlowe's "If thou wilt live with me and be my love." Marlowe's shepherd, like Daphnis, offers "all the pleasures" that "valleys, groves, hills, fields,/ Woods, or steepy mountain yields." Marlowe's shepherd also resembles Corydon. Indeed, all three offer the enticement of pastoral scenes and Arcadian vistas where the mind can be moved. Like Barnfield's Ladon, Marlowe's shallow river makes musical delight; and like Corydon and Daphnis, the passionate shepherd offers gifts familar now: "Beds of roses,/ And a thousand fragrant posies, and a cap of flowers, and a kirtle,/ Embroidered all with leaves of myrtle." Marlowe is far less prodigal in his use of the Virgilian imagery than Barnfield, but the principle is the same: if "all these pleasures may thee move,/ Come live with me and be my love."

Marlowe's poem is spoken by a man to a woman, or so literary history has insisted. But there are problems with this unquestioned assumption. Virgil and Barnfield wrote about homosexual love; Marlowe was not specific. But had he wanted a nymph instead of a shepherd, why did he not supply one? Why the teasing omission? The passionate shepherd will give "gowns" and "kirtles," but these were generally worn by students, who were always male, and sometimes by women. Some texts have the couple watching the "shepherd's swains" dancing and singing; other texts have "shepherd swains." If the latter, why should the nymph who is the delight of the passionate shepherd encourage still another swain? If the former, it needs little comment to see that the shepherd's swains were male, since *swain* was primarily used to signify a male lover.

Putting all linguistic oddities aside, Marlowe's poem is very much in that homosexual tradition exemplified by Virgil's *Eclogue,* and very much representative of the literature that finds "groves, hills and fields" part of the geography of Arcadia. Is it an accident that Marlowe asks his lover to "come live with me and be my love," and Corydon implores Alexis to "but live with me in our rude fields?"

These three poems show how lovers have traditionally repaired to Arcadia and wild retreats, there to lament or implore or celebrate their love. The discussion that follows will document this tradition and elaborate upon some of the constituent parts of the Arcadian ideal as represented in works of the specifically homosexual imagination.

II

The Arcadian garden as a safe haven appears startlingly in two works, one American, the other British. In *Joseph and His Friend*, written by the American poet and novelist Bayard Taylor in 1869, Arcadia is described as:

> a great valley, bounded by hundreds of miles of snowy peaks; lakes in its bed; enormous hillsides, dotted with groves of ilex and pine, orchards of orange and olive; a perfect climate, where it is bliss enough to breathe, and [where there is] freedom from the distorted laws of men, for none are near enough to enforce them. If there is no legal way of escape for you, here, at least there is no force which will drag you back, once you are there: I will go with you, and perhaps, perhaps. . . .[6]

The speaker, Joseph, says to his friend Philip: "We should be outlaws there, in our freedom! — here we are fettered outlaws" (p. 216). The two man determine that the time has not yet come for them to enter into their great valley, their Arcadia. But in the fullness of the vision, and against every canon of Victorian rectitude,

> they took each other's hands. The day was fading, the landscape silent, and only the twitter of nestling birds was heard in the boughs above them. Each gave way to the impulse of manly love, rarer, alas! but as tender and true as the love of woman, and they drew near and kissed each other. As they walked back and parted on the highway, each felt that life was not wholly unkind, and that happiness was not yet impossible. (p. 217)

Earlier in the book, Joseph met Philip when both were in a train wreck. Joseph's response to Philip's handsome face, and the intimacy that develops between them, are at odds with the fact that the plot of the book ostensibly has nothing to do with homosexuality. Rather, it is a midcentury novel of manners, detailing Joseph's misery in a loveless first marriage and his eventual happiness in a second (with, it ought to be noted, the look-alike sister of his friend Philip). But aside from the fact that much of Taylor's poetry is specifically homoerotic, his reference to "manly love" (a code word in Whitman and the nineteenth-century British Uranian poets) and his play upon the biblical story of David and Jonathan, whose love was "passing the love of women" as Philip and Joseph's is "rarer, alas, but as tender and true as the love of woman," provide a distinctly homosexual atmosphere that is only reinforced by the lengthly appeal to the happy-valley imagery, the happy valley as a place where two men can be free and "live as outlaws." The "great valley," of course, is Arcadia, the secret garden where their love can be consummated, far from the "distorted laws of men."

Whereas *Joseph and His Friend* presents itself as a novel of hetero-sexual life but possesses a text full of homosexual implication, E. M. Forster's *Maurice* (1913/1971) is a homosexual love story. It is also about the discovery of homosexuality and the search for the Ideal Friend. Once the discovery is made, accepted, and ratified, and the friend finally found, Maurice and Alec enter into their Arcadia. Forster calls this "the greenwood." Maurice sought the greenwood because "he was an outlaw in disguise."[7] Perhaps, he mused — this after the certain discovery of his homosexuality — "among those who took to the greenwood in old times there had been two men like himself — two. At times he entertained the dream. Two men can defy the world" (p. 137). Maurice and Alec (is this Corydon's Alexis?) do indeed escape to the greenwood at the end of the book, and Forster tells us that they went there to seek a "cave in which to curl up . . . a deserted valley for those who wish neither to reform nor corrupt society, but to be left alone" (p. 254).

Though *Maurice* is a homosexual love story and *Joseph and His Friend* is not, in both, at the center of the desire of each hero and in-deed at the most emotionally charged moment of the book, the Arcadian image dominates and illuminates the text. That this is not an accidental image can be seen in two American novels from the mid twentieth century.

Gore Vidal's *The City and the Pillar* (1948) and Nial Kent's *The Divided Path* (1949) both offer images of a happy valley, a secret green-wood. Here, "men can be completely alone in their own private world."[8] Here, "complexes and disturbances seem all shed away."[9] One dweller in Arcadia could be "free and natural, completely himself . . . filled with love to overflowing";[10] another feels "at peace, as if he were a part of the day. There was nothing to worry him."[11] In each book, the cli-mactic scene is the same: the hero is at a rustic, lakeside cabin with his current friend, who is somewhat unaware of the passion he stirs. Their hours together are lovingly described:

> They could swim without clothes here . . . and Jim, when he
> looked at Bob's strong white body did not envy, rather he felt a
> twinship, a similarity, a warm emotion he could not name.
>
> — *The City and the Pillar* (p. 22)[12]

> They seldom wore more than shorts . . . and Paul often went
> without even those during the day. When they walked to and from
> the pool, Michael loved to watch the way the sun came through
> the leafy roof here and there and fell on Paul's bare skin, bright
> flecks sliding across the burnished bronze body as it moved with
> Arcadian naturalness. . . . Michael felt protective and adoring as if
> Paul were his child as well as his god. And both were at peace.
>
> — *The Divided Path* (p. 179)

In Arcadia, where there is peace, the feelings between men partake of
the mythology of homosexual life. Jim's feeling of "twinship" with
Bob, Michael's adoration of Paul's godlike "Arcadian naturalness," and
his protective impulse toward Paul, are emotions that are felt properly
only in happy valleys like these. Jim's feelings invoke the myth of
Narcissus but also recall that moment in Plato's *Symposium*, one of the
great repositories of original homosexual myth, when Aristophanes describes the origin of man. There were originally three species: male,
female, and androgynous. To punish their pride, the gods divided them
in half, dooming them to walk the earth, always looking for their other
halves: women for women; men for men; and of the androgynous, the
man for the woman. Aristophanes slyly suggests that this explains why
there are three sexual preferences. Vidal, probably knowingly, echoes
this moment when he mentions Jim's feeling of twinship with Bob. In
Plato, the feeling is described thus:

> They who are a section of the male, follow the male. . . . when
> they reach manhood they are lovers of youth. . . . but they are
> satisfied if they may be allowed to lives with one another un-
> wedded; and such a nature is prone to love and ready to return
> love, always embracing that which is akin to him. And when one
> of them meets with his other half, the actual half of himself . . . the
> pair are lost in an amazement of love and friendship and intimacy
> and one will not be out of the other's sight. . . . Yet they could
> not explain what they desire of one another.[13]

For Jim, the feeling of twinship is precisely that Platonic moment of "an
amazement of love," and like his Platonic counterparts, his "warm emotion he could not name" is similar to their inability to "explain what they
desire of one another."

Platonic, or at least Greek, is the implication of Michael's feelings in *The Divided Path*. He feels protective of his friend, as if Paul were a child, yet adores him like a god. So too the lover as he contemplates his beloved in Plato's description in the *Symposium* is inspired to protect the beloved and teach him, for by Greek tradition the lover is older and more experienced than the beloved. The beloved is a god, though, as Plato points out, "the lover is more divine: because he is inspired by God" (p. 19). The god, of course, is Eros, offspring of the Heavenly Goddess, who presides over homosexual love. Pausanias describes it in the *Symposium*:

> The offspring of the Heavenly Aphrodite is derived from a mother in whose birth the female has no part. She is from the male only; this is the love which is of youths. . . . those who are inspired by this love turn to the male, and delight in him who is the more valiant and intelligent in nature. . . . he who gives himself to a lover because he is a good man, and in hope of being improved by his company, shows himself to be virtuous . . . than which there can be nothing nobler. This noble in every case is the acceptance of another for the sake of virtue. This is the love which is of the Heavenly Goddess, and is heavenly, and of great price to individuals and cities. . . . (p. 19)

Michael feels both protective and adoring because he is inspired by that heavenly love, which is homosexual, virtuous, and spiritually uplifting. Perhaps the most impressive paradigm of the feelings that Jim and Michael express is found in "Death in Venice," where Mann describes Aschenbach's mixed response to the beautiful Tadzio:

> The sight of this living figure, virginally pure and austere, with dripping locks, beautiful as a tender young god, emerging from the depths of sea and sky, outrunning the element — it conjured up mythologies, it was like a primeval legend, handed down from the beginning of time, of the birth of form, of the origin of the gods. With closed lids Aschenbach listened to this poesy hymning itself silently within him. . . . Afterwards, Tadzio lay on the sand and rested. . . . And even when Aschenbach read . . . he was conscious that the lad was there. . . . It was almost as though he sat there to guard the youth's repose. . . . And his heart was stirred, it felt a father's kindness. . . .[14]

My point is that in Arcadia the hidden feelings of common day can bloom into the complex manifestations of homosexual mythology. The sun casting its burnished gleam on the "Arcadian naturalness" of a bronzed body invokes feelings too deep to name.

But these emotions are more than the stuff of myth, they are sexual as well. In the face of the promise of Arcadian safety, Joseph and his friend exchange a plighting kiss. In the greenwood Maurice and Alec can find their love. At their lakeside cabin, Jim and Bob can wrestle down by the water, lovers in the sacred grove, in a scene freighted with the myth and metaphor of homosexual discourse.

> Jim, his face dry, stretched out beside Bob, lay close to him. "I'm hot," he said. "It's too hot a night to be wrestling." Bob laughed and suddenly grabbed him. They clung together a moment, wrestling. Jim was suddenly conscious of Bob's body. He pretended to wrestle and then both stopped moving on the blanket still clinging to each other. Jim was aware of Bob's body as never before. In the back of his mind half-forgotten dreams began to come alive, began to seek consummation in reality. Neither moved for a minute, their arms around each other, smooth chests touching, breathing fast and in unison. Abruptly Bob pulled away. For a moment their eyes met. Then deliberately, gravely, Bob shut his eyes and Jim touched him, for so it always happened in those dream nations: without words, perfect encounters beyond earth's precise turning . . . no time, no knowledge but the present, the bright moment in each other's arms. Half to half and the whole created. When eyes are shut the true world is born within. Their bodies in accord, all secret imaginings shared at last . . . and Jim no longer himself. No longer separate, no longer the lost half of a broken god, became the other. And now they were complete, finished, their original divinity restored.
>
> — *The City and the Pillar* (pp. 27-28)

All of this occurs in a moment of wrestling, near rape, and love, on the banks of a river in Arcadia, by the waters, perhaps, of an American Ladon.

Jim and Bob are united in a sexual union that far transcends mere sexuality in the same way that the imaginings of homosexual literature and its tradition far transcend the merely sexual event: they turn the lust of life into the lessons of legend. Only in Arcadia can this consummation genuinely be found. In the happy valley, in the safety of the greenwood, the divided self can be reunited. The search for the Ideal Friend, object of so many homosexual stories and lives, is successfully ended.

III

We have seen that in Arcadia, whether manifest as a fair pastoral, a leafy grove, the greenwood or a great valley, lovers can tell their love or ratify it. One facet of this is when the garden is the scene for a revelation of homosexuality, sometimes to another, sometimes as an admission to one's self.

In the American novel *Imre* (1906) written by Xavier Mayne — a pseudonym for the novelist, critic, historian, and student of homosexuality Edward Prime Stevenson, whose remarkable book *The Intersexes* (1908) was the first American history of homosexuality — this truth is uttered clearly and without equivocation.

Oswald, the narrator, loves the darkly handsome Imre, an army officer. Oswald determines to confess his homosexuality to Imre, whatever the cost. Oswald is an American, Imre a Hungarian. The novel is set in Hungary, itself a mysterious land by Yankee standards, a land far removed, as Oswald says, from the oppressively Anglo-Saxon morality of America, where, in Oswald's words,

> is still met, at every side, so dense a blending of popular ignorances, of century-old and century-blind religious and ethical misconceptions, of unscientific professional conservativism in psychiatric circles, and juristic barbarisms; all, of course, accompanied with the full measure of British and Yankee hypocrisy toward the daily actualities of homosexualism. By comparison, indeed, any other lands and races — even those yet hesitant in their social toleration or legal protection of the Uranian — seem educative and kindly; not to distinguish peoples whose attitude is distinctly one of common sense and humanity.[15]

Thus, Oswald/Mayne denounces "those brutes" and "the distorted laws of men" that so disturb the speakers in Taylor's *Joseph and His Friend*. It is to escape such a world that Oswald has chosen to spend his time in Hungary, a sexual exile from his native land.

The time comes, as it must in classic tales of homosexual revelation, when Oswald can no longer wear a mask and hide the truth from Imre. For the purposes of this revelation, the author sends Oswald and Imre into a symbolic Arcadian garden, an ancient park outside the city, which fulfills the Arcadian requirement of being far from the haunts of men. The park is "itself . . . almost a forest, so large it is and so stately are the trees. Long wide alleys wind through the acacias and chestnuts," and "the public is not admitted" to this bower. In the midst of the garden is a monument to the devotion of two soldiers, Lorand and Egon. The one died avenging the death of the other: two hearts, as

Oswald says, "that after so ardently beating for each other are now but dust" (pp. 80 ff.). Like Vidal, Mayne is not unfamiliar with classical literature, and if the reader is not reminded of the monument set up by the Greeks to honor the lovers Harmodius and Aristogeiton, at which other lovers swore their fidelity to each other, then an allusion to Achilles, who avenged the death of his lover, Patroclus, will tease us into thought.

Oswald awaits the moment to declare himself and, he hopes, his love for Imre. "We made a detour around the lonelier portion of the park. . . . Not a sign of life . . . not a sound except a gentle wind . . . melancholy and fitful. We two might have been remote . . . not within twenty minutes of a great city" (p. 96). A few steps away rose the memorial to "the unforgettable memory of Lorand and Egon." Here, safe in the isolated greenwood, before the monument to the dead lovers, Oswald and Imre stand wrapped in a mythic moment, Oswald waiting for courage and inspiration.

At last he reveals his homosexuality and his love. He sits in the garden and waits for Imre to respond. "Full darkness was now about us. The stillness had so deepened that the ceasing of my own low voice made it the more suspenseful. The sweep of the night-wind rose among the acacias. The birds of shadow flitted about us. The gloom seemed to have entered my soul — as Death unto Life. Would Imre ever speak?" (p. 151).

Speak he does, though his response is neither what Oswald hoped nor what he expected:

> "If I could . . . my God!" Imre said, "If only I could! . . . say to thee what I cannot. Perhaps some time . . . forgive me thou breakest my heart. . . . Not because I care less for thee as my friend. . . . No. We stay together, Oswald. We shall always be what we have become to each other. Oh we cannot change, not through all our lives! Not in death. . . . Oh Oswald, that thou could'st think that I would dream of turning away from thee . . . suffer a break between us two, because thou art made in thy nature as God makes mankind. . . . We are what we are. . . . Friendship between us? Oh whether we are near or far! Forever! Forever! Yes, by God above us, by God in us. Only for the sake of the bond between us from this night, promise me that thou wilt never again speak of what thou hast told me of thyself — never unless I break the silence." (pp. 151 ff.)

He will break the silence, and his emotional and somewhat incoherent speech will be explained later when he confesses his own homosexuality and love for Oswald. At the end of the book the two are united in the "friendship which is love, the love which is friendship" (p. 205) and propose to spend their lives together in their happy valley of love. But as in the other books, the emotional climax of the book occurs in the Arcadian garden. There can be no doubt that in this garden Imre, without directly saying so, has plighted his eternal bond with Oswald. Only Oswald mentions homosexuality; indeed Imre urges him not to speak of it again, "unless I break the silence." Which of course he does. But there in the garden before the lovers' shrine he has already said what needs to be said. The place and the circumstances have told the story, the symbols have ratified and clarified words unspoken.

This moment in *Imre* is a classic of its kind. The content is obliquely, though certainly, sexual. Corollary images from the classical locations of homosexual myth and literature are invoked. And the moment itself, for Oswald, is liberating, indeed transforming. It is a plighting of vows, but most of all it is an epiphany, for the observant reader will see that in this Arcadian garden a wedding song has been sung.

One of the most striking evocations of this kind of epiphanic moment is the great scene in "Death in Venice" where Aschenbach, in a revelatory instant mixed with both horror and joy, declares his love for Tadzio. Fleeing from the verandah of the hotel, fleeing from the "fatal gift" of his lover's smile, he enters the dark garden.

> Aschenbach received that smile and turned away with it as though entrusted with a fatal gift. So shaken was he that he had to flee from the lighted terrrace and front gardens and seek out with hurried steps the darkness of the park at the rear. Reproaches strangely mixed with tenderness and remonstrance burst from him: "How dare you smile like that! No one is allowed to smile like that!" He flung himself on a bench, his composure gone to the winds, and breathed in the nocturnal fragrance of the garden. He leaned back, with hanging arms, quivering from head to foot, and quite unmanned he whispered the hackneyed phrase of love and longing — impossible in these circumstances, absurd, abject, ridiculous enough, yet sacred too, and not unworthy of honor even here: "I love you." (p. 51)

The dark garden should by now be a familiar site; the nocturnal fragrance should recall Corydon's laurel and sweet myrtle, Marlowe's thousand fragrant posies, Oswald's park of chestnuts and acacias, Joseph and his friend amid the groves of ilex, pine, and orange. Aschenbach is "quite unmanned" as he leans back, quivering in near-orgasmic exhaustion. His arms hang loose, so different from the rigid picture we have of him at the beginning of the story: "'Aschenbach has always lived like this' — here the speaker closed the fingers of his left hand to a fist —

'never like this' — and he let his open hand hang relaxed from the back of his chair" (p. 9).

In the garden Aschenbach finds the courage to declare his love, indeed is suddenly and stunningly aware of it, and thus of his own homosexuality. In the eyes of the world in which he has so long and rigidly lived and which he has so long and brilliantly served, his love for Tadzio must seem ridiculous, abject, absurd. But in the garden, the archetypal myths of the homosexual imagination come crowding round and support him, for "even here" his love is "sacred" and "not unworthy of honor."

In discussing *Joseph and His Friend*, I said that the Arcadian image can be used as a signpost to explicitly indicate homosexual content, even though there has been no specific mention of the subject earlier in the work. Arcadia serves the same function for Mann, for although there can be no doubt about Aschenbach's feelings for Tadzio by the time the garden scene is reached, Aschenbach himself is remarkably unaware of his latent homosexuality until precisely that moment. The observant reader, however, schooled in the method of homosexual literary discourse, has understood all along what was going on.[16]

"Death in Venice" is in its largest sense a tale of conflict between the demanding and limited virtues of a Christian morality, which would consider homosexuality abject and would scorn it as ridiculous and absurd, and the freer, open morality of classical paganism as represented for Aschenbach by Greek homosexuality, which would declare his love honorable and sacred.

Thus, at the end of the story, rather than reading it as defeat and tragedy, we must see it as a triumph. In the last pages Tadzio, transmuted into a divinity by the imagination of Aschenbach, beckons the dying artist to final rest and unity with perfect beauty, which Tadzio has come to represent. Tadzio stands there

> with his face turned seaward . . . he paced there divided by an expanse of water from the shore . . . a remote and isolated figure, with floating locks out there in sea and wind, against the misty inane. . . . he turned from the waist up . . . and looked over his shoulder at the shore. The watcher sat there just as he had sat that time in the lobby of the hotel when first the twilight grey eyes had met his own. . . . it seemed to him that the pale and lovely summoner out there smiled at him and beckoned; as though with hand lifted from his hip, he pointed outward as he hovered on before in an immensity of richest expectation. (p. 74)

With a hieratic gesture, like an archaic god, Tadzio invites Aschenbach to him, Goethe's eternal feminine here transformed to a vision of homosexual love, for it was the moment in the garden that finally allowed Aschenbach to know the meaning of his passion for Tadzio, the boy, the image of perfect beauty, the god, Aschenbach's way to knowledge. Aschenbach dies here, but not in disgrace or tragically, but rather transcendently. In the *Symposium*, once again, the meaning of his death is made clear:

> Drawing towards contemplation of the vast sea of beauty, he will create many fair and noble thoughts and discourses in boundless love and wisdom, until on the shore he grows and waxes strong. . . . he who, ascending from earthly things under the influence of true love begins to perceive beauty, is not far from the end.[17]

A description, certainly, of the life, and death, of Aschenbach.

IV

Aschenbach stands on the edge of a vast sea of beauty, invited into an immensity of richest expectation. We will see in what follows that the rites of the sea, of purification and transformation by water, are one of the central rituals of Arcadian life. With this ceremony will go symbolic union: that marriage of which Plato speaks, celebrated now in Arcadia. We have seen it in its most poetic form in the pages of "Death in Venice." But we have also seen something of the symbolic event in *The City and the Pillar* and *The Divided Path*: the sexual union is consummated only after a baptismal dip in the swimming hole.

In Forster's *Room with a View* (1908), the Reverend Beebe accompanies George and Freddy for a swim. The two handsome, naked young men cavort in the water, the clergyman stands on the shore. Beebe has been described as one who was, "for rather profound reasons," somewhat "chilly toward the other sex."[18] Eventually he joins the young men in the water. As he stands on the edge of the pool, he observes, "We despise the body less than women do. But not until we are comrades shall we enter the garden" (p. 134). For him, perhaps, the "garden" is Eden and his reference is biblical. But for Forster, the use of the image of water and the garden, and the use of the word *comrades*, invoking as it does numerous variations on "the manly love of comrades," can only be a clear indication of Beebe's homosexual meaning, another case of the subtext defining the innocent text.

Beebe makes his pronouncement, and then strips and swims. He smiled, "flung himself at them, splashed them, ducked them, kicked them, muddied them, and drove them out of the pool" (p. 139). As Forster explains it: "It had been a call to the blood, and to the relaxed will, a passing benediction whose influence did not pass, a holiness, a spell, a momentary chalice of youth" (p. 141). The religious language is no accident. This moment transforms Beebe and releases his homosexual impulses; and as such, in the garden where they can be comrades, it is a religious rite. Now that Beebe is purified, he can be a comrade with George and Freddy and then, presumably, enter the garden.

Scenes of boys bathing are unquestionably a genre of homosexual art and literature. Tuke's celebrated painting *August Blue* (1894), a picture of four boys, nude and sunbathing in a boat on the river, was the occasion of several poems by English Uranians.[19] Alan Stanley's "August Blue" and Charles Kains-Jackson's "Sonnet on a Picture by Tuke" are examples; one of the best is Frederick Rolfe's melodic "Ballade of Boys Bathing." A prime example of the genre was printed in *The Artist*, a magazine that devoted itself, especially under the editorship of Kains-Jackson, to homosexual poetry and fiction. This was S. S. Saale's sonnet of 1890, which links the miracle of transformation by water, a kind of homosexual baptism, to legends of Greek mythology.

> Upon the wall, of idling boys in a row
>   The grimy barges not more dull than they,
>   When sudden in the midst of all their play
> They strip and plunge into the stream below:
> Changed by a miracle, they rise as though
>   The youth of Greece burst on this later day
>   As on their lithe young bodies many a ray
> Of sunlight dallies with its blushing glow.
> Flower of clear beauty, naked purity,
>   With thy sweet presence olden days return,
>   Like fragrant ashes from a classic urn,
> Flashed into life anew once more we see
> Narcissus by the pool, or 'neath the tree
>   Young Daphnis, and new pulses throb and burn.[20]

The dull boys are transformed into Grecian youths and the grimy urban Thameside into a paradise resplendent with rural and Arcadian sunlight, the same sunlight that will later shine, incidentally, on the burnished body of Paul in *The Divided Path* as he walks with "Arcadian naturalness." If the poet recalls the pool of Narcissus, and Daphnis in his grove, so too are we reminded of Tadzio, who in "Death in Venice" will rise from the water "with dripping locks, beautiful as a tender young god" (p. 33).

The homosexual content of Saale's sonnet lies not in any overt sexuality but, first, in a code that includes phrases like "clear beauty," "sweet presence," and "naked purity"; second, in references to homosexual myth (Narcissus and Daphnis); and last, in the dominant metaphor of the poem, the transformation by water, turning dull boys into lithe ephebes. Similarly, such elements of homosexual discourse can be found in poetry even less obviously homosexual in content. For Gerard Manley Hopkins, the homosexual discourse was one that exerted considerable fascination and produced no inconsiderable pain and evasion. But in his "Epithalamion,"[21] an unfinished poem ostensibly written in celebration of heterosexual marriage, the dominant metaphor and attending imagery are concerned with just those matters under discussion here. Though Hopkins tacks onto the end of the poem a few incomplete and not entirely clear lines — perhaps fragmentary — about wedlock and spousal love, they are half-hearted and do not have the passionate force of the homosexual elements of the bulk of the poem.

To begin, Hopkins invokes the "hearer" to "hear what I do." Though the image is conventional in its invocation of a muse at first consideration, a muse is generally thought of as the inspirer, not the hearer. Not to put too fine a point on it, we might be reminded that in Greek custom and poetry the beloved youth was called the "hearer" and his lover the "inspirer." As Hans Licht, the pseudonymous Paul Brandt, notes in *Sexual Life in Ancient Greece*: "In the Dorian dialect, the usual word for the lover was . . . the 'inspirer,' which contains the hint that the lover, who indeed was responsible for the boy in every connection, inspired the young receptive soul with all that was good and noble. . . . with this the Dorian name for the loved boy, the 'listening, the intellectually receptive,' agrees."[22]

For his hearer, Hopkins the inspirer conjures up a truly wondrous greenwood. "Make believe," he says,

> We are leafwhelmed somewhere with the hood
> of some branchy bunchy bushybowered wood
> Southern dene or Lancashire clough or Devon cleave,
> That leans along the loins of hills, where a candy-colored
> > where a blue-brown
> Marbled river, boisterously beautiful, between
> Roots and Rocks is dance and dandled, all in froth
> > and water
> > blowbells, down.

In the river, "boys from the town" are bathing. "It is summer's sovereign good." Into this noisy scene comes a "listless stranger" who watches and is so inspired by the "bellbright bodies," the "garland of their gambols flashes in his breast/ Into such a sudden zest," that he

hies to a pool neighboring; sees it is the best
    There; sweetest, freshest, shadowiest;
Fairyland; silk-beech, scrolled ash, packed sycamores
    wild wychelm, hornbeam fretty overstood
By.

While the boys from town bathe in the real world, the listless stranger's pool is in Fairyland, surely Arcadia, a happy valley surrounded by Virgilian forests and fragrant with Marlovian posies.

Of course, the listless stranger is one with the unhappy Corydon. And, like the boys in Saale's sonnet, and like the Reverend Beebe, he will strip and plunge into the miraculous pool.

Off with — down
    he dings
His bleached both and woolen wear:
Careless these in colored wisp
All lie tumbled-to; then loop-locks
Forward falling, forehead frowning, lips crisp
Over fingers teasing task, his twiny boots
Fast he opens, last offwrings
Till walk the world he can with bare his feet. . . .

Striding naked, in command of the world in sudden liberation, he dives into the water and into communion with the bathing boys and with the innocence of the happy valley:

Here he will then, here he will the
    Flinty feet kindcold element let break across his limbs
Long. When we leave him, froliclavish, while he looks about
    him, laughs, swims

The image is striking. In one pool the naked boys frolic; in the next, the stranger. The naked stranger is inspired by the beauty of the boys; he enters the secret garden, Fairyland, and dives into the pool of miracles. He is transfigured. No longer listless, he is "froliclavish." He laughs and is liberated, purified by water.

"What is this delightful dene," Hopkins asks. "This is sacred matter that I mean." His answer is that the delightful dene is "wedlock." "What is water," he inquires. The answer: "Spousal love." The answers are curiously out of context in a poem where a naked male stranger is revived from his spiritual decline by the sight of bathing naked boys and in which he is drawn into refreshing communion with these boys in a baptismal pool, this all taking place in our now-classic homosexual Arcadian grove.

Hopkins compounds the confusion at the end with a fragmentary observation: "Father, mother, brothers, sisters, friends? Into fairy trees, wild flowers, wood ferns/ Ranked round the bower." This is distinctly unhelpful; in fact, I think, deliberately misleading. Yet he tells the truth when he says that "This is sacred matter that I mean." For the poem describes one of the sacred rituals of Arcadia: wedlock. The poem celebrates a moment of revelation in the greenwood where young men and boys are united in spousal love, where the listless stranger is transformed by the purifying waters of homosexual passion. The poem is an epithalamion indeed, and we are hearers to Hopkins' inspirer if we only have the ears.

V

All of the elements of the Arcadian metaphor come together in two poems by Whitman, "In Paths Untrodden" and "These I Singing in Spring." Like Corydon, who seeks out his "beeches with their shady summits" to sing his passionate song, or like Hopkins' "listless stranger" who seeks out the "sweetest, freshest, shadowiest" pool, Whitman, who elsewhere is the "solitary singer," seeks out "paths untrodden,/ In the growth by the margins of pond waters" (p. 112). His purpose in finding this isolated retreat is to "escape from the life that exhibits itself," and "from all the standards hitherto published, from the pleasures,/ profits, conformities,/ Which too long I was offering to feed my soul." In this place he is alone, "away from the clank of the world."

Two elements are present here: the world of real life, which demands a certain conformity of appearance, and the world of the spirit, which is ill fed by the standards of that world. Physical and spiritual yearnings, then, call Whitman to his untrodden paths, his hidden pond waters. The typical Arcadian paradigm is again established: the lonely retreat, and the miraculous pool. Why does he come here? Like all the others, "in this secluded spot I can respond as I would not dare elsewhere" (p. 112). But what is it that he would not dare to speak of amidst the conformity of the real world? Three things: "standards not yet published," the fact that he "rejoices in comrades," and that "strong upon me" is "the life that does not exhibit itself." That all three of these are references to homosexuality has been ignored by many critics, denied by several, and should be perfectly clear to all. The most obvious phrase, "rejoices in comrades," had such a general homosexual use in the nineteenth century that its meaning is almost unavoidable, even if Whitman did not make it even more clear at the end of the poem and in other poems in the "Calamus" group, such as "For you O Democracy," with its refrain "by the love of comrades,/ By the manly love of comrades" (p. 117). More oblique than this are "the standards not yet published" and the "life that does not exhibit itself." Obvious to any gay person, the standards not published are the standards of homosexual life and all its works, manners, and feelings. The "standards hitherto published," standards of heterosexual morality, are not useful to the soul of a man like Whitman. The standards of his own soul, the qualitites that make him homosexual not only in sexual orientation but in sensibility — what we now call gay — are not, indeed cannot be, openly published. Similarly, the "life that does not exhibit itself" is certainly Whitman's phrase for the hidden gay sensibility, and it is the life, necessarily secret and secretive, that any nineteenth-century homosexual had to lead. But not only that, it must also be the life of the spirit that Whitman has had to conceal, and which he reveals in his poems, especially in this poem, a manifesto declaring his homosexuality and its purpose. This hidden life, he says dramatically, "contains all the rest," a singular statement revealing Whitman's deep awareness of how homosexuality informs, and becomes a dominating metaphor for, each individual life. That all this cannot be spoken in the real world demands that he repair to this secluded spot.

Like Corydon inspired to song in his fastness, Whitman is "resolv'd to sing no songs to-day but those of manly/ attachment" (p. 112). Here, surrounded by "tongues aromatic" — the calamus — and of course all that other fragrant verdure we have seen in so many other Arcadian moments, he discovers the purpose of his life and the reason for his homosexuality: to bequeath "hence types of athletic love." (These types are of course his poems about homosexual love. "Athletic love" was to become another nineteenth-century commonplace standing for homosexuality.[23]) His mission is to sing the songs of manly attachment and, like the Grecian inspirer, to "proceed for all who are or have been young men," that is, to be the spokesman for all those who have not dared to speak, to educate them into the proper meaning of the virtuous homosexual life. To do this, he determines to undertake the breathtaking task of telling the "secrets of my nights and days," to be the celebrant of the "need of comrades." For Whitman, the experience in the garden frees him and sets him upon his appointed path: a creator spirit, come from paths untrodden to sing the most remarkable coming-out poem in our literature.

But if Arcadia serves as the scene for personal discovery and revelation, we have seen that it is also the place where a spiritual voyager can find a safe haven with others like himself and celebrate their common rites. So, in "These I Singing in Spring" (p. 118), we find Whitman talking of what Hopkins called "sacred matter," what Forster described as "a holiness, a spell, a momentary chalice of youth." Whitman begins the ritual by collecting tokens "for lovers." He asks: "Who but I should understand lovers and all their sorrows and joy?/ Who but I should be the poet of comrades?" The search for tokens, we recall, is common to many of the works we have examined; the tokens are the wedding gifts that Corydon, the passionate shepherd, and Daphnis collected. His search for tokens leads Whitman into the "garden of the world." And soon, he says, "I pass the gates" into the world of the greenwood. The magic of pastoral rules, "along the pond-side . . . far, far, in the forest." He had thought himself alone, but "soon a troop gathers round me." This is his troop of bathing boys, his ideal friends. He distributes his tokens to them, moss from the live oak (which, as he has noted elsewhere in "I Saw in Louisiana a Live-Oak Growing," "Makes me think of manly love"), lilac, pine, and sage, tokens like those Corydon brings to his Alexis. The significant moment, the moment of revelation — here nearly a eucharistic climax — comes when he draws from the water the aromatic calamus root, symbol of phallic homosexuality, physical and spiritual. Whitman is reminded now of *his* lover, "him that tenderly loves me, and returns again never to separate from me." Memory and desire flood in as he offers the calamus to his troop of young men in a sacred ceremony. This calamus is the "token of comrades. . . . Interchange it youths with each other! never render it back." So complex is this moment that it combines communion in both a spiritual and a religious sense — in wedlock, of Whitman to his troop of young men and of Whitman to his lover who will soon return, and in a plighting of vows: "Interchange it youths! never render it back." The vow is to eternal fidelity not only to one another but to the homosexual life itself, for the calamus is the symbol of that life.

Of all the moments of climax and communion that we have seen in various manifestations in the Arcadian garden, this is the most intense because it is the most highly charged with ritual and myth. There, in the greenwood, in the "far, far forest," which Whitman describes as redolent with "twigs of maple and a bunch of wild orange and chestnut,/ and stems of currants and plum blows, and aromatic cedar," this natural incense rising to heaven, Whitman celebrates his erotic communion. Like Hopkins' "riot of . . . boys from town," Whitman's acolytes are a "thick cloud of spirits." They stand in Arcadia at its altar, next to the water of calamus, Whitman's Ladon. Whitman distributes his sacred token, the sacrament of calamus. Hopkins was specific: this cleansing by water means wedlock and is sacred matter. Whitman is equally clear: the calamus he draws from his pond-side is given "only to them that love as I myself am capable of loving." The poet has bound himself and his troop of friends by tokens and sacred oaths to the love of comrades. His words are the testament; calamus is the symbol and outward sign of that inward grace which can only be found in the leafy greenwood bower of a secret Arcadia.

VI

I hope that this paper will suggest to other students some areas for exploration in the examination of that term which seems to be so real to all of us who engage in the pursuit of gay history, but which so often seems difficult to define precisely: *the gay sensibility*. For surely the mythology and the symbolic acts of our literature contribute not only to the texture of that sensibility but to its definition as well.

Concerning the subject of this essay, it may be said that the myth of Arcadia is almost a quasi-religious requirement of the human psyche, in all climes and cultures, and whatever the sexual preference. But for gay people — or homosexuals, or Uranians, or whatever name we have used for ourselves at various times in history — Arcadia has seemed to be a special kind of metaphor, relevant to the conditions of our lives and spirits. We have adapted it to our own needs, to express the yearnings and secret desires of a sexual, emotional, and intellectual minority, embellishing it with the products of our pen. Thus, while the Arcadian myth is only one element in the much larger tapestry of the homosexual imagination, it is a myth that speaks directly to our minds and hearts.

NOTES

[1] Walt Whitman, *Leaves of Grass,* ed. Sculley Bradley and Harold Blodgett (1965; rpt. New York: W. W. Norton, 1973), p. 112. All references to Whitman hereinafter are from this edition.

[2] Sometimes the implicit approaches the explicit. For example, in 1873, Walter Pater included an essay on Johann Winckelmann in his book *The Renaissance.* In what is one of the earliest, if oblique, references to the homosexual imagination, Pater notes that Winckelmann's "affinity for Hellenism was not merely intellectual. . . . The subtler threads of temperament were inwoven in it, as proved by romantic, fervent friendships with young men" (Walter Pater, *The Renaissance* [1873; rpt. New York: Modern Library, n.d.], p. 158). As an epigraph for this essay, Pater inscribed: "Et ego in Arcadia fui" (p. 147).

Some years before, John Addington Symonds had found himself involved in a fervent friendship with a young man. The youth was named G. H. Shorting, and we are told he had long and curling yellow hair. Symonds pursued Shorting, as he said, because he detected that they both shared similar tastes. "Arcadian tastes," he called them (Phyllis Grosskurth, *The Woeful Victorian: A Biography of John Addington Symonds* [New York: Holt, Rinehart and Winston, 1964], p. 58). Oscar Wilde, writing to Douglas from his prison cell, referred to "Sicilian and Arcadian airs" to get around the censors (Rupert Hart-Davis, ed., *The Letters of Oscar Wilde* [New York: Harcourt Brace, 1962]). See Wilde's remarkable letter to Douglas (pp. 423-511), which is an evocation of the themes of the homosexual sensibility.

[3] Virgil, *Eclogues II*, trans. H. Rushton Fairclough, Loeb Classical Library, quoted in *Eros: An Anthology of Male Friendship*, ed. Alistair Sutherland and Patrick Anderson (New York: Citadel Press, 1963), p. 83.

[4] The poetry of Richard Barnfield (1574-1627) can be found in Sutherland and Anderson, and in my anthology *Hidden Heritage: History and the Gay Imagination* (New York: Irvington Press, 1980), pp. 141 ff.

[5] Christopher Marlowe, *The Complete Poems and Translations*, ed. Stephen Orgel (1971; rpt. Harmondsworth: Penguin, 1973), p. 209. All references to Marlowe's poetry are to this edition.

[6] Bayard Taylor, *Joseph and His Friend* (New York: 1870), p. 216. All references to the novel are to this edition. For an excellent discussion of Taylor's presumed homosexuality, see Robert K. Martin, *The Homosexual Tradition in American Poetry* (Austin: Univ. of Texas, 1979), pp. 97 ff.

[7]E. M. Forster, *Maurice*(New York: New American Library, 1971), p. 135. All references to the novel are to this edition.

[8]Nial Kent, *The Divided Path* (New York: Greenberg, 1949), p. 179. All references to the novel are to this edition.

[9]Kent, p. 179.

[10]Kent, p. 179.

[11]Gore Vidal, *The City and the Pillar* (New York: Signet/New American Library, 1948), p. 24. All references to the novel are to this edition.

[12]When Vidal revised the book in 1965, he changed this passage to read: "When Jim looked at Bob's body, he felt as if he were looking at an ideal brother, a twin. . . ."; interesting in light of my comments to follow.

[13]Plato, *Symposium*, trans. Benjamin Jowett (New York: Pocket Books, n.d.). The Jowett translation, available in many editions, should always be compared to later, and more frank, translations, such as that by Walter Hamilton in the Penguin Classics series. Hamilton renders the passage that Jowett translates as "they hang about men and embrace them" as: "they love men throughout their boyhood, and take pleasure in physical contact with men." In this essay all references are to the Jowett translation as the most familiar to most readers. I quote from the selection in Fone, p. 19.

[14]Thomas Mann, "Death in Venice," in *Death in Venice and Other Stories*, trans. H. T. Lowe-Porter (New York: Vintage, 1954), pp. 33-34. All references to the story in the text are to this edition.

[15]Xavier Mayne [pseud. of Edward Prime Stevenson], *Imre: A Memorandum* (Naples: 1906). Best found in the Arno reprint of 1975, from which all references are taken. See pp. 80 ff. for Imre/Mayne's views on homosexuality.

[16]Homosexual images abound from the beginning. The original of the garden is seen in Aschenbach's early vision, a garden "swollen, monstrous, rank," phallic in its suggestions (p. 5). The strange traveler in the cemetery stares at him with a bold glance, which Aschenbach takes for hostility, but which, from a homosexual standpoint, contains the seeds of sexual invitation. Aschenbach's ideal hero is likened to Sebastian. (St. Sebastian was the subject of a recent film in which his rumored homosexuality was exploited. A subject for painters, among them Giovanni Bazzi, Sebastian seems to have found a special place in the gay imagination. See Tennessee Williams' *Suddenly Last Summer* as an example.) On the boat to Venice, the obviously homosexual old man, described as "goat bearded," offends Aschenbach. But he is clearly what he is, and if more were needed, he wears a red cravat, a symbol of homosexuality. (The red cravat as a sign of homosexuality is attested to in a 1915 letter of Havelock Ellis', who notes that in America "it is notable that of recent years there has been a fashion for a red tie to be adopted as a symbol of inverts as their badge. . . . 'It is red,' writes an American correspondent, himself inverted, 'that has become almost a synonym for sexual inversion. . . .'" See Jonathan Katz, *Gay American History* (New York: Thomas Y. Crowell, 1976), p. 52. That the old man and Tadzio both wear red ties ought to be considered in light of this letter, roughly contemporaneous with Mann's story.) As he nears Venice, it is the homosexual poet Von Platen whom Aschenbach thinks to quote, recalling the *Venetian Sonnets* of that poet, explicitly homosexual in their content, indeed celebratory of Von Platen's love for a young gondolier. The gondolier whom Aschenbach engages insists that the "seignore will pay," which Aschenbach takes as a threat, but which reminds us that Venetian gondolieri were notoriously loose with their sexual favors, and often for money. From the moment Tadzio is encountered wearing a red tie, the allusions to classical homosexuality arise unbidden but unchecked in Aschenbach's imagination. Tadzio reminds him of the noblest moment of Greek sculpture. Is that Eros? His twilight-gray eyes stare at Aschenbach. The eyes of Achilles? Tadzio is literally surrounded by Platonic references — to the *Symposium*, to the *Phaedrus* — and images of Zeus and Ganymede, Apollo and Hyacinth, and Narcissus are invoked. All of this leads to that scene in the garden, when what has been clear to the reader finally becomes clear to Aschenbach.

[17]Plato, p. 26.

[18]E. M. Forster, *A Room with a View* (London: 1955), p. 38. All references to the novel are to this edition, which is cited in Jeffrey Meyers' illuminating essay on Forster in his equally illuminating book, *Homosexuality and Literature (1890-1930)* (London: Univ. of London/Athelone Press, 1977), pp. 90 ff.

[19]The best book on the English Uranian poets and prose writers is *Love in Earnest* by Timothy d'Arch Smith (London: Routledge and Kegan Paul, 1970).

[20]S. S. Saale, "Sonnet," quoted in *Sexual Heretics*, ed. Brian Reade (New York: Coward McCann, 1970), p. 228.

[21]Gerard Manley Hopkins, *Poems and Prose: A Selection*, ed. W. H. Gardner (Harmondsworth: Penguin, 1953), p. 85. All references to Hopkins are to this edition.

[22]Hans Licht [pseud. of Paul Brandt], *Sexual Life in Ancient Greece* (London: Routledge and Kegan Paul, 1932), p. 415.

[23]The phrase appears often as a euphemism for homosexuality. Pater's essay, "The Age of Athletic Prizemen," from *Greek Studies* (1895) suggests it, and Forster in *Maurice* has Maurice know the "impossibility of vexing athletic love" (p. 111).

Edward Carpenter and the Double Structure of *Maurice*

Robert K. Martin, Ph.D.

Maurice remains E. M. Forster's least appreciated novel largely because it is also his least understood novel. Because of the wide attention paid to the book's revelation of Forster's homosexuality, readers have not accorded it the serious attention they have paid to Forster's other works. The novel has been taken simply as a plea for homosexual rights on the part of a homosexual writer. And, as a didactic work, it has been thought to lack the qualities of subtlety and irony that mark Forster's other novels.

Despite Forster's acknowledgment that *Maurice* "was the direct result of a visit to Edward Carpenter,"[1] readers have not fully explored the significance of that source. It has regularly been supposed that the novel is concerned primarily with an opposition between homosexuality and heterosexuality and that the views expressed by Clive in the first half of the book may be taken to represent the author's.[2] In fact, the novel opposes two kinds of homosexuality — one that is identified with Cambridge and Clive, and one that is identified with Alec and the open air — and uses the opinions on homosexual love expressed by Clive to indicate a stage in Maurice's development, but one that does not represent the author's concept of the final stage of development: this Maurice can achieve only through the encounter with Alec. *Maurice* is not a plea for homosexual rights, but an exploration of the growth in awareness of a homosexual protagonist, who moves from a false solution to a truer one.

The novel is divided into roughly equal parts, each of which is then again divided in two, to provide the four parts identified by Forster. The first half of the book is devoted to the Maurice-Clive relationship, to suburban life, and to Cambridge. Similarly, the second half of the book is devoted to the Maurice-Alec relationship, to the opposition of gentry

Robert K. Martin, who was born in Bryn Mawr, was educated at Wesleyan University and at Brown University, where he received a Ph.D. in American Civilization. He is now Associate Professor of English and Director of Graduate Studies in English at Concordia University in Montreal. He is the author of *The Homosexual Tradition in American Poetry* (Texas, 1979) and co-editor of *E. M. Forster: Centenary Revaluations* (Macmillan, 1982).

35

and servants, and to the country house, Penge. The first is dominated by Plato and, indirectly, by John Addington Symonds and the apologists for "Greek love";[3] the second is dominated by Edward Carpenter and his translation of the ideas of Walt Whitman. The two sections run almost exactly parallel: Part I ends with Maurice entering Clive's window in response to his call; Part III concludes with Alec entering Maurice's room in response to a similar call. Part II concludes with dawn, the hoped-for new light that ironically brings the death of the love between Maurice and Clive; Part IV ends with sunset, the apparent darkness that ironically brings life and the surivival of the love of Maurice and Alec.

Although Forster's concept of homosexuality was not fully developed until he had absorbed the ideas of Carpenter, some of the elements that are present in *Maurice* can be traced back at least a decade earlier. For instance, the story "Ansell," probably written in 1902 or 1903, treats in abbreviated version some of the important themes of the later novel. Ansell himself recurs in *Maurice* as George, the garden boy about whose departure Maurice's mother lies and who serves as a foreshadowing of Alec. By the time of the composition of this story, Forster had already come to see a possible link between a homosexual love that crossed class barriers and the questioning of the assumptions based on class, including the expectation of worldly success.[4] Although we do not know the exact date at which Forster first read Whitman's poetry (the first diary mention we know of is for 1907), the story is similar in its implications to a number of poems from the "Calamus" sequence, notably "When I heard at the close of the day" with its opposition of the satisfactions of a personal love to those of fame.[5]

During the early years of his awareness of himself as a homosexual, Forster was concerned with understanding the nature of a homosexual literary tradition. Signs of this are evident in *The Longest Journey*, his novel conceived in 1904 and published in April 1907. The allusion to Theocritus, whom Rickie "believed to be the greatest of Greek poets,"[6] underscores the novel's ironic contrast between the actualized pastoral of Stephen, the "real" shepherd, and the pseudo-Greek spirit of late-Victorian England and its public schools. Rickie fails to understand Theocritus' significance as a poet of pastoral love between two men, but the reader makes use of the allusion as a way of measuring Rickie's lack of self-knowledge and the gap between Theocritus' time and the present. The reference to Shakespeare's Sonnet CXVI, when Rickie is reported to think "he wished there was a society, a kind of friendship office, where the marriage of true minds could be registered,"[7] serves to heighten and dignify Rickie's plight, as well as to remind us of the way in which homosexual art can be turned to the purpose of a heterosexual society.

Forster's means of establishing a homosexual tradition was the one that has often been followed: he made a list of famous homosexual authors. Such a list is in part a gesture toward the alleviation of the radical loneliness that may confront the homosexual following the acknowledgment of his or her own nature. It is also the raw material out of which can be built a sense of history, an understanding of how others have dealt with a similar situation. Because Forster limited his listmaking to homosexual artists, it is clear that he was especially aware of the problems he would face if he were to deal with his homosexuality in his art (as he had begun to do in a conscious manner in *The Longest Journey*). Forster's list (an entry in his diary for New Year's Eve 1907) is given in part in a footnote in Furbank's biography. Furbank terms it simply "a further book list," but a glance at the list makes its real purpose clear. The names are: Sturge Moore, A. E. Housman, Symonds, Pater, Shakespeare, Beddoes, Walt Whitman, E. Carpenter, Samuel Butler, Fitzgerald, Marlowe.[8] Forster's reading during this period was directed in part toward discovering a homosexual literary tradition. What he found in his own time was largely the schoolboy novel, with its celebration of a wistful and impossible love between boys. He knew at least four examples of such novels: A.E.W. Clarke's *Jaspar Tristram*; H.N. Dickinson's *Keddy*; H.O. Sturgis' *Tim*, published anonymously, and Desmond Coke's public school and college novels, pseudonymously published as by "Belinda Blinders." Something of their spirit may well have contributed to the Cambridge scenes of *The Longest Journey* and *Maurice*. Forster's knowledge of this tradition contributes to our recognition that the homosexual allusions and implications of *The Longest Journey* were intentional. The schoolboy novels display a characteristic emphasis on hopeless love, one which Forster retained for *The Longest Journey* but abandoned for *Maurice*.

What sent Forster back to this material six years later was his celebrated visit to Edward Carpenter and George Merrill at Milthorpe. It was this visit that caused Forster to, as it were, rewrite *The Longest Journey*. In its new version the character of Ansell is transformed into Clive, and that of Stephen into Alec. As in the earlier version, it is neither Cambridge nor Sawston that shall prevail, but Wiltshire (Penge is on the border of Wiltshire and Somerset, and Sawston is not unlike Alfridge Gardens in its embodiment of suburban values). Rural England, under the surface of its county families, retains a heritage that is close to that of rural Greece, as the characters of Stephen and Alec demonstrate. What Carpenter's influence meant for Forster was a reexamination of the homosexual tradition he had been constructing, and a revision of it. In the first half of *Maurice* the attitudes of Symonds prevail: homosexuality is defined as a higher form of love, and its spiritual superiority is preserved by its exclusion of physical consummation. In the second half of the book, which presents homosexual love as viewed under the influence of Carpenter, homosexuality is seen to include physical love, and whatever superiority it may possess over heterosexuality is now related to its social consequences, to its provision of an outlaw status for even its most respectable adherents. It seems likely that in depicting these two aspects to Maurice's development Forster is working out of his own life. For it was surely Carpenter more than anyone who helped Forster to an awareness of his own need for a relationship at once spiritual and physical.

The first half of *Maurice* is concerned with tracing the false vision of an idealized homosexuality. We perceive its falseness, however, only after we have followed Maurice through his sense of confusion and his apparent salvation in the arms of Clive. By adopting a narrative method that is related to James's "point of view," but with considerably more authorial intrusion, Forster forces the reader to follow Maurice up his wrong path and to feel with him the pain that ensues upon its dead-ending.

Part I illustrates the unreliability of school and university as guides to conduct in the sexual realm. The first chapter, for instance, exposes Mr. Ducie as a pious fraud, who asserts a brave sexual honesty but is actually embarrassed at the thought that someone may find his sexual diagram in the sand. Maurice knows enough to recognize Ducie as a liar and coward, but not enough to know the truth about sexuality. Thus the act of betrayal, when Ducie promises enlightenment but offers none, opens a world of darkness: "the darkness that is primeval but not eternal, and yields to its own painful dawn" (p. 9). Teachers cannot give Maurice the light that he needs, and when Ducie invites Maurice *and his wife* to dinner in ten years' time, he not only expresses the conventional assumption that everyone is heterosexual, but also prepares for one of the central ironies of the book. For it is precisely ten years later that Maurice meets Alec, and although the two do not take Ducie up on his invitation, they do meet him in the British Museum.[9] On that occasion Mr. Ducie gets his facts wrong again, calling Maurice Wimbleby, and Maurice finally renounces his past, his previous identity, by momentarily assuming Alec's name. Cambridge provides no higher standard of intellectual integrity: at the Dean's translation class, a passage is omitted because it is "a reference to the unspeakable vice of the Greeks" (p. 42). The same Dean will send Maurice down because he sees it as his duty "to spoil a love affair" between two students when he has the chance (p. 70). One of the ironies on which Forster insists throughout this section is that such attitudes persist in a culture that is officially so classicizing. Maurice, we recall, gave the Greek Oration on his school's Prize Day, delivering a speech in praise of war ("The Greek was vile: Maurice had got the prize on account of the Thought," p. 18) and receiving a copy of Grote's *History of Greece* as his prize. Thoroughly inbued with things Greek, and thus bolstering its own imperialism and militarism, English culture has nonetheless totally ignored the most striking fact about Greek society: its institutionalization of homosexual relationships.

As Maurice comes to recognize the inadequacy of education as a moral guide, he also comes to an understanding of his own sexual nature. This nature has been present since his earliest memories and is manifested in his two dreams, the one of the naked garden boy leaping over the woodstacks and the other of a face and a voice saying "That is your Friend."[10] It is also present in his schoolboy crushes, and it reasserts itself in his recognition of his need for friendship with Risley. Although he is not sexually attracted to Risley, he recognizes that the two share something, even though he is not yet able to give a name to it. Clive suggests that Maurice read *The Symposium*, but even this is apparently not enough to transform his suburban soul. His rejection of Clive, however, leads him to reexamine himself and come to terms with his own nature. He acknowledges the degree of self-deception that he has engaged in: his agony "worked inwards, till it touched the root whence body and soul both spring, the 'I' that he had been trained to obscure, and, realized at last, doubled its power and grew superhuman" (p. 51). This rediscovery of the personal self below the social self leads him to his resolve: "He would not — and this was the test — pretend to care about women when the only sex that attracted him was his own. He loved men and always had loved them" (p. 53).[11] Part I concludes with the dramatization of what we would now call Maurice's "coming out." But, because of his education, in which sexuality remains clandestine and unspoken, his emotional coming out is not accompanied by a similar physical expression. Clive remains his only model, and Clive's model is Plato. Thus the groundwork is laid by the false climax of Part I for the developing disaster of Part II.

Clive's expression of their love to Maurice in Part II reflects the language of the late nineteenth-century apologists for homosexuality. It is an argument derived essentially from *The Symposium*: "I feel to you as Pippa to her fiancé, only far more nobly, far more deeply, body and soul . . . a particular harmony of body and soul that I don't think women have even guessed" (p. 81). For Clive this higher love depends upon the renunciation of physical passion: "The love that Socrates bore Phaedo now lay within his reach, love passionate but temperate, such as only finer natures can understand . . ." (p. 89). The snobbishness of his responses is evident and seems an accurate depiction of the mainstream of homosexual defense at the turn of the century, and indeed up until the very recent past. The failure of Maurice's relationship with Clive provides an opportunity for Maurice to develop beyond these attitudes. Homosexuality, as expressed by Clive and as lived by Maurice and him, is a state reserved for a tiny élite of those with highly developed sensibilities. It effects no change in the homosexual. It encourages misogyny — Clive is, Forster tells us, even more misogynistic than Maurice. It allows the life of the "suburban tyrant" (p. 92) that Maurice is about to become. Its only concession to itself is a small part of time, apportioned off and reserved for the lover:

> But every Wednesday he slept at Clive's little flat in town. Weekends were also inviolable. They said at home, "You must never interfere with Maurice's Wednesdays or with his weekends. He would be most annoyed." (p. 93)

Despite Maurice's resolve not to go back on his nature, he lives his life as if he were heterosexual. Homosexuality remains a small, secret vice at the heart of an otherwise conventional life.

Although it is Clive's conversion to "normal" sexuality that brings an end to Maurice's dream for a time, everything has led the reader to expect such a failure. Even those images that seemed most positive are, upon closer inspection, often ironic. Take, for instance, the ride in the cycle and side-car. The apparently ecstatic prose conceals a sense of warning: "They became a cloud of dust, a stench, and a roar to the world, but the air they breathed was pure, and all the noise they heard was the long drawn cheer of the wind" (p. 66). In the self-absorption of their love, they fail to see the consequences of their action. Their reliance upon a machine, something that creates dirt, noise, and stench, should warn us of Forster's wry use of this scene. The escapade comes to an end when "the machine comes to a standstill among the dark black fields" (p. 67), Forster's cold term ("machine") signaling the opposition between nature and the products of an industrial society. Clive's recollection of the scene completes the irony: "Bound in a single motion, they seemed there closer to one another than elsewhere; the machine took on a life of its own, in which they met and realized the unity preached by Plato" (p. 71). The absurdity of the motorcycle and its side-car as image of the Platonic egg warns us of the inadequacies of this kind of "poeticizing" idealism as a guide to behavior, just as Ansell's realism (in *The Longest Journey*) ought to have served as a warning to the idealism of Rickie.

If the second section of the novel is devoted to an exploration of homosexual love in the atomosphere of late-Victorian Cambridge, the third part turns to an investigation of lust, the element totally excluded from the earlier relationship. Two episodes help to remind Maurice of his own sexual desires: once when he sees Dickie Barry asleep, "embraced and penetrated by the sun" (p. 134), and a second time when a handsome French client invites him to lunch. On the second occasion

Maurice's refusal to respond to the invitation is due to the influence of the Clive relationship: "The ethereal past had blinded him, and the highest happiness he could dream was a return to it." This past includes the rule that "their love, though including the body, should not gratify it" (p. 139), and so he is prevented from realizing the possibilities that confront him. Clive, too, although embracing heterosexuality, retains a prudishness about sexuality that makes his marriage shallow: "He never saw her naked, nor she him. They ignored the reproductive and digestive functions. [Here one should recall Maurice's nursing of Clive during his illness, which includes cleaning out his chamber pot. Their love does provide something of a triumph over squeamish respectability, at least for Maurice — Clive prefers a trained female nurse.] He had never itched to call a spade a spade, and though he valued the body the actual deed of sex seemed to him unimaginative, and best veiled in night. Between men it is inexcusable, between man and woman it may be practised since nature and society approve, but never discussed nor vaunted" (p. 151).

Maurice's visit to Penge demonstrates the extent to which he is unmoved by his sexuality. He remains an unbearable snob, and his snobbery is directed ironically at the man who will become his lover. His hard-heartedness is a response to his own misery: unwilling to face his own situation, he develops a philosophy of toughness that takes his personal defenses and applies them to the world. One may help the poor, he asserts, but only because poverty may injure society. Not because one loves the poor: that kind of soft-heartedness he leaves to the priest, Mr. Borenius. As Glen Cavaliero has remarked, Maurice confronts the "four guardians of society — the schoolmaster, the doctor, the scientist and the priest. All four in different ways condemn him, and not one of them can offer any help."[12] The irony of Mr. Borenius as an exponent of the gospel of love, while Maurice and Alec are about to make actual love in the Russet Room, is delightful, and it anticipates the central irony of "The Life to Come." Penge itself serves two simultaneous functions: as a house it represents the values of the English upper middle classes, values that are in serious disrepair but nonetheless muddle on in their unthinking, oppressive way; but as a place Penge is part of the English landscape and provides a way back into the natural world. Maurice is called outside by the scent of the primrose bushes and accidentally bumps into Alec. When he returns to the house, his head is covered with pollen.

The final scenes of Part III indicate a major change in direction. The first two parts were, as we saw, dominated by the image of dawn. Light was seen as a positive figure toward which Maurice was groping, and yet the only dawn that came was the one that culminated Part II, Clive's vision of his new heterosexuality. In the encounter with Alec, Maurice becomes aware of a new darkness: "not the darkness of a house which coops up a man among furniture, but the darkness where he can be free!" (p. 178). It is the darkness that calls Maurice to sensuality, the darkness that allows for Alec's visit to Maurice's bed. The light that prevails over their room at Penge is not of the sun but the moon. As Maurice's pollen-covered head indicates, the transformation in Maurice is in part a shift from Apollo to Dionysus, from light to darkness, from sun to moon, from science to art, from head to heart.

The Dionysian spirit evoked by Alec is subversive of all the values Maurice had lived by. He recognizes that events at Penge have paralleled those at Cambridge ("Risley's room had its counterpart in the wild rose and the evening primroses of yesterday, the side-car dash through the fens foreshadowed his innings at cricket," p. 191). But the episodes with Clive have not served to question any fundamental assumptions of society or even of their own lives. The affair with Clive was, in the common phrase, just a phase. The affair with Alec goes far deeper and is far more disturbing:

> . . . all that night his body yearned for Alec's, despite him. He called it lustful, a word easily uttered, and opposed it to his work, his family, his friends, his position in society. In that coalition must surely be included his will. For if the will can overleap class, civilization as we have made it will go to pieces. (p. 191)

The cricket game reestablishes the fundamental class structure of England, momentarily overturned by the night Maurice and Alec have spent together. Maurice comes to realize that his sympathies will finally be with his lover, not with his class (just as in his famous statement, so often used against him, Forster asserted his loyalty to his friend over his country). Maurice's love for Alec frees him from the stifling values of middle-class England and offers him the possibility of spiritual growth. Maurice confronts this when he sees the King and Queen passing and, following convention, removes his hat. The choice he sees is between the office and Sherwood Forest. It is Alec who provides the occasion, and the courage, to choose the Forest.[13]

The novel thus depicts three stages in Maurice's development. In the first, Maurice comes to accept homosexuality as an idealized friendship, as the expression of a pure and spiritual love. In the second he moves toward the acceptance of lust in the physical expression of homosexuality. In the final stage he begins to accept the social and political consequences of homosexuality. In this final stage he realizes that the outlawed state of the homosexual provides the privilege of a radical perspective on society. By creating a hero who is completely unexceptional, Forster calls attention to the possibility that homosexuality may provide growth for even the most conventional. Forster came to recognize the importance of this third stage largely through the influence of Carpenter. As we have seen, Forster was already aware of Carpenter by 1907, if not earlier; and he had an apparently intuitive grasp (based on personal experience) of the possible connections between homosexuality and democracy. Such views were by no means common at the time Forster was writing. They were limited almost exclusively to Whitman and his English disciple Carpenter. But Forster's visit to Carpenter, and his reading of him and Whitman, provided the basis for a novel that would attempt not to analyze the passage of a man from confused or repressed homosexuality to a blissful ideal homosexuality, but to juxtapose that development with another, much more significant one from the homosexuality of the *fin de siècle* aesthetes to the robust political homosexuality of Whitman and Carpenter.

A brief examination of *Love's Coming of Age* will shed some light on the role Carpenter played in the conception of *Maurice*. Carpenter's essay "Man the Ungrown" seems particularly pertinent. In it he concerns himself with "the men of the English-speaking well-to-do class" whose learning stops after public school. These men are, in Carpenter's analysis, permanent schoolboys who continue to run society by the rules of their school days. These men see no reason for equality in marriage, since for them, according to Carpenter, "it seems quite natural that our marriage and social institutions should lumber along over the bodies of women, as our commercial institutions grind over the bodies of the poor and our 'imperial' enterprise over the bodies of barbarian races."[14] The character of Clive is particularly influenced by Carpenter's analysis. He is Forster's illustration of the "ungrown" man, who has never learned to question any of the values of his class. Clive's marriage in *Maurice* is an illustration of the marriage of such a man. The novel's final words, "[he] returned to the house, to correct his proofs and to devise some method of concealing the truth from Anne" (p. 231), illustrate not the failure of marriage, but the failure of such a marriage, based on inequality and ignorance. Thus Norman Page's complaint that "it is surely a limitation of Forster's that he finds himself unable simply to make a place for the acceptance of homosexual love as an equal to heterosexual love, but must claim that it is superior and thus involves himself in the disparagement of marriage"[15] seems less than fair. The novel clearly rejects the idea of the superiority of homosexuality, an idea that is specifically Clive's and derived from Plato, while keeping the idea that homosexuality may provide the occasion for a growth in spiritual awareness. It is not, of course, that heterosexuals are denied the possibility of such growth; it is that they lack the impulse toward it, and that the institutions of heterosexuality, such as marriage, specifically work against growth. Marriage in Carpenter's view is linked to property, whereas homosexuality exists outside of class and ownership. Maurice's realization, "They must live outside class, without relations or money; they must work and stick to each other till death" (p. 233), is pure Carpenter — and, in turn, pure Whitman: recall the closing stanza of "Song of the Open Road":

> Camerado, I give you my hand!
> I give you my love more precious than money,
> I give you myself before preaching or law;
> Will you give me yourself? will you come travel with me?
> Shall we stick by each other as long as we live?

To the ungrown man of the middle class, Carpenter opposes the energetic workman, who provides "sympathy and affection" lacking in the upper classes. Something of this analysis lies behind the depiction of Alec, although there is also a great deal of Forster's personal mythology (after Alec, "now he knew very well what he wanted with the garden boy," p. 191) and something of the mythological structures one finds in other novels of this period (Alec as Dionysus or Pan). But above all, Carpenter gave him personal testimony to a love between two men, a love that had survived by moving outside society and through which a man of the upper middle classes had come to question the dominant image of homosexuality presented by the homosexual apologists.

Edward Carpenter thus brought an end to Forster's search for a homosexual tradition. For Carpenter seemed to create his own tradition, to offer a world where the homosexual could build a new social order. In the crucial passage in which Clive and Maurice discuss the role of desire in beauty and oppose Michelangelo to Greuze (copies of Greuze turn up in Dr. Barry's office, along with a Venus de Medici), Forster writes, "Their love scene drew out, having the inestimable gain of a new language. No tradition overawed the boys. No convention settled what was poetic, what absurd" (p. 83). Page has complained that this passage "works against"[16] the Greek references, but he ignores the way in which the novel itself works against these references. They are Clive's, not Maurice's, although Maurice will adopt them for a time, just as Michelangelo is an appropriate enthusiasm of Clive's, as of Symonds'. Whitman and Carpenter were the means by which Forster came to go beyond those traditions. Do Alec and Maurice have a cast of David in the boathouse? One assumes that their love does not require such appeals to authority, which would in any case be contrary to its spirit, in which two men face the world alone, free to create their lives as they please. That is the revolutionary part of *Maurice*, not its homosexuality, and it was that which Carpenter praised in his congratulatory letter to Forster: "I am so glad you end up on a major chord. I was so afraid you were going to let Scudder go at the last — but you saved him and saved the story, because the end tho' improbable is not impossible and is the one bit of real romance — which those who understand will love."[17] That "major chord," Forster's "happy ending," which he found "imperative," is a sign of Maurice's growth from the false values of Clive to the truer values of Alec. Successfully transforming the conventions of marriage fiction, Forster moves his Austen-like protagonist toward wisdom through courtship and concludes with a marriage that seals his moral growth. It was Carpenter who confirmed Forster in his sense of the "new" homosexual and who proposed the terms for Forster's dual perspective on homosexual love.

NOTES

[1]E. M. Forster, *Maurice* (Toronto: Macmillan, 1971), "Terminal Note" (1960), p. 235. All further citations are to this edition, a Canadian printing of the Edward Arnold edition, and are indicated in the text.

[2]One example of this confusion may be seen in Glen Cavaliero's complaint that although Maurice's relationship with Clive "disguises his true nature instead of revealing it," Forster "appears to endorse it for more than it proves to be worth" (*A Reading of E. M. Forster* [London: Macmillan, 1979], p. 134). An earlier, and more hostile, view is expressed by Jeffrey Meyers, who calls *Maurice* "a *roman à thèse* whose aim is to defend homosexual love" (*Homosexuality and Literature 1890-1930* [Montreal: McGill-Queen's Univ. Press, 1977], p. 101). His essay on *Maurice* repeatedly confuses Clive's and Maurice's statements.

[3]On Symonds, see Jeffrey Weeks, *Coming Out: Homosexual Politics in Britain, from the Nineteenth Century to the Present* (London: Quartet Books, 1977), pp. 47-56, and Symonds' *A Problem in Greek Ethics* (1883). In an 1893 letter to Carpenter, however, Symonds praised homosexuality as a leveler of social classes. The "nobler" view of homosexuality was one of the most striking aspects of the Uranians. See Timothy d'Arch Smith, *Love in Earnest* (London: Routledge & Kegan Paul, 1970).

[4]See my essay on "Ansell": "Forster's Greek: From Optative to Present Indicative," *Kansas Quarterly* IX (Spring 1977), 69-73. It is worth noting, given the emphasis in *Maurice* on the protagonist's being twenty-four years old when he meets Alec, that Forster was twenty-four in 1903, the probable year of composition of "Ansell."

[5]See my *The Homosexual Tradition in American Poetry* (Austin: Univ. of Texas Press, 1979).

[6]E. M. Forster, *The Longest Journey* (New York: Vintage Books, 1962), p. 4.

[7]Forster, *Journey*, p. 69.

[8]P. N. Furbank, *E. M. Forster: A Life* (New York: Harcourt, 1978), I, p. 159, n. 1. An examination of the actual diary entry reveals Forster placed a small question mark above Sturge Moore, and marks whose significance is unclear above Symonds, Shakespeare, and Butler. Above this list in the diary, but not reprinted by Furbank, is another list of four names: A. E. W. Clarke, Desmond Coke, H. N. Dickinson, Howard Sturgis. All of them are authors of schoolboy novels. Below the main list is a third list, on three lines: Tuke/ Luca Signorelli? Michelangelo, Cellini/ Loti. There are marks above Signorelli and Cellini. (Forster's diary is in King's College Library, Cambridge.)

[9]The scene in the British Museum treats comically the schoolmaster's ignorance of sexuality by referring to the statue of the five-legged Assyrian bull, a joke not unlike that of "The Classical Annex." It also takes the British Library to task, calling it "supposedly catholic" (p. 209), an apparent reference to the library's refusal to include Carpenter's *The Intermediate Sex* in its catalogue until forced to do so in 1913, the year of the first composition of *Maurice*.

[10]One source of this dream, as well as of the dawn imagery, is almost certainly Kenneth Grahame's *The Wind in the Willows*. Grahame is another example of the idealized, ethereal homosexuality that Maurice will grown beyond. Grahame's domestic/prophetic voice may be the source of the ecstatic prose that is partially parodied in *Maurice*.

[11]Again the analogies to Whitman are striking. Many poems in the "Calamus" sequence deal with the discovery of the real self beneath the facade of a social self. And the image of the root

I stared, then saw the light:
"Somewhere a Father Figure shakes his rod

At sons who have not sired a child?
Through our own spirit we can both proclaim
And shuffle off the blame
For how we live — that good enough?" . . .[2]

For the doctor, perhaps, but that very night Freud himself beseeches JM
and DJ via the board not to give away the key to their natures — and the
earthlings decide "never to forego, in favor of/ Plain dull proof, the
marvelous nightly pudding" ("Ephraim," p. 76).

If DJ and JM are the living principals of the drama, their counterparts
in heaven are their much-missed and dearly loved friends W. H. Auden
and Maria Mitsotáki. For two of the three volumes it seems Maria is the
only woman, much less the only heterosexual member of the quartet —
until in *Scripts for the Pageant* we learn she is an avatar of none other
than Plato! I'm not sure her guise as Maria is now meant to be dismissed
and forgotten; indeed JM continues to address her as *Maman* and she
goes on calling JM and DJ her ENFANTS. I suspect she's rather like one
of those Eastern deities who can be worshiped in whatever form is
more congenial to the devotee — as the male Avalokitesvara in India
or the goddess Kuan-Yin in China. As a matter of fact (or fancy), the
many rebirths every soul must undergo in Merrill's cosmos somewhat
undermine gay identity or women's consciousness as watertight subjec-
tivities and plunge one and all into the promiscuity of collective humanity. Nevertheless, the quartet of scholars in the trilogy who set out to
fathom the secrets of the universe, who master the lessons of God,
Nature, and the great angels — these students are three gay men and
one woman, Plato-as-Maria. The dead pair, Wystan and Maria, are on
the most courtly and affectionate terms with each other; they in turn
figure somewhat as parents to JM and DJ — parents and patrons and
guiding lights. The sort of love expressed all around — decorous,
teasing, edifying, at turns witty and grave — this love seems to me a
utopian vision of love, a vision most often glimpsed these days by
homosexuals, one that draws on the energies of both family love and
romantic love but transforms that vitality into something new, a sublime
sort of friendship. In *Mirabell* we watch that dramatic transformation
take place.

The human quartet is receiving instruction from 741, a bat; at an
unexpected moment the bat announces (in the capital letters of the ouija
board): "MY ASPECT WAVERS   YR KINDNESS KEEPS ME IN THIS
NEW FORM." JM asks, "You talk as if we saw you. *What* new form?"
and Maria announces: "MES ENFANTS HE HAS TURNED INTO A

PEACOCK."[3] Later, Wystan Auden explains that the transformation has occurred because of the crosscurrents of love among the four human beings: ". . . IF MM & I/ IMAGINE U, YOU US, & WHERE THE POWERS/ CRISSCROSS WE ALL IMAGINE 741 . . ." (p. 65). This exchanged crossfire of affectionate imaginings, of soundings and reverberations, of flashings and reflections — this exchange is the most exalted sort of love of comrades, a love enacted under the motto that to be is to be perceived. Mirabell (as 741 is renamed after his transformation) has chosen to appear as a peacock to the four friends precisely because that kind of bird is "SOMEWHAT ATHENIAN," i.e., queer (p. 64).

The most memorable and irrepressible minor characters are also lesbian or gay — Marius Bewley, Chester Kallman, Robert Morse, The Blessed Luca Spionari, Gertrude Stein and Alice Toklas. Indeed, we learn that in heaven there's an Athenian club "where you can get a drink and read/ The underground newspapers." Plato and Wystan are its "cochairpersons."[4] Merrill's whole tale is a bit like Proust's, in which virtually everyone turns out to be queer.

In Merrill this insistence is not whimsical (nor is it in Proust). It is not a sniggering insinuation, but a straightforward if somewhat bizarre consequence of a theory. The old religions, we learn, have worn out and will soon be replaced by the new faith of literature, "THAT FLAT WHITE PRINTED PAGE" (*Scripts*, p. 164). The high priest of this new religion, the Scribe, is necessarily homosexual. As 741 explains:

> LOVE OF ONE MAN FOR ANOTHER OR LOVE BETWEEN
>   WOMEN
> IS A NEW DEVELOPMENT OF THE PAST 4000 YEARS
> ENCOURAGING SUCH MIND VALUES AS PRODUCE THE
>   BLOSSOMS
> OF POETRY & MUSIC, THOSE 2 PRINCIPAL LIGHTS OF
> GOD BIOLOGY. LESSER ARTS NEEDED NO EXEGETES:
> ARCHITECTURE   SCULPTURE   THE MOSAICS & PAINT-
>   INGS THAT
> FLOWERED IN GREECE & PERSIA CELEBRATED THE
>   BODY.
> POETRY   MUSIC   SONG INDWELL & CELEBRATE THE
>   MIND . . .

A few lines later, 741 goes on to say:

> NOW MIND IN ITS PURE FORM IS A NONSEXUAL PASSION
> OR A UNISEXUAL ONE PRODUCING ONLY LIGHT.
> FEW PAINTERS OR SCULPTORS CAN ENTER THIS LIFE OF
>   THE MIND.

> THEY (LIKE ALL SO-CALLD NORMAL LOVERS) MUST
>   PRODUCE AT LAST
> BODIES   THEY DO NOT EXIST FOR ANY OTHER PURPOSE
>
> *(Mirabell,* p. 62)

Science, music, and literature, those celebrations and expressions of pure mind, will become the reigning religions in the future.

I'm not sure how many modern readers, even gay and lesbian readers, will feel comfortable with these formulations, which conceive of homosexuality as "nonsexual passion" and of heterosexuality as a stud service. If 741 propounds these grandiose and out-of-date theories, JM and DJ have a humbler and more amusing theory as to why they've been chosen as the means for justifying the ways of God to man:

> The blue room of an evening. Luminous
> Quiet in which a point is raised. DJ:
> What part, I'd like to ask Them, does sex play
> In this whole set-up? Why did They choose *us*?
> Are we more usable than Yeats or Hugo,
> Doters on women, who then went ahead
> To doctor everything their voices said?
> We haven't done that. JM: No indeed.
> Erection of theories, dissemination
> Of Thought — the intellectual's machismo.
> We're more the docile takers-in of seed.
> No matter what tall tale our friends emit,
> Lately — you've noticed — we just swallow it.
>
> *(Mirabell,* p. 60)

Still another explanation is presented later: that childless homosexuals become the natural transmitters of wisdom to the next generation — as spiritual, since never biological, parents. Even more ingenious is the imagery derived from printing that Wystan uses to make this point:

> KEEP IN MIND THE CHILDLESSNESS WE SHARE   THIS
>   TURNS US
> OUTWARD TO THE LESSONS & MYSTERIES   IT IS A
> FINE POINT: THE TYPE U SET JM, INVERTED &
>   BACKWARD,
> IS YET READ RIGHTSIDE UP ON THE BIOLOGICAL PAGE
>
> *(Mirabell,* p. 122)

The message JM is encoding in this poem may make more sense to his readers than to himself, since, as Auden puts it, "FOR THE LOVE/ U EXPERIENCE IS NOT THE STRAIGHTFORWARD FRONTAL LOVE/ MANY READERS INFER . . ." (*Mirabell*, p. 122). The "inversion" of homosexual love and experience, in short, can be read as a straightforward, right-side-up message by heterosexuals.

Perhaps the most striking insight of the trilogy is that each soul is cloned from a limited supply of original souls. In many cases an earlier soul must be doled out in small portions to many different new creatures. Still more remarkably, an individual can acquire *new* "soul densities" even after he or she is alive and in midcareer. This sense of sudden metamorphosis and rebirth, of radical transformation of the self, is more available to a gay poet than a straight, I'd contend — more available to someone who has had to invent his or her sexuality than to someone who has merely conformed to convention. Even more fundamentally, anyone who is gay and conscious must live with an abiding mystery, his or her own inexplicable but unremitting and incorrigible desires; intimacy with this mystery prepares the poet for the greater mysteries of the ouija board. The gay man, for example, is less guarded, less resisting, more humorous, pliable, resilient in his brushes with the cosmos, since he has been raised in that finishing school of social comedy, gay life, where he has learned to speak in the dialect of dialectics. Hegel taught us that all thinking is negation, the crucial second term that precedes synthesis. Negation begins when we begin to question "nature" and common sense, as any homosexual must do.

The current of gay sensibility also influences the tone of Merrill's trilogy, or rather supplies one note in the complex chord it sounds, a chord worthy of Scriabin, bristling with sharps and flats, an augmented eleventh flung across several octaves. Luca, Chester, and Robert are camps of the highest and most scandalous ingenuity. When Chester is told he'll soon be reborn as a black African boy, he says:

WAIT ANOTHER 16 YEARS & SEE
WHO CRUISES U IN YR PITH ELEGANT
HELMETS. . . .

(*Mirabell*, p. 103)

Mirabell himself is ceaselessly witty, as when he says that Einstein has declared Ephraim, or E, to be "any Emcee's equal, even squared" (*Mirabell*, p. 172). JM in his relaxed narrative voice can mention in passing that a huge papyrus meadow looks like an assemby of "frightwigs" ("Ephraim," p. 96). Wystan tells JM to expect a visit from Plato just before Plato is due to be reborn:

I DARESAY HE'LL LOOK IN B4 HE GOES
PERFUMED LIKE MOTHER IN HER PARTY CLOTHES
KISSING THE SMALL INCIPIENT ASTHMATIC
GOODNIGHT. . . .

(*Scripts*, p. 137)

(Here, of course, not only the tone is gay but also the figure of Proust, a writer Merrill made the subject of his college thesis and whom he'd invoked in many earlier poems.) But Merrill's wit, even his specifically gay wit, is too prodigal and celebrated to require further citations (oh, just one more, in which a Japanese painting is referred to as the usual "SWIRLS BEFORE PINE"; "Ephraim," p. 80).

Merrill has praised Dante for employing a mixed diction, an eclectic style, one that allows Dante his "touching, first-person particularity." Something similar can be said of Merrill's own diction, which in its range expresses in miniature the diversity of the universe. The gay wit in particular functions as a worldly vocabulary designed to deflate the pompous and to domesticate the sublime. If we *trust* Merrill, the modern prophet, we do so because he's not only prophetic but also mocking, campy, irritable, childlike, satiric.

I don't want to make too much of the gay aspects of the trilogy, which is, after all, a masterpiece of universal appeal and implication. But it does strike me, as a gay critic, as heartening that the social and linguistic resources of contemporary gay experience have been drawn on so freely and naturally in this great work. In earlier books Merrill usually sidestepped any explicit reference to homosexuality; even lovers were ambiguously addressed in direct discourse (the famous "you" strategy). In the trilogy, by contrast, Merrill has felt free to present the homosexual artist as a privileged being — as indeed from Merrill's and Proust's own luminous examples we conclude he certainly must be, at least once in every generation.

NOTES

[1]"DJ: A Conversation with David Jackson," *Shenandoah*, 30, No. 4 (1979), 25-44.
[2]"The Book of Ephraim," in *Divine Comedies* (New York: Atheneum, 1976), p. 74.
[3]*Mirabell: Books of Number* (New York: Atheneum, 1978), p. 63.
[4]*Scripts for the Pageant* (New York: Atheneum, 1980), p. 23.

Don Leon, Byron, and Homosexual Law Reform

Louis Crompton, Ph.D.

The origin of the anonymous poem entitled *Don Leon*, written in the 1830s but known to us only in an edition of 1866, is one of the mysteries of English literary history. The title page describes the work as "A Poem by Lord Byron, Author of Childe Harold, Don Juan, &c., &c. and Forming Part of the Private Journal of His Lordship, Supposed to Have Been Entirely Destroyed by Thos. Moore," but it is less and more than this. Byron had died in 1824 and his memoirs were burned shortly after by a committee of friends and other interested parties.[1] The author and publisher of *Don Leon* were clearly trying to attract attention by pretending that the poem was part of the destroyed manuscript, but this claim was obviously not meant to be taken seriously. The numerous references in the text to parliamentary events of the thirties would have immediately informed any knowledgeable reader of that period that the poem had been written after Byron's death. By the sixties, these blatant anachronisms were less obvious; in fact, the man who republished it in 1866, William Dugdale, had at first believed the poem was genuinely Byron's.

The publication history of *Don Leon* is almost as obscure as its authorship, which has been keenly debated.[2] We know that a version was in print before 1853 because in that year a correspondent signing himself "I. W." refers, in *Notes and Queries*, to "a poem (about 1500 lines) which professes to be written by Lord Byron, is addressed to Thomas Moore, and was printed abroad many years since." To identify the work, he quotes the opening line of *Don Leon*.[3] But the earliest extant copies are from the 1866 edition of Dugdale, a publisher notorious chiefly for his pornographic titles. When, then, did the poem first appear? The extensive (more than ninety) notes on homosexual history and literature provide some hints, since many cite dated sources. Of these the greatest number (nine) draw on material published in 1833. Six of these are

---

Louis Crompton is Professor of English at the University of Nebraska, Lincoln. His study *Shaw the Dramatist* received the Phi Beta Kappa Christian Gauss award for 1969. He has published "Gay Genocide: From Leviticus to Hitler" in *The Gay Academic*, ed. Louie Crew, and "Homosexuals and the Death Penalty in Colonial America" and "The Myth of Lesbian Impunity: Capital Laws from 1270 to 1791" in the *Journal of Homosexuality*.

53

references to an important book, *A Free Examination*, which we shall discuss later, but one of the others cites no fewer than six newspaper articles on arrests for homosexual offenses in that year.[4] Given the ephemeral interest of these items it is likely that the notes were first written up in 1833. This suggests that some version of the poem existed at that time. It is implied that the annotator is a person different from the poet; occasionally he corrects him. Notes 31, 66, and 67 give magazine or newspaper reports belonging to 1836. The poem may have been emended or enlarged then, as the text contains one reference to an event in 1836. Perhaps the first edition appeared at that time. An even likelier year is 1842, since note 27 speaks of "its being now 1842," which would hardly make sense unless immediate publication were envisioned.[5]

The poem is an impressive effort, running to more than fifty pages; the notes are almost as long again. Written with great verve and energy, its expression is concentrated and its ideas carefully organized. Though it is not the literary masterpiece it has been called, it is a work of real literary significance. It has generally been described as a satire in the tradition of Byron's *English Bards and Scotch Reviewers, The Curse of Minerva*, etc., but its rhymed pentameters surpass Byron's polemics in substance, force, and interest. Obviously, the author had given many years of thought to his subject. Though *Don Leon* purports to be an account of the homosexual side of Byron's life and provides much accurate information about his pederastic love affairs with Robert Rushton, John Edlestone, and Nicolo Giraud, this is not, eventually, where the center of interest lies. The poem is in fact a rhymed pamphlet in favor of homosexual law reform that incorporates a pseudoautobiography and erotic *jeux d'esprit*. Granted that satire has always been a loose and accommodating form, these diverse strands of *Don Leon* make it unique in English literature.

But why should an unknown poet have produced such a document in or about 1833? The answer lies in the plight of England's homosexual minority, who at that time faced the threat of hanging. On the Continent, Russia, Austria, Prussia, and Tuscany had all, late in the eighteenth century, adopted reform codes that dropped the death penalty for sodomy; France had decriminalized adult homosexual relations entirely in 1791.[6] In England a campaign to mitigate the rigors of a very severe criminal code began in 1808 under the leadership of Sir Samuel Romilly.[7] However, no real advance was made in reducing the large number of capital offenses (over two hundred) until Parliament appointed a Committee of Inquiry into the State of Criminal Law in 1819. The debate that led to the appointment of the committee showed a significant contrast in liberal and conservative positions on homosexuality and the law. Lord Castlereagh, who opposed setting up the committee, divided crimes into two classes: those indicating "deep moral depravity or national degradation," such as murder, rape, and "assaults with the attempt to commit unnatural offenses"; and lesser crimes, such as those against property.[8] (Here it is worth noting that "assaults" meant, not actual acts of sodomy, which were then capital, but often merely cases of what we would now call solicitation, which at the time were punished by fines and imprisonment. That Castlereagh should have ranked these with murder was typical of English hysteria on the subject.) The more liberal Sir James Mackintosh drew the line differently. He made three classifications: first, the worst crimes, murder and acts likely to cause death; second, arson, armed robbery, piracy, and "other offenses . . . which it would be painful to specify"; and finally, larceny and fraud.[9] Disappointingly, the report of the committee of 1819 made many recommendations but left untouched the question of sexual crimes. Some progress was made under Sir Robert Peel, who as home secretary in Wellington's cabinet in the twenties succeeded in reducing the large number of capital crimes against property. After the Reform Bill of 1832, the chances of abolition were enhanced when Lord John Russell replaced Peel at the Home Office and appointed a new panel of commissioners with Benthamite views in 1833.

The question foremost in the mind of the *Leon* poet was whether the new commissioners would recommend removal of the death penalty for homosexuality. The law was anything but a dead letter. In 1819–25 some fifteen men were hanged, in 1826–30, seven; there was one hanging in 1831, two in 1833, four in 1834, and two in 1835 — a total of about eighty since the beginning of the century if we include a score of naval hangings (the last of which took place in 1829).[10] If Parliament ranked even an attempted homosexual act as a "crime of national degradation," there was little hope; if Parliament followed Mackintosh and distinguished it as a crime of lesser import, there was a chance for abolition. The prognosis did not look good. There was, for one thing, the ominous continuation of executions; moreover, in 1828 Peel had actually sponsored a bill that made conviction in sodomy cases easier. In the eighteenth century it had been necessary to prove both penetration and emission to convict; now it was proposed to make proof of penetration alone sufficient. The debate on the 1828 measure makes curious reading. Peel referred to homosexuality only as the crime "*inter Christianos non nominandum*" and recommended reducing the "two kinds of proofs" to "one," without giving any more specific indication as to what he was talking about.[11] Such was the reticence of the day.

With the passage of the Reform Bill in 1832 and the election of a more liberal parliament the next year, most oppressed groups in England hoped for some relief from traditional abuses. Nonconformists had been relieved of disabilities by repeal of the Test Act in 1828, Catholic Emancipation had come in 1829, and it was expected that the reformed

House of 1833 would crown decades of agitation by ending black slavery (which it did). But the year turned out to be a bad one for homosexuals, and the *Leon* poet's rhetoric is mixed with more rage and despair than hopeful expectations. The poem opens with a strong protest against hangings and police entrapment:

> Thou ermined judge, pull off that sable cap!
> What! Can'st thou lie, and take thy morning nap?
> Peep thro' the casement; see the gallows there:
> Thy work hangs on it; could not mercy spare?
> What had he done? Ask crippled Talleyrand,
> Ask Beckford, Courtenay, all the motley band
> Of priest and laymen, who have shared his guilt
> (If guilt it be) then slumber if thou wilt;
> What bonds had he of social safety broke?
> Found'st thou the dagger hid beneath his cloak?
> He stopped no lonely traveller on the road;
> He burst no lock, he plundered no abode;
> He never wronged the orphan of his own;
> He stifled not the ravish'd maiden's groan.
> His secret haunts were hid from every soul,
> Till thou did'st send thy myrmidons to prowl. . . . (1-16)

The "sable cap" is, of course, the black cap English judges put on when they were about to pronounce sentence of death. The particular hanging that seems to have aroused the poet is that of Captain Henry Nicholas Nicholls on 12 August 1833. The *Times* had published details of his trial a week earlier; when it reported the hanging, it mentioned a companion of Nicholls, similarly charged, who had committed suicide.[12] The annotator of *Don Leon* preserves only the thinnest pretense that Byron had written these lines: "In reading the opening of this poem, it would almost seem that the author of it had in his eye Mr. Justice Park [who pronounced sentence on Nicholls] were it not that the supposed date of the poem would imply an anachronism" (note 1). The poet goes on to remind us that capital laws against housebreaking and robbery without violence have been repealed and asks, by implication, whether consensual sodomy seems as threatening. He is also outraged at the use of plainclothesmen who insinuate themselves at homosexual rendezvous and invite solicitations.

Despite the differences of style and rhetoric, the concerns of the *Leon* poet inevitably suggest comparison with Bentham's arguments for reform in his manuscript notes and essays of 1774, 1785, and 1814-16.[13] The topicality of the poem and its preoccupation with parliamentary matters link it with another contemporary publication of mysterious provenance.

This is the legal study already noted, *A Free Examination into the Penal Statutes, xxv Henr. VIII, cap. 6, and v Eliz. c. 17*, i.e., England's historical sodomy laws. The book is ascribed to "A. Pilgrim &c. &c.," presumably a pseudonym. Henry Ashbee in his *Index Librorum Prohibitorum* describes a copy bearing the date "London, 1833," though he suggests that it was "printed probably in Paris." He also gives a fuller version of the title, which indicates that it was "*addrest to Both Houses of Parliament.*"[14] Presumably this was a kind of legislator's brief on the subject of homosexual law reform. It must have been a work of some substance if the reference to "page 771" in note 30 to *Don Leon* is not a misprint. Note 24 tells us that "it is become very scarce," which suggests that it was not widely distributed. No copy has been described in the twentieth century. Since it appears to have been the first book on homosexuality ever published in English, the loss to gay scholarship is very considerable. We can derive some idea of its scope and tone from the quotations in the *Leon* notes and in Ashbee. First, Pilgrim's estimate of Europe's homosexual population, radical for its age, seems closer to the statistics of Kinsey than to the conservative guesses of Bentham. Though the laws in England are most often enforced against the poor, he conjectures "that the taste has been in all ages that of the most distinguished individuals, and that we might count perhaps as many delinquents in the great continental cities now, as there were in Athens, or in ancient Rome."[15] On the historical side, he notices Aristotle's statement that homosexuality was encouraged among the Cretans for Malthusian ends and gives a summary of Roman law and a description of Roman manners (notes 76 and 24). Pilgrim laments the reiteration of such names as Tiberius, Nero, Caligula, and Heliogabalus in homophobic polemics and protests the prejudicial omission of any reference to the legion of "the virtuous, the brave, the generous and the temperate" who shared the same orientation (note 24). *A Free Examination* also draws the inevitable comparison between French tolerance and English harshness and decries the credulity that in England led men to follow uncritically religious laws that decide "our very destiny and existence" (note 8).

If "A. Pilgrim" is a murky and unknown figure, the identity of the *Leon* poet is also veiled in mystery. G. Wilson Knight, who in 1954 first rescued the poem from disreputable obscurity, has suggested that it is by a playwright-poet Byron knew and caroused with, George Colman, the younger.[16] Byron, who came to know Colman through their work at Drury Lane Theatre, celebrates this wit and conviviality in his journals. The parallels in vocabulary and moral attitudes between *Don Leon* and some of Colman's own satires are striking, but ascriptions of authorship based on stylistic similarities are always tenuous. There is also the question of Colman's age and ill health — he died in 1836 at 73. Doris

Langley Moore has argued against Colman's authorship on these and other grounds and has hinted at another candidate.[17]

Indeed, all we can say with certainty about the *Leon* poet is that he had a clever (and sometimes highly erotic) wit, a talent for writing forceful couplets, and as we shall see, a remarkable knowledge both of Byron's pederastic interests and of parliamentary debates and personalities in the years 1824-33. The poem itself is full of ideas and information, though when it speaks of Byron one cannot always tell how much is factual and how much imagined. Since the kaleidoscopic turns of thoughts are so many that even someone who has read it two or three times may have only a confused recollection of its structure and logic, a fairly extended summary may be valuable. It will also communicate, as no other approach can, the concentrated energy of the poem. Because the *Leon* poet purports to be speaking in the person of Byron, I shall refer to him as Byron in this résumé. Note, however, that the pseudo-Byronic mask is often casually dropped in the argumentative sections.

After the opening protest (quoted above), Byron begs Moore to give a sympathetic ear to his "swelling rage" and to print his thoughts unaltered. (This is almost the only reference in the text to the pretense that the poem has some connection with the famous memoir.) England, he complains, tolerates the most open forms of prostitution but condemns "poor misogynists" to the gallows and vilifies them incessantly in the press. The Sodom story is urged against them, though many other ancient cities have vanished without anyone's interpreting their disappearance as instances of divine displeasure. The venial clergy approve only those unions that bring them marriage or baptismal fees, and are blind to a love that will "Produce no other blossoms than its own" (126).

Even during his teens, Byron tells us, he was aware of an instinct that drew him to other boys. Social custom allowed him to express his love for such young women as Mary Chaworth and Margaret Parker, but not these other longings. Now, looking back, he realizes that his feelings for boys like his page Robert Rushton, which once passed for lordly patronage, had a sexual element:

> Full well I knew, though decency forbad
> The same caresses to a rustic lad;
> Love, love it was, that made my eyes delight
> To have his person ever in my sight. (169-72)

At Cambridge, he feels alienated from the common revels and longs for a kindred soul, who might return his affection. He hears John Edlestone singing in the choir, and friendship ripens into love:

> Oh! 'tis hard to trace
> The line where love usurps tame friendship's place.

Friendship's the chrysalis, which seems to die,
But throws its coils to give love wings to fly. (219-22)

He is tormented by the intensity of his emotions and struggles to understand them. Moral law opposes his desires, but to him they seem natural,
since they spring from his inner being. He begins to question traditional
standards — after all, he is not about to ruin a virgin, betray a husband,
or beget a bastard. He seeks to divert himself from these anxieties by
losing himself in the pleasures of classical poetry but is inadvertently
driven back to the question. Horace, he discovers, loved youths, Virgil
sighed for Alexis, Socrates and Plato spoke openly of kissing ephebes,
and Plutarch praised the love of Epaminandos for Cephidorus. He rejects
these loves as pagan perversions, but when he turns to the history of
Christianity, he discovers such attachments again in the lives of popes,
devotees, kings, scholars, jurists, and poets —

Nay, e'en our bard, Dame Nature's darling child,
Felt the strange impulse, and his hours beguiled
In penning sonnets to a stripling's praise,
Such as would damn a poet now-a-days. (315-18)

Obviously, "the great, the wise, the pious, and the good" have had the
same susceptibility. In alarm he rejects books and history as morally
dangerous guides. But untutored schoolboys take the same path even if
they are "in *Justine* unread." This may be better, however, than their
risking disease through harlotry. School authorities should quietly ignore
such "illicit play": only fools would make a public issue of it.

Edlestone dies (the poem is inaccurate in making this occur before
Byron left England for Greece in 1809), and weary of Cambridge, Byron
seeks the freedom of the East:

Love, love, clandestine love, was still my dream.
Methought there must be yet some people found,
Where Cupid's wings were free, his hands unbound
Where law had no erotic statutes framed,
Nor gibbets stood to fright the unreclaimed. (423-27)

(We now know, of course, that Byron did indeed have such thoughts
in mind when he sailed for the East.[18]) The account of Byron in Greece
is particularly full and striking. In Constantinople he is excited by the
traditional tourist visit to taverns with dancing boys but hides his feelings
from his friend Hobhouse, affecting to be horrified. He feels alienated
from his countrymen and is relieved when he parts from Hobhouse at
Zea. Byron warmly praises the latter's political work for radical causes
in England but himself follows other pursuits: "A demon urged, and

with Satanic force / Still goaded on" (494-95). He is enraptured by
the historical associations of Athens, swims at Piraeus, moves to a
monastery, and then takes up residence in the nearby Lantern of Demos-
thenes.[19]

While searching through the ruins of the city he is invited home by a
citizen. There the man's son attends the guest in Oriental fashion. Byron
is struck by the boy's beauty, courts him, and is urged by the father to
take him as his page. He tries to cultivate the boy's mind, gazes on him
with affectionate lust while he sleeps, and cares for him with tender
solicitude. The dual fires of poetic inspiration and carnal desire rage in
him. Though he has met the Macri sisters, they inspire him only poeti-
cally; his real passion is for this boy (Nicolo Giraud, who is named in
line 678), who finally gratifies him in the convent cell: "So boldly I set
calumny at naught,/ And fearless utter what I fearless wrought" (690-91).
(Letters have come to light in the present century to confirm this detail.[20])
There follows a description of how the then Waiwode (or mayor) of
Athens was attended by a beautiful catamite on public occasions; such
openness is common at every level of Turkish society.

The *Leon* poet, now dropping any effort to relate his plea to the
experiences of the historical Byron, at this point embarks on a frank
apology for homosexuality. First, Malthus has dramatically shown the
danger of overpopulation, which must breed starvation if not controlled.
One must take into consideration the great diversity of sexual tastes.
Some men (like the English ambassador to Constantinople) are born
exhibitionists. Others seek cunnilingus, flagellation, or fellation from
women. Incest and lesbianism are not uncommon. Some women have
died to preserve their virginity, but others, like the Countess of Bless-
ington, have risen to wealth and social prominence by judiciously losing
theirs. When bench and pulpit reiterate endlessly the view that the sexual
behavior of the English is morally superior to other nations, they are
hypocritical, and never more so than when, in the case of homosexuality,
they give the impression

> That self-condemned, decried, ineffable,
> Innominate, this blackest sin of hell,
> Had fled dismayed to some Transalpine shore
> To sully Albion's pudic cliffs no more. (854-57)

The press exposes arrested men with cruel glee and titillates its readers
with scabrous police reports. The rich and secure feign horror, never
taking into account what may have led a man into these paths: perhaps
he was corrupted when young; perhaps he shrank from the idea of se-
ducing a woman; perhaps he was ugly or shy, or averse to the ribaldry
or diseases of harlots.

Every rank of English society is involved. The average British soldier or tar is a priapist prone to take his pleasure where he finds it. Teachers relish flogging half-naked schoolboys. Parliament itself is not immune. Looking into the future, Byron prophesies that a member famed for his learning and book collecting will be forced to flee the country and later will be cruelly maligned in a libel suit brought by a father against an editor for having linked his son's name to the exile's. Another, a young officer who fought in Sicily, will be tragically drawn into the case. A third member, a pious advocate of prison reform and Negro rights, will also face the bitterness of exile. The poet complains indignantly that Peel's revisions of the law have worsened matters. Liberal legislators like Richard Martin, who led the movement to protect animals from cruelty, and legal reformers like Sir James Mackintosh remain callously indifferent to the plight of homosexuals.

Near the Speaker's chair where Charles Manners-Sutton presides and waits for his peerage, sits Sir Stephen Lushington, whom Byron curses for having turned Lady Byron against him. He recalls some of his happy moments with his wife; in a bedroom colloquy he describes Moslem manners to her and pictures the life of harem women and the Turks' passion for boys. Annabella expresses curiosity, and Byron enlightens her about Anacreon, Virgil, and Catullus. She is somewhat shocked but allows him to practice anal relations (which he extols) with her, because her pregnancy makes ordinary relations awkward. Later, when they are estranged, Annabella is pressed to reveal this secret, and friends use it to separate her from her husband.

After a second appeal by Byron to Thomas Moore to tell the truth and not bowdlerize his life, if Moore should ever write it, the poem abruptly flashes back to Parliament to cast a spotlight upon another figure, a friend (William Bankes) whom Byron had known since his college days. Despite his wealth, the fame of his travels, and his high social standing, Bankes will eventually suffer Byron's fate. Bankes's friend Peel, when he passes Bankes's darkened house and remembers what a staunch supporter he has been in Parliament, may then regret his failure to reform the law.

In conclusion, Byron bitterly recalls what abuse he suffered as a man after being praised so highly as a poet. But England is not the universe: her prejudices cannot stand before the light of reason. God's law is higher than Parliament's; it is as outrageous to persecute sexual as religious heresy. Then with a final impish gesture the poet ends with a series of crude and exuberant epigrams on the pleasures of anal intercourse.

Don Leon is remarkable for the challenge it posed to contemporary prejudices against homosexuality, and for the new facts it purported to give about Byron's life. Who the source of these facts was we do not know. Possibly, like Colman, the poet was a confidant of Byron's. Friends of Byron's may have enlightened him, or he may have met someone who either knew Byron in Greece or picked up gossip there. Thomas Moore, whose *Life* of Byron appeared in 1830, had described Byron's attachments to Rushton, Edlestone, and Giraud but was careful to represent them as romantic friendships and nothing more. We now know from many sources that these affairs had a sexual element. G. Wilson Knight speculated extensively on this possibility in 1957 in *Lord Byron's Marriage*. The thorough researches of Leslie Marchand and Doris Langley Moore have provided conclusive documentary evidence in the form of Byron's letters from Greece to Hobhouse, Hobhouse's marginalia to Moore's *Life,* Lady Byron's memoranda, etc.[21]

There are, however, material facts the *Leon* poet was not aware of. He did not realize, for example, that the "Thyrza" lyrics were elegies on the death of Edlestone; and he had no inkling of Byron's love, during the final months of his life, for the fifteen-year-old Loukas Chalandrutsanos. But he goes far beyond Moore in providing details about Byron's first stay in Greece. Moore does not mention the visit to Galata or (of course) the consummation in the monastery. We have confirmation of the first from Hobhouse's journals and of the second from Byron's "Greek epistles," as he called them. It appears that the *Leon* poet had some informant who knew the Athenian scene: in note 40 the story of the Waiwode is ascribed to Lord Plymouth. But he is not always accurate here: he errs, for instance, in representing Nicolo Giraud as living with his father rather than with his brother-in-law.

Whatever its source, the story is worked out with much sensitive detail. The gradations by which ardent friendship melts into erotic awareness are depicted with some subtlety. It is difficult to think of any comparable description of the awakening of homosexual feeling in English literature before the twentieth century. As a portrait of an adolescent struggling toward self-awareness *Don Leon* compares with Forster's *Maurice*, which was not written till eighty years later. But where Forster in his novel gives us the psychosexual development of two young men who are, respectively, a classical scholar and a conventionally minded businessman, *Don Leon* shows us the awakening of a sensual poet.

The sympathetic dramatization of the stages by which Byron realized his feelings for the male sex works in two ways — as a biographical revelation, and as a rhetorical device to moderate homophobic sentiment by showing the anguish of a sensitive boy. The "argument from antiquity" is cleverly handled by having Byron discover the truth about Greek and Roman society in his reading. The "great men" argument is less adroitly managed; the catalogue is set forth effectively, but hardly as a boy's discoveries. The lines on Shakespeare bear some relation to a comment on the sonnets made by Byron and recorded by George Finlay during the poet's last days in Greece.[22]

As for the sociological arguments for tolerance, it is interesting to compare these to Bentham's. There is the same citing of Malthus (who did indeed list "unnatural acts" as a check to population: "Economists, who seek the world to thin,/ 'Tis you who teach this so named deadly sin" (775-76). Both protest strongly against the sensationalism and virulence of the British press. Bentham had complained in his notes of 1816 that

> A battery of grape shot composed of all the expressions of abhorrence that language has given or can give birth to is by each newspaper and every other periodical kept continually playing upon this ground. No wonder that down to this instant no man with the torch of reason in his hand should have found nerve enough to set foot on it. Miscreant! You are one of them then! Such are the thanks he would receive, such the bad thanks which any man who should attempt to carry upon this part of the field of morality those lights to which all other parts are open ever could or even now can rationally expect to receive.[23]

Like Bentham, the *Leon* poet also argues that homosexuality is less of a social evil than extramarital pregnancies and adultery and is thus less dangerous than illicit heterosexual relations. Bentham, in a prospectus to a proposed book on homosexuality addressed to William Beckford, painstakingly enumerated every kind of sexual conduct, heterosexual and homosexual, he could think of in order that prejudice might be "perplexed and weakened" by their sheer numbers.[24] The *Leon* poet does something similar, dwelling on a variety of heterosexual techniques, some of which border on the bizarre. This is perhaps the least acceptable part of the poem: there is something offensive in his lubricious bandying of names and initials. Where Bentham presents his list in a scientific spirit with dry logic, the *Leon* poet writes with a smirk that is rather reminiscent of Martial; his approach is too much like blackening the kettle to brighten the pot.

Another detail likely to puzzle the modern reader is the use, in this passionately antihomophobic poem, of virulently homophobic language. This diction is hard to explain. In other contexts such language might be explicable on rhetorical grounds. A debater in the public arena in that age, given the force of popular sentiment, might have adopted abusive language to allay suspicions about his own tastes. Or he might have felt that arguments for less-harsh legal punishment came with more effect from someone who expressed moral horror at homosexual behavior. So strong was the taboo on discussion that many nineteenth-century writers, even in a scholarly legal or historical context, seem to have felt that homophobic abuse was a necessary coin to be paid for the privilege of touching even briefly on a forbidden topic. So Bentham felt compelled to use pejorative language (totally at odds with his feelings) in his manuscript essay of 1785, and so, too, Byron in the famous lines on Beckford he had at first intended for *Childe Harold*.[25] But these considerations would hardly seem to hold in the case of the anonymous *Leon* poet, who frankly celebrates the joys of same-sex intercourse. To find this enthusiasm coupled with references to homosexuality as a "morbid lust," "sport obscene," "rank disease," "impure delinquency," etc., is puzzling. G. Wilson Knight explains the anomaly as an attempt at "balance," but the effect is more like a linguistic, if not moral, schizophrenia.

It is also difficult, since the chief aim of the poet is to change the reader's mind about capital punishment, to account for the explicit eroticism of some of the later pages. Though it is a minor element, there is enough in this vein to have tempted most nineteenth-century readers to dismiss the production as a mere essay in pornography, as the Victorians understood the term. This must have drastically limited its circulation and weakened its impact on all but the least prudish. One possibility is that the more glaring passages — the bedroom scene and the final peroration — were not added until 1842, by which time all hopes for homosexual law reform, as we shall see, had been finally laid to rest. Perhaps the author felt that, given the circumstances, the only channels of distribution open to him were under-the-counter sales in shops dealing in erotica. This may have prompted him to add these passages. Ironically, spicy details, which, under Victorian law, would themselves have justified the pamphlet's destruction by the authorities, in fact preserved it, since the erotic sections seem to have been what motivated Dugdale to print his version.

Some of the contrasts with Bentham, both in tone and argument, result from the change that took place in the political situation between the Regency (when Bentham did most of his writing) and the 1830s. In 1818, when Bentham finished his most extensive notes in favor of the decriminalization of sodomy, criminal law reform in England was still in the future. By 1833, the death penalty had been abolished for scores of offenses. This movement in the Commons and the Lords had aroused, for homosexuals, both hope and despair. The poem is consequently full of minutiae relating to Parliament and parliamentarians. Though these create many obscurities for the modern reader, they also give the poem substance and reality. *Don Leon* contains detailed accounts of four members who found themselves embroiled with or threatened by the law in homosexual scandals, and a fifth is mentioned in the notes. The men whose fates the poet and annotator limn at some length were Richard Heber, James Stanhope, Henry Grey Bennett, Baring Wall, and William Bankes.

Richard Heber, the bibliophile, was a friend of John Cam Hobhouse. Via Hobhouse, Byron sent his compliments from Ravenna to Heber upon his election as member from Oxford in 1821.[26] When Heber died in exile in 1833, the English press was full of lengthy obituaries, most of which ignored or made only veiled references to his ostracism. Walter Scott had praised him as "Heber the magnificent" for his library, rendered him thanks in the notes to the Waverley Novels, and celebrated their friendship in the sixth canto of *Marmion*.[27] Heber's collection of early English books was regarded in his day as the most impressive ever assembled; he left eight houses full of volumes in England and on the Continent. The details of his case are obscure. Scott noted that "his life was compromised but for the exertions of Hobhouse under Secy of State who detected a warrant passing through the office."[28] Forewarned, Heber fled to Brussels. Next year, rather than face the publicity of an election, he resigned his seat. Scott, who had wondered at his disappearance, confided in his journal for 25 June 1826 that a friend had

> mentioned to me last night a horrid circumstance about a very particularly dear friend who lately retired suddenly and seemingly causelessly from parliament. He ascribed [it] to his having been detected in unnatural practices — I hope there may be doubts of this though he spoke very positively and the sudden and silent retreat from a long wishd for seat look[s] too like truth. God, God whom shall we trust!! Here is learning, wit, gaiety of temper, high station in society and compleat reception every where all at once debased and lost by such degrading bestiality. Our passions are wild beasts. God grant us power to muzzle them.[29]

Scott, who shared the common British prejudices of the day, seems not to have reflected that it was an arbitrary social taboo that had driven Heber from England.

Some dim and indirect light on the circumstances of Heber's flight glimmered in the press. On May 14, *John Bull* published a typical clever-vicious notice: "We understand that Mr. Heber's complaint (for which he has been recommended to travel upon the Continent) is an overattachment to *Hartshorn*."[30] The *Leon* poet puns on the name of the aromatic (sal volatile) in his verse, and note 63 tells us that "Mr. Heber's shame was brought to light in consequence of an action for libel, instituted by Mr. Hartshorn against the editor of a newspaper, wherein pointed allusions were made to a supposed intimacy between Mr. Heber and Mr. Hartshorn's son." In a very detailed account of his scholarship and politics, published on the occasion of Heber's death, the *Annual Register* reported: "In the year, 1831 he returned to England, but not into the society which he had left; for rumors had been in circulation degrading to his moral character. With the exception of his visits to the auction-rooms and booksellers' shops, he lived entirely secluded among his books at Pimlico or Hodnet."[31] Scott never attempted to communicate with him.

The identity of the next parliamentary portrait in *Don Leon* is less clear. Note 65 speculates that the "youth with courtly manners" who had fought in Sicily was "probably the Honourable James Stanhope," the younger brother of Leicester Stanhope, Byron's colleague in the Greek wars. He is described as "the intimate friend of Mr. Heber, [who] soon after the disclosures made concerning the latter gentleman, hung himself in an outhouse in Caen Wood." The *Times* for 8 March 1825 contains a long article on Stanhope's suicide but does not hint at its cause. Since the date is earlier than Heber's flight, it is possible that the identification is wrong.

The antislavery crusader whom the *Leon* poet chided for his failure to take up homosexual law reform was Henry Grey Bennett, member for Shrewsbury and a friend of Hobhouse. An active debater, Bennett suddenly disappears from the pages of Hansard in the mid twenties. The parliamentary sketches in *Don Leon* are all introduced, rather awkwardly, as prophecies by the omniscient Byron; one ends with a couplet: "An exile to a foreign land he'll fly,/ Neglected live, and broken-hearted die" (986-87). Since Bennett did not die till June 1836, these lines have caused a debate about the date of their composition. Knight has suggested that here we have a genuine anticipation by the *Leon* poet of Bennett's demise, rather than a post facto one. Doris Langley Moore has objected to this as unlikely. However, a date of 1836 for the poem as a whole seems to me too late.

At the end of this lengthy section on Parliament Byron is made to spy Charles Manners-Sutton in the Speaker's chair. Sutton is decried as a timeserver who "Counts Ayes and Noes to make himself a peer" (1040). It has been assumed that these lines were written after March 1835, when Sutton was elevated to the Lords. But Sutton's obvious desire for a peerage had been a political issue as early as 1833. At the opening of the reformed Parliament, it had been expected that Sutton would retire as Speaker of the House. But when his hoped-for peerage was not forthcoming, Sutton stayed in the post, a move that gave some offense, since he had opposed the Reform Bill.[32] The jibe might thus have been penned any time after January 1833; probably soon after, as it is hard to imagine so ephemeral a matter would have engaged the poet's attention after the controversy had died down.

Another homosexual episode involving a member of Parliament is mentioned only in the notes. In February 1833, Baring Wall, the member for Guilford, was accused by a policeman, whose testimony was explicit and detailed, of making sexual advances late at night in Harley Street.[33] Wall was tried for the crime of "attempting to commit an unnatural offense," but the jury refused to believe his accuser and Wall served in the House till 1852. However, the year 1833 seems to have been a bad one for legislators in relation to such accusations, for in June another respected member of long standing faced a similar charge. This was William Bankes, who for many years had been on close terms with Byron. When he was at Cambridge, Byron called Bankes his "collegiate pastor, and master, and patron" and often joined Bankes and Charles Skinner Matthews, another homosexual friend, in Bankes's rooms.[34]

During his first year at Trinity College, Byron identified Bankes and Edward Long as his closest intimates. In 1807, when Byron was about to publish his juvenile poems, he submitted them to Bankes's judgment and took his harsh criticism in good part.[35] Five years later their paths crossed again under ironic circumstances: Bankes proposed to Annabella Milbanke shortly after Byron had made his first proposal, and like him was turned down. He then went on an eastern journey that lasted some eight years. Byron wrote recommendations when his friend proposed to visit Albania and, impressed by Bankes's scholarly discoveries, took a vicarious pride in his "perilous researches."[36] "Bankes is a wonderful fellow," Byron wrote to his publisher John Murray in 1820, "there is hardly one of my School and College Contemporaries that has not turned out more or less celebrated"; "I love and esteem him."[37] That same year, Byron, who generally avoided English visitors during his exile in Italy, wrote a warm invitation to Bankes to join him in Ravenna to celebrate the carnival of 1820. When Bankes returned to England, his country house in Dorset became a showplace for antiquities, including a famous obelisk, and was often visited by the Duke of Wellington, who was a close personal friend.[38] From 1822 to 1826 Bankes sat in Parliament as the member for Cambridge; later he was elected as the representative from Marlborough and then from Dorset.

On 7 June 1833, he was arrested and accused of sexual misconduct with a guardsman in a public convenience near the House of Commons. According to the *Times*, the police station where Bankes and the soldier were held overnight was surrounded by an angry crowd early in the morning. "Long before the hour of commencing business, at least 2,000 persons had assembled," and when the soldier was brought up the police escort "had the greatest difficulty in keeping the mob off. The yells and execrations of the crowd were tremendous."[39] Such hostile mobs of thousands were commonplace in London when news of arrests on homosexual charges circulated; seventeen years earlier between thirty and fifty thousand had been drawn to the pillorying of the Vere Street coterie.

The crowd objected loudly to being excluded from Bankes's hearing and shouted, "It's because he's a rich man!" The magistrate, intimidated by the multitude, or recollecting the flight of the Bishop of Clogher and the uproar it had occasioned a decade earlier, set bail at the immense sum of £12,000 (about $300,000 in today's currency). When the soldier left the court, a sergeant of his regiment, the Coldstream Guards, seized the cap from his head and tore off the lace.

The trial was postponed till December, perhaps in the hope that feeling would subside. Wellington, who had witnessed the Clogher affair at close hand, must have felt alarmed. Given British traditions, Bankes's conviction might have led to the hanging of a Tory member of Parliament at a moment when radical sentiment still ran high. The strategy adopted was the one that had succeeded in the case of Wall — to over-awe the jury with character witnesses. Wellington himself testified. So did Samuel Rogers, Dr. Butler (the headmaster of Harrow), and the high bailiff of Westminster; the earls of Callaghan, Liverpool, and Brecknock; Lords Burglesh, Cage, Cowley, and Stuart; and a number of members of Parliament. The jury, duly impressed, found the men not guilty and "without the least stain on their character."[40] Eight years later, when Bankes was again arrested for a similar offense, he followed in Byron's footsteps by retiring to Venice, where he died in 1855.

Don Leon was written to forward the cause of homosexual law reform, but the movement (if it can be called that) did not prosper. The Commission on Criminal Law appointed in 1833 issued their report on 20 June 1836. They recommended reducing capital offenses to eight crimes, all of which (except sodomy) involved violence or danger to life. Though they tabulated the statutes of ten American states, none of which made sodomy capital for the first offense, their one reference to homosexuality was a single sentence: "A nameless crime of great enormity we, at present, exclude from consideration."[41] A bill to abolish the death penalty for rape and sodomy passed the Commons in 1841 (where the debate touched only on rape), but sodomy law reform was killed in the Lords. On 17 June, the Earl of Wicklow argued that if the Lords passed such a law, "they would lower themselves in public opinion; for as the organ of the public voice, they would sanction what the people of this country would never confirm — that sodomy and rape were not crimes of so heinous a character as to deserve death." Next day, the Earl of Winchelsea proposed an amendment to retain capital punishment for homosexuality alone. "Their Lordships, he was convinced, would do great violence to the moral feelings of a very large class of the community, if they exempted this crime from the penalty of death."[42] As a result, though executions ceased in 1835, over two hundred homosexuals were sentenced to hang in the next twenty years. In some years the number of such sentences exceeded those for murder. In 1861, a comprehensive measure consolidating and revising portions of the English criminal law was passed, and the death penalty for sodomy was reduced to life imprisonment, a sanction that remained unchanged for more than a century.

Though it is impossible to speak with real certainty of the author and the date of *Don Leon*, certain considerations do suggest themselves. First, it seems altogether likely that, whatever touches were added later, the poem was completed substantially in its present form sometime in the late summer or early fall of 1833. The two cases that seem to have provoked the work were the arrest of William Bankes in June and the execution of Nicholls in August. The Bankes episode may have suggested to the poet that members of Parliament would now be ready to listen to reform arguments, since a distinguished member of the lower house had become a victim of the law. The earlier case of Baring Wall was omitted from the poem, since, though he had faced an ordeal in many ways parallel to Bankes's, he had been acquitted. Because Bankes's own acquittal in December made his case moot as well, it is likely that the section of the poem devoted to Bankes (which is very near the conclusion) was finished before his trial took place. There is also the curious fact that the list of arrests for 1833, in note 56, includes cases that occurred in February, April, May, June, and early August, but none later. Probably, then, the note was compiled in late August or shortly afterwards.

As for the author, one is struck by his minute knowledge of details pertaining to the Commons. He notes, for instance, that Stephen Lushington sat near the Speaker, and that the "youth with courtly manners" (who may or may not have been Stanhope) shared the same row with the "elder Bankes," i.e., Bankes's father. No one who had not frequented the House often and been closely familiar with its membership would have been aware that these two obscure parliamentarians sat in the same row, or could have told the reader that James Brogden spoke in a shy manner at certain moments (as in line 1020). If the author was not an elected representative he was certainly someone whose duties or interests brought him into close relation with Parliament. Given his passionate commitment to homosexual law reform, it seems likely that he had some contact with the coterie of reformers who compiled *A Free Examination* in 1833. His intimate knowledge of Byron's life also suggests that if he had not known Byron, he was at least a confidant of some friend of his. Possibly this friend was William Bankes himself, who, on visiting Byron in Italy on the way home from his eastern travels in 1821, may have exchanged confidences with him.

But whoever he was, the *Leon* poet has left us a unique document. No further candid discussion of Byron's homosexuality appeared in English until 1935, when Peter Quennell published his *Byron: The Years of Fame*. Not only did the *Leon* poet set forth the main facts about Byron's homosexuality a full century before Byron's more conventional biographers dared to broach the subject, he also wrote, in a form that is telling and powerful, the earliest published protest against homosexual oppression in England that has survived and the first plea for understanding.

That so much mystery attends the poet's efforts is an indication of the extreme caution reformers in England felt they must use when the laws on homosexuality were at issue. In France the merits of law reform had been discussed openly by Voltaire and others in the eighteenth century. When a new national code was drawn up in Germany during its unification in the 1860s, the arguments for decriminalization of sodomy were openly debated. But none of Bentham's voluminous writings saw the light of day in nineteenth-century England, nor do we have evidence that they were known to others. A public stance in favor of even so moderate a step as the dropping of the death penalty was regarded as too radical to risk. Homophobia, with the English, was in that age so pronounced a national trait that publication and debate were precluded. To uncover the roots of this striking phenomenon is a challenge to social historians.

NOTES

[1]Doris Langley Moore gives a full account of this episode in *The Late Lord Byron* (Philadelphia: J. B. Lippincott Company, 1961), pp. 12-45.

[2]See G. Wilson Knight, "Who Wrote 'Don Leon'?" *Twentieth Century,* 156 (1954), 69-79; Chapter v of his *Lord Byron's Marriage* (New York: MacMillan, 1957); and Doris Langley Moore, *Lord Byron: Accounts Rendered* (London: John Murray, 1974) pp. 445, 449-53. An edition of *Don Leon* published in 1934 by the Fortune Press was suppressed; a facsimile of this edition appears in *A Homosexual Emancipation Miscellany c. 1835 - 1952* (New York: Arno Press, 1975). References in the present article are to the earliest known edition, *Don Leon: A Poem by the late Lord Byron* (London: For the Booksellers, 1866).

[3]*Notes and Queries,* 7 (1853), 66.

[4]The notes that cite *A Free Examination* are 8, 24, 30, 42, 53, and 68; the arrests are listed in note 56; the other press citations for 1833 are in notes 1 and 88.

[5]Other notes with material dated later than 1833 mention an arrest in 1841 (88); cite newspapers for 1844 (3), 1849 (first note numbered 51), 1850 (7,26), 1853 (88, 92), and 1856 (second note numbered 51); and refer to the 1853-56 edition of Moore's *Memoirs* (5, 6, 15, 30, 34) and to an *Athenaeum* article of 1859 (92). Note 88 appears to speak of William Bankes as still alive; he died in 1855.

[6]See Leon Radzinowicz, *The Movement for Reform,* Vol. I of *A History of English Criminal Law and Its Administration from 1750* (London: Stevens, 1948), pp. 286-97.

[7]Radzinowicz, p. 313.

[8]1 March 1819; Great Britain, Parliament, *Parliamentary Debates* (London: Hansard, 1819), XXXIX, col. 747.

[9]2 March 1819; *Parliamentary Debates,* XXXIX, col. 790. When he edited his speech for publication, Mackintosh changed his deliberately vague phrase to the more explicit "certain serious sexual offenses." "Speech on Moving for a Committee to Inquire into the State of Criminal Law," *Miscellaneous Works* (New York: D. Appleton and Company, III, 1873), 529-30.

[10]See *Tables Showing the Number of Criminal Offenders Committed for Trial or Bailed . . . in the Year 1836,* cited in Louis Crompton, "Gay Genocide: From Leviticus to Hitler," *The Gay Academic,* ed. Louie Crew (Palm Springs, Calif.: ETC Publications, 197[7]), p. 91. For statistics

on naval hangings, see Arthur N. Gilbert, "Buggery and the British Navy," *Journal of Social History,* 10 (1976), 72-98.

[11]5 May 1828, *Parliamentary Debates,* NS XIX, col. 354.

[12]*Times,* 5 Aug., p. 4, col. 2; 13 Aug., p. 4, col. 2.

[13]Bentham's notes of 1774 are as yet unpublished; they are contained in boxes 73 and 74a of the Bentham manuscript collection in the department of Rare Books and Manuscripts of the D. M. S. Watson Library at University College, London. His essay of 1785 has been transcribed and published by the present author in the *Journal of Homosexuality,* 3 (1978), 389-405, and 4 (1979), 91-107. Excerpts from the 1814-16 manuscripts are included in an appendix, "Bentham on Sex," to C. K. Ogden's edition of *The Theory of Legislation* (New York: Harcourt Brace, 1931), pp. 473-97. I plan to give a detailed account of these writings (which run to over five hundred pages) in a monograph on Byron and homosexuality, of which this article forms a part.

[14]Pisanus Fraxi [pseud. of Henry Ashbee], *Index Librorum Prohibitorum,* Vol. I of *Bibliography of Prohibited Books* (1877; rpt. New York: Jack Brussel, 1962), p. xxxiv, n. 46.

[15]Fraxi, p. 339.

[16]"Colman and 'Don Leon'," *Twentieth Century,* 159 (1956), 562-73.

[17]*Lord Byron: Accounts Rendered,* pp. 449-55. For the suspected author, see Moore's *The Late Lord Byron,* pp. 211-13. Moore implies the author was a Mr. Paternoster, of Madras, who contributed to a Byron monument fund in 1826 and then quarreled with the committee.

[18]See his letter to Charles Skinner Matthews, written before embarking at Falmouth, 22 June 1809, in which Byron speaks of the "hyacinths" he expects to find and enjoy in Asia; *Byron's Letters and Journals,* ed. Leslie Marchand (Cambridge: Belknap Press, 1973), I, 207.

[19]Note 31 explains that the poet is wrong on this point. Byron did not live in the Lantern, although he occasionally wrote poetry there.

[20]See Byron's letter to Hobhouse from Patras, 4 Oct. 1810; *Byron's Letters and Journals,* II, 23.

[21]Marchand, *Byron: A Biography* (New York: Alfred A. Knopf, 1957), I, 90n; Moore, "Byron's Sexual Ambivalence," *Lord Byron: Accounts Rendered,* pp. 437-59.

[22]"People talk of the tendency of my writings, and yet read the Sonnets to Master Hughes." *His Very Voice and Self: Collected Conversations of Lord Byron,* ed. E. J. Lovell, Jr. (New York: Macmillan, 1954), p. 552.

[23]24 March 1816; Bentham manuscripts, box 74a, folio 168.

[24]"General Idea of a Work," 1817; box 161a, f. 16.

[25]"To Dives," *Works of Lord Byron,* ed. E. H. Coleridge (London: John Murray, 1898), VII, 7.

[26]12 Sept., *Byron's Letters and Journals,* VIII, 207.

[27]*Dictionary of National Biography.*

[28]10 July 1826, *The Journal of Sir Walter Scott,* ed. W. E. K. Anderson (Oxford: Clarendon Press, 1972), p. 170. Anderson identifies the undersecretary as John Cam Hobhouse, but it was in fact Henry Hobhouse, his cousin.

[29]*Journal of Sir Walter Scott,* p. 162.

[30]*Journal of Sir Walter Scott,* p. 162.

[31]*Annual Register . . . of the Year 1833* (London: Baldwin and Cradock, 1834), p. 246*.

[32]*Annual Register . . . 1833,* p. 3.

[33]*Annual Register . . . 1833,* pp. 314-19*. Wall's case is mentioned as number 5 in note 56.

[34]Letter to John Murray, 19 Nov. 1820; *Byron's Letters and Journals,* VII, 230.

[35]*Byron's Letters and Journals,* I, 110-12.

[36]Letter to Bankes, 20 Nov. 1819; *Byron's Letters and Journals,* VI, 243.

[37]31 Aug. and 7 Oct. 1820; *Byron's Letters and Journals,* VII, 168, 195.

[38]A. L. Rowse, *Homosexuals in History* (London: Weidenfeld and Nicolson, 1977), pp. 120-25.

[39]8 June, p. 6, col. 5.

[40]*Annual Register . . . 1883,* p. 169*.

[41]Great Britain, Parliament, *Second Report from His Majesty's Commissioners on Criminal Law, 20 June, 1836,* pp. 33, 112.

[42]*Parliamentary Debates,* 3rd ser., LVIII, cols. 1557, 1568.

Stoddard's Little Tricks
in *South Sea Idyls*

Roger Austen, M.A.

In 1873 American readers had come to expect certain ripely romantic qualities in books about travel to foreign lands, and perhaps even a certain overripeness when these books described life in the tropics. Exotic sights, sounds, smells, and tastes were to be vividly re-created so that armchair travelers could escape for a few minutes into the only paradise they would know this side of Heaven. In *South Sea Idyls,* Charles Warren Stoddard gave these readers all the lushness they could desire, plus a dollop of dreamy homoeroticism, which, astoundingly, hardly anyone seemed to recognize as such.

Stoddard first went to the South Seas in 1864, as the twenty-one-year-old "Boy Poet of San Francisco." Hoping to recover his equilibrium after an emotionally devastating year at Oakland's Brayton Academy, Stoddard did much more than that — he found love in the arms of Kane-Aloha on the island of Hawaii. Returning to San Francisco, he occupied himself during the next few years by publishing a slim volume of pastel poems and seeking refuge in the bosom of the Roman Catholic Church. In 1868 he sailed again to Hawaii, as a free-lancer for the San Francisco *Evening-Bulletin*. From Hawaii he wrote to Walt Whitman that he was acting as his "nature" prompted him in a way he could not "even in California, where men are tolerably bold." In 1870 Stoddard went to Tahiti for a few months, hoping to gather material for sketches that, along with those he had been writing about Hawaii, he planned to gather together in a book under the title *South Sea Bubbles*. In 1872 he went to Hawaii once more. On his return to San Francisco, Stoddard's friends Bret Harte, Ambrose Bierce, and Joaquin Miller paved the way for the publication of *South Sea Idyls*, both here and in England.

Down through the years, relatively sophisticated literary critics have persisted in pegging *South Sea Idyls* as merely an airy, humorous travelogue, which, though containing an extraordinary number of good-looking, naked young males, is essentially sexless in its point of view.

Roger Austen is an Assistant Lecturer at the University of Southern California. He is the author of *Playing the Game: The Homosexual Novel in America* (1977) and is a contributing editor of the *San Francisco Review of Books*. He is currently engaged in research on D. H. Lawrence.

Granted, Stoddard's homoeroticism doesn't dominate every one of the sixteen sketches included in the book. In "The Chapel of the Palms," for example, he devotes himself to one of his other pet themes — the beautiful, self-sacrificing lives of Roman Catholic priests who have found a certain enviable serenity in their service to the church. Nor is there anything very sexual in "The Last of the Great Navigator," which simply recalls the final days of Captain Cook on Hawaii. But in most of the pieces, either in the background or the foreground, there is at least one handsome young pagan who captures Stoddard's eye or heart or both. For instance, in "Taboo" the narrator is not so much interested in his misshapen companion as he is in the perfectly shaped, "naked and superbly built fellows" who shinny up a greased pole, or in the sight of the hundred young bucks in their war canoes, all "stripped to the skin and bareheaded," their "brawny bodies glistening in the sun as though they had been oiled. . . ." In "Joe of Lahaina" the young man's significance can hardly be overlooked.[1] One night, spying Joe in the moonlit ocean, Stoddard is so struck by the scapegrace's "fresh and joyous physique" that he realizes "how the old Greeks could worship mere physical beauty and forget higher forms." Soon the Stoddard persona and Joe set up "housekeeping" — which "*is* good fun," including as it does the sensual evening ritual of drinking cocoa milk, eating bananas, and then going "to bed, because we had nothing else to do." But of all the tales in this book, perhaps the greatest degree of homoeroticism can be found in "Chumming with a Savage," based on the 1869 visit to Molokai, and "Pearl Hunting in the Pomotous" and "In a Transport," both based on the 1870 trip to Tahiti.

In "Chumming with a Savage," Stoddard and Kana-ana give themselves up to nearly every sensual delight imaginable. They sleep together in a huge Elizabethan bed, its posts charmingly festooned with wreaths, as if for their honeymoon. Kana-ana, it seems, will not let Stoddard alone.

> Again and again, he would come with a delicious banana to the bed where I was lying, and insist upon my gorging myself. . . . He would mesmerize me into a most refreshing sleep with a prolonged and pleasing manipulation.[2]

After their prodigal time together, Stoddard tears himself away from this young savage, who has loved him "more than anyone else can."

In the much more fanciful "pearl hunting" story, Stoddard is impressed by a pearl diver who looks like a "wild Hercules" and whose name is Hua Manu. After the native swims up to Stoddard's schooner, hearts are exchanged during a Romeo and Juliet "balcony scene." The tale ends melodramatically on a tiny desert island, where "Romeo" gives up his life for his new-found bosom friend. Unlike Melville's *White Jacket, Redburn,* and *Billy Budd,* "In a Transport" suggests that shipboard romances between men can be fun. Here the cast of characters includes ten "bold" young French sailors on a training ship, a shameless first officer who is the "happy possessor" of a "tight little African" named Nero, and the Stoddard persona, who spends most of his time hugging Thanaron, a French sailor whose "handsome little body" everyone on board loves to squeeze. His intimacies with Thanaron were such, Stoddard hints, that "by the time we sighted the green summits of Tahiti, my range of experience was so great that nothing could touch me further" (p. 297).

While Stoddard's unabashed delight in seeing and touching and being touched by handsome, naked males seems rather obvious to us now, at the same time it is understandable that *South Sea Idyls* caused few eyebrows to be raised a hundred years ago. The combination of innocence and ignorance of nineteenth-century readers was a key factor, of course, but another was Stoddard's half-shrewd, half-bumbling technique of constructing sentences and paragraphs so as to cover his tracks with confusion. The governing pattern in the following examples of this "technique" can be compared with a squirrel venturing out, farther and farther, to the leafy end of a branch. When swaying signals danger to the squirrel's brain, it stops short and leaps back to safety as nimbly as it can. Likewise, instead of crossing out and revising passages of telltale homoeroticism, Stoddard in his lazy way merely retreated, hoping he could scurry back to safety under a mindless barrage of misleading explanations.[3]

The first example is taken from the paragraph in "Chumming with a Savage" that shows Stoddard getting into bed with Kana-ana for the first time.

> Over the sand we went, and through the river to his hut, where I was taken in, fed, and petted in every possible way, and finally put to bed, where Kana-ana monopolized me, growling in true savage fashion if anyone came near me. I didn't sleep much, after all. I think I must have been excited. (p. 4)

Excited? Now he *is* in trouble. But rather than crossing out that last sentence, he gropes about for some suitable basis for the excitement. The paragraph continues:

> I thought how strangely I was situated: alone in a wilderness, among barbarians; my bosom friend, who was hugging me like a

young bear, not able to speak one syllable of English, and I very
shaky in a few bad phrases of his tongue.

The explanation that he is distressed at the thought of sleeping among
barbarians is belied by his being among hospitable Hawaiians who pose
no threat to him at all. Nor under normal circumstances could a sudden
awareness of impending language difficulties be strong enough to induce
the emotion of excitement. Most revealing of all, though, is the fact that
he has carelessly dropped his mask in midflight. By including "who was
hugging me like a young bear," Stoddard betrays the true cause of
excitement during his willy-nilly search for a camouflage.

In another example from this tale, Stoddard is still in bed, now peer-
ing at the sleeping body of Kana-ana:

> He lay close to me. His sleek figure, supple and graceful in repose,
> was the embodiment of free, untramelled youth. You who are
> brought up under cover know nothing of its luxuriousness. How I
> longed to take him . . . (p. 26)

What Stoddard goes on to say is surely about the last thing he must
have had on his mind. After describing, in euphemistic terms, the joys
of being naked, he turns right around and suggests they go to America
and put on some clothes:

> . . . over the sea with me, and show him something of life as we
> find it. Thinking about it, I dropped off into one of those delicious
> morning naps.

In midparagraph in "Pearl Hunting in the Pomotous," Stoddard again
realizes he has tipped his hand. During the "balcony scene," Hua Manu
begins "making vows of eternal friendship," vows that are "by no means
disagreeable" to the narrator now playing Juliet. But why are these vows
not disagreeable, or, rather, why are they so agreeable? Is it the beauty
of the native's Herculean physique that nudges the narrator into recipro-
cating? No, Stoddard wants us to believe, it is Hua Manu's intimidating
size:

> He was big enough to whip any two of his fellows, and one likes
> to be on the best side of the stronger party in a strange land.
> I reciprocated!
> I leaned over the stern-rail . . assuring the egg-boy that my
> heart was his if he was willing to take it at second-hand.[4]

A final example will be cited from "In a Transport," which is surely
one of the most lavender pieces of prose written by anyone in the

nineteenth century. In the following paragraph, Stoddard wants to show both the cause and the effect of the ship's crew and passengers being "unmanned" as they catch sight of Tahiti:

> There was something in the delicious atmosphere, growing warmer every day, and something in the delicious sea, that was beginning to rock her floating gardens of blooming weed under our bows, and something in the aspect of *Monsieur le Capitaine* . . . that unmanned us; so we rushed to our own little cabin and hugged one another . . . (p. 297)

Stoddard seemed to realize that the conjunction *so* was not strong enough to stand alone in explaining why he and Thanaron were hugging each other. What motivation, precisely, had they? How to finish this sentence in order to satisfy or at least confound the reader?

> . . . lest we should forget how when we were restored to our sisters and our sweethearts, and everything was forgiven and forgotten in one intense moment of French remorse.

This conclusion is, of course, the most feeble nonsense. The last clause about forgiveness is so devoid of meaning as to be almost gibberish, and what could be more lame than the idea that men need to hug each other just to keep in practice? Nonetheless, the spray of words following "lest" no doubt convinced nineteenth-century readers that the narrator and Thanaron were embracing for reasons that, not being perfectly clear or convincing, were therefore meant to be quaintly amusing.

South Sea Idyls does not have the wit to amuse us today, but in 1873 a great many people apparently found this book awfully funny. In terms of its homosexual overtones, they were almost obliged to. Because the magazine reviewers refused to believe that Stoddard had any serious interest in hugging French sailors or going to bed with naked savages, they decided these aspects of the book represented nothing more than Stoddard's attempt to have his little joke.

The reviewer in the *Nation* pegged Stoddard as a "California humorist" who wrote in the tall-tale vein of Bret Harte and Mark Twain. *South Sea Idyls*, said this reviewer with East Coast condescension, "was amusing with a dreamy sort of amusement, which we suppose is the proper color for California humor to take upon itself in the tropics."[5] In the *Atlantic Monthly* review (unsigned, but apparently written by William Dean Howells), it was mentioned that Stoddard professed to be an "unrepentant prodigal son"; but surely, the reviewer added, Stoddard's prose of unrepentance was merely a part of the overall "drollery." The "amiable French midshipmen and lieutenants" who hug and kiss each other during "In a Transport" were regarded as amusing, and the tale was cited as a good example of the author's "airy humor." Altogether, the *Atlantic* critic said in summary, *South Sea Idyls* was a welcome "addition to the stock of refined pleasures" from which cultured readers could choose.[6]

During the last one hundred years nearly everyone who has written for publication about this book has been unable, or unwilling, to recognize the pervasive undercurrent of sexuality for what it is. Either through obtuseness or chagrin, most commentators have preferred to dwell on the safer aspects of the idyls and to ignore Stoddard's hints of "adhesiveness" altogether.[7] Writing about Stoddard in *The Times of Melville and Whitman,* American literary historian Van Wyck Brooks echoed the sentiments of William Dean Howells. Howells had termed Stoddard's tales the "lightest, sweetest, wildest, freshest things that ever were written" about the South Seas, and Brooks agreed that Stoddard was a master of the picturesque detail. What is missing as Brooks sketches a panorama of all that Stoddard loved best in the tropics?

> He loved the dreamy days of calm in the flowering equatorial waters, the booming of the surf on the beaches, the clashing of the palm-fronds, the twilight glow on the yellow shores . . . the groves with their seventeen shades of green. . . .[8]

Scrupulously airbrushed out of this panorama are all the lovable young males who scamper in and out of *South Sea Idyls.*

And these young men are also ignored, of course, when Catholic critics have tried to sum up the book. It is true, wrote Father Francis O'Neill in a 1917 issue of *Catholic World*, that Stoddard took a fancy to a "dear little velvet-skinned, coffee-colored chum" named Kana-ana, but Stoddard's motivation was probably just his "boundless sympathy" for all humanity.[9] These tales "remain the most popular of Stoddard's books," O'Neill claims, "for in them is blended tranquil, yet enthusiastic joys, soul stirring pathos and a spiritual vision that counts the trappings of artificial living not worth striving for."

When Franklin Walker wrote *San Francisco's Literary Frontier* in 1939, it seemed that someone was finally summoning up the courage to say the obvious about *South Sea Idyls.*

> The emphasis in this unusual picture of island life is not on the customary brown maidens with firm breasts, lithe limbs, and generous impulses, but on strong-backed youths, human porpoises who drive their canoes through the mists of the storm and share their joys and sorrows with the prodigal from California.[10]

But what was the precise appeal of these "strong-backed youths?" Was it not their equally interesting torsos and limbs, and their equally generous impulses? Walker, not daring to complete his sentences with a parallel cataloguing of the youths' attractions, retreats behind a Stoddard-like barrage of innocuous information that is essentially irrelevant.

Just a few years ago an even more reticent critic — a professor of English at the University of Pittsburgh — wrote of Stoddard and *South Sea Idyls* in almost exclusively heterosexual, or at least sexless, terms. Granted, Robert Gale does perceive a little bit of "miscegenating" going on between that French officer and his black servant in the middle of "In a Transport," but Stoddard himself is thought never to have "miscegenated." In summing up the author's "favorite pleasures" in *South Sea Idyls*, Gale counts just three: "lonely observing and luscious eating — his word pictures here would inspire a half-dozen latter-day Gauguins — and lying in bed late, alone again and sometimes almost with a death fixation."[11] One could argue that Stoddard wasn't always alone as he slept in and that he derived enormous pleasure from the cuddly companionship of his lively bedpartners. But, no, Gale will have none of it.

A noteworthy exception to all these examples of blindness or squeamishness or wrongheadedness is the commentary Edward Prime Stevenson wrote at the turn of the century. This pioneering homosexual propagandist, writing as "Xavier Mayne" in *The Intersexes*, was quick to recognize Stoddard's "predilections" for what they were. In his chapter on "philarrhenic literature" in America, Stevenson reprints a passage from "Chumming with a Savage" as a fine example of Uranian prose.[12]

Shortly before his death, Stoddard wrote another tale of his trip to Tahiti, "The Island of Tranquil Delights," which was published in 1904. In it he seems to be expressing his gratitude to the beautiful, tender-hearted Tahitians (using a tone of voice that John Horne Burns was to adopt when he described the simpatico Italians in *The Gallery*):

> I was a stranger in their midst . . . they pitied me for the sorrows I had known . . . the suffering I had endured . . . for the indelible scars I bore in form and feature, these the unmistakable evidences of civilization. . . . They were beautiful . . . they were olive-tinted and this tint was of the tenderest olive. . . . They had the gift and the voice and the eyes of love. . . .[13]

Here Stoddard seems to be announcing what he wasn't quite ready to spell out in 1873. And yet, between the lines and in spite of all of the back-pedaling, the message of *South Sea Idyls* is abundantly clear. If one is willing to look beyond conventional descriptions of "seventeen shades of green" and the pleasures of "luscious eating," one can see that Stoddard's message is a joyous celebration of "coming out," thanks to the obliging young pagans of the South Seas who had the "gift and the voice and the eyes of love."

NOTES

[1]From a biographical point of view, "Joe" is also of special interest. In the Huntington Library is a letter Stoddard wrote on 15 Oct. 1901 to his friend Dewitt Miller, who wanted to know which of the South Sea fellows had been "Greek" as defined by John Addington Symonds. Joe of Lahaina, Stoddard replied, was the one "most inclined that way," though he was also interested in girls, being at what James Whitcomb Riley fondly called the Red Pecker Age. Stoddard perceived that Riley himself might be "inclined that way."

[2]*South Sea Idyls*, 2nd ed. (New York: Scribners, 1892), p. 32. My page references throughout are to this edition of the book. In keeping with the streamlined punctuation of the twentieth century, I am dropping the original hyphen between *South* and *Sea*.

[3]One of the reasons why Stoddard was not a first-rate writer is that he lacked the capacity to shape a soft, oozing first draft into a sharp, hard-hitting, polished product. As Carl Stroven has noted in his doctoral dissertation on Stoddard, "he was an 'inspirational' writer, who composed freely only during moments of the creative impulse and who seldom knew whither his pen was bound" (Duke Univ., 1939).

Stoven's dissertation is invaluable for anyone studying Stoddard. It includes an appendix containing Stoddard's diaries (written in Hawaii during the early 1880s), which overflow with lovelorn lamentations. At this time Stoddard was caught up in a painful sort of triangle: he was in love with young Charlie Deering, who was in love with Mrs. Belle Strong (Mrs. Robert Louis Stevenson's daughter), who flirted — along with Stoddard — with any good-looking naval officers who were stopping over in Honolulu. Dr. Stroven's kind cooperation has assisted me greatly in my research, and I am much in his debt.

[4]P. 139. Ambrose Bierce, who called this tale "outrageous," was one of Stoddard's contemporaries who saw through all of the camouflage. "You lie enormously — unconscionably," Bierce teased in a letter on 2 Feb. 1874 (now in the Huntington) after reading the book. At this time tolerantly aware of his friend's penchant for falling in love with "nigger boys," Bierce later broke with Stoddard. In 1909 Bierce told poet George Sterling that he objected to Stoddard's not being "content with the way God had sexed him." See M. E. Grenander's "Ambrose Bierce and Charles Warren Stoddard: Some Unpublished Correspondence," *Huntington Library Quarterly*, 23, No. 2 (1960), 261-292.

[5]*Nation*, 18 Dec. 1873, p. 411.

[6]*Atlantic Monthly*, Dec. 1873, p. 742.

[7]Somewhat more approvingly than Ambrose Bierce, Walt Whitman was also able to recognize the "adhesive" tone of Stoddard's affections, but again this recognition was expressed in a private letter rather than a printed review. After "Chumming with a Savage" was printed in the *Overland Monthly*, Stoddard mailed a copy with compliments to his favorite American poet. In April 1870, Whitman responded by saying that he found the tale "nourishing" and he "warmly" approved of Stoddard's "adhesive nature, & the outlet thereof." But, Whitman added, couldn't Stoddard stop being so airy and come down to earth and start writing about the "hard, pungent, gritty" aspects of American life? As it turned out, the answer was no. Whitman's letter can be found in Jonathan Katz, *Gay American History* (New York: Thomas Y. Crowell, 1976), pp. 507-08.

[8]Van Wyck Brooks, *The Times of Melville and Whitman* (New York: Dutton, 1953), p. 271.

[9]Francis O'Neill, O.P., "Stoddard, Psalmist of the South Seas," *Catholic World*, July 1917, p. 512. In another Catholic publication (*Ave Maria*, 22 May 1909), a friend of Stoddard's named George James tried to come to grips with this subject. Writing shortly after Stoddard's death, James asked, "How could a man of such culture . . . ever so demean himself to live" and sleep with the savages? James answered that Stoddard had essentially been attracted by the spiritual qualities of his island chums: "He saw the inner and beautiful things of the soul — the purest affection, the devotion, the simplicity, the tenderness, the gentleness, the innate poetry and instinctive religious feeling of the child of Nature."

[10]Franklin Walker, *San Francisco's Literary Frontier* (Seattle: Univ. of Washington Press, 1939), p. 273.

[11]This quote is taken from p. 14 of Gale's 49-page pamphlet *Charles Warren Stoddard*, which was published by Boise State University in 1977 as part of the Western Writers Series. Perversely obdurate, Gale again reveals his imperceptiveness when he turns to Stoddard's 1903 novel, the equally homoerotic *For the Pleasure of His Company*. Remarking on the word *Affair* in the novel's subtitle, Gale terms it a "teasing misusage," since the hero loves only things, not women. (Once

more the hero's favorite pleasures, Gale tells us, are neatly threefold: books, seafood, and the moonlit San Francisco Bay.) Unobserved by Gale, who apparently doesn't understand that homosexuals, like heterosexuals, can have "affairs," Stoddard's autobiographical hero has at least two in this novel: one with "Foxlair" (based on the charming, mysterious Samuel Wylde Hardinge, the ex-husband of Belle Boyd, Civil War spy for the Confederacy) and another with "Roscius" (based on Eben Plympton, an impetuous homosexual who became a rather famous Broadway actor). In reviewing Gale's pamphlet in *American Literary Realism* (Autumn 1978), M. E. Grenander observes that Gale skirts the issue of Stoddard's sexuality to the extent "that the reader might miss it entirely. Yet it was a central force in Stoddard's life . . .," p. 334.

[12]Edward Prime Stevenson [Xavier Mayne], *The Intersexes: A History of Similisexualism as a Problem in Social Life* (1908; rpt. New York: Arno Press, 1973), pp. 383-86. Much more recently one other American writer has dealt perceptively with Stoddard. Although *Land's End* (1979) is a novel, California literary historian Kevin Starr obviously did considerable research in the Bancroft before creating his cameo character of Stoddard. For instance, readers of this novel are given a turn-of-the-century glimpse of Stoddard and his "kid," Kenneth O'Connor, at St. Anthony's Rest in Washington, D.C., just as they were in real life.

[13]The Tahitian men are described in passing on pp. 26-31 of *The Island of Tranquil Delights*, which was published by Herbert B. Turner in Boston. In this volume Stoddard is much more daring in describing his romantic adventures in Tahiti than he was when writing *South Sea Idyls*. He insists that he was abducted *often*. "Was I not seized bodily one night," he asks rhetorically, "one glorious night and . . . borne down the ravine by a young giant, sleek and supple as a bronzed Greek god, who kept me captive in his Indian lodge till I surfeited on breadfruits and plantain and cocoanut milk? And then did we not part with a pang — one of those pangs that always leaves a memory and a scar? And this happened not once, but often. . . ." Whether these steamier passages in the later book should be regarded as an accurate memory of the uncontrollable lusts of Tahitian males or merely as evidence of a wistful old man's tendency to exaggerate the past is hard to say.

Henry James:
Interpreting an Obsessive Memory

Richard Hall

The rules by which texts may be interpreted, within what theoretical frameworks the reader may explore a novel or play or poem, have become increasingly vague in recent years. The notion of a "correct" reading, as well as an unquestioned "value," has tended to disappear. The job of interpretation is seen as unending, and radical reinterpretations of standard works appear regularly. These readings may be set beside previous ones; thus, relativism becomes a component in critical discourse, allowing each reader to go his or her own way provided a responsibility to the text is met in terms of image, tone, contemporaneity, etc.

Although this process grants theoretical freedom to an interpreter, who may measure a work by psychological or moral structures quite alien to the author's, in actual practice there are limits to such freedom. These limits may constrain a critic politically, economically, or socially without ever being publicly acknowledged.

For example, Marxist, Maoist, or anarchist readings of texts may be so dangerous to one's career, or so unlikely to be published, that the critic is, in effect, prevented from offering them. In the same way, breaches of sexual taboos may be so unwelcome that the critic is prohibited from developing them. This constraint has been noticeable where homosexuality is concerned — in readings of texts by Whitman, Thoreau, Hawthorne, for example — though there is some indication that a new freedom of discussion is now permitted. New freedom has not, however, been granted to critics who would like to violate deeper and darker taboos, such as those involving incest (whether homosexual or heterosexual), a central theme in the life and work of Henry James.

The process of censorship where the homosexual imagination is concerned has been well documented in the special edition of *College*

Richard Hall has authored fiction (*The Butterscotch Prince*, 1975; *Couplings: A Book of Stories*, 1981), as well as several popular plays and a great many articles and reviews. From 1976 to 1982 he was a contributing editor (books) for *The Advocate*. He is a member of the National Book Critics Circle, the first openly gay critic to be so honored, as well as of American Pen. He is presently working on a full-length study of the relationship between Henry and William James.

English (1974) edited by Louie Crew and Rictor Norton.[1] The antigay bias may take many forms, all described in detail by Crew and Norton in their opening editorial: the destruction of homosexual texts, the deletion of homosexually relevant information from existing texts, the heterosexualization of texts after initial publication, the deliberate overlooking by scholars of texts that might lead to homosexuality, the unavailability in libraries of overtly gay materials, negative appraisals of works whose gay content cannot be avoided, and — most subtle of all — the refusal to discuss the homophobic prejudice that created the whole situation in the first place.

It has become increasingly apparent, since publication of the Crew/Norton article, that the antigay bias in academia can best be countered by the progay bias of homosexual critics.

I have made these prefatory remarks because it is not only certain biographical and textual data about Henry James that I wish to present here but also the treatment of it by the major Jamesian of our era, Leon Edel. Edel's handling of the material, which he unearthed and put together in one of the great biographies of our time, illustrates in complex and subtle ways the problems facing both the nongay and the gay critic. Not only literature is involved but the sociology of literature. The interpretation of Henry James by Leon Edel illustrates in miniature what taboos, artifices, and self-deceptions have been employed by literary critics since the genre began with Samuel Johnson's *Prefaces to Shakespeare*.

The "problem" of Henry James has always intrigued me — the problem being a certain biographical weightlessness despite the enormous accretion of letters, journals, workbooks, etc., and a sexual reticence that leaves a puzzling emotional vacancy at the center of his life and the lives of his fictional protagonists. James's sexual dormancy has given rise to numerous explanations, including impotence, physical injury, and hormonal dysfunction. In recent years arguments emphasizing his homosexuality have been put forward by gay critics, despite a certain lack of concrete evidence.

It became clear to me, however, soon after finishing the fifth and last volume of Edel's biography, that James's apparent asexuality derived not from repressed homosexuality, injury, or hormonal dysfunction but from a profound and lifelong fixation on his brother William, older than he by sixteen months. This fixation had preempted Henry's undoubted homosexual feelings and constituted the core of his affective life.[2]

This theory of homosexual incest brought me to the attention of Edel, who confirmed my ideas. "Your entire chain of evidence is certainly convincing to me. . . . The subject of incest has been neglected and in my volumes is only implicit; if I were writing these volumes today I would indeed make much more of this."³ Later, in a personal interview in New York, he remarked to me, "Once we agree on Henry's love fixation on William, that explains a lot of things. . . . You've opened up something that would make me want to reread James from beginning to end."⁴

The promptness with which Edel accepted my views surprised me until I read some of his theories of literary biography. He has stated:

> . . . in our quest for the life-myth we tread on dangerous speculative and inferential ground that requires all of our attention, all of our accumulated resources. For we must read certain psychological signs that enable us to understand what people are really saying behind the faces they put on, behind the utterances they allow themselves to make before the world.⁵

In short, Edel wants to find the hidden truth, the face behind the mask. His is the approach of an artist and a Freudian psychologist, ferreting out unconscious motives, as long as the hypotheses offered can be based on data, to some extent.

And yet — and this is the key question — if this is indeed Edel's intention, why did he not uncover the libidinal nature of the relationship between Henry and William James? Why was it only "implicit" in his biography, which is another way of saying not seen and not commented on? He has been steeped in the James family since the early 1930s, when he earned his doctorate at the Sorbonne with a dissertation on the plays of Henry James. He has edited the novels, tales, plays, letters, and assorted personal papers of the Master. He is co-compiler of the major bibliography. Given his interest in psychological speculation and his belief (unlike that of some critics) that biography can be used to illuminate texts and vice versa, one would expect that the central libidinal relationship between the brothers would have been apparent to him at an early date. It was not. Edel left the sexual dormancy at the center of Henry's life largely unexplained, for which he was criticized by more than one reviewer. How to explain, then, this timidity in a biographer who stated to me, "I try to operate without any bias, I do not sit in judgment on my subject. . . . Other biographers, yes, they have sexual hang-ups and so on; I don't think I have."⁶

I believe this inability to see — and it must be considered unconscious, not conscious — has two roots, personal and social. On the personal level, Edel is (by his own admission) heterosexual. Thus he lacks the experience that would equip him to imagine a certain kind of eroticism, to believe in its possibility, and to seek the empirical evidence to support his belief. As a result of his historical, social, and personal background, he lacks what Heidegger called *Vorverständnis*, preunderstanding. Once the evidence was presented to him — my summing-up based on his own researches — Edel seized it instantly, which is to his credit. But he was not empowered by his own life and experience to see an erotic component in the relationship between the two brothers. His psychic terrain was not coextensive with theirs, and his powers of insight or imagination did not permit him to take that last synoptic leap into the most daring conjecture.[7]

On a macro, or social, level inhibition also carried the day. While homosexuality might be discussed with greater freedom during the writing of the later biographical volumes (all were written between 1950 and 1971), homosexual incest was another matter. It incorporates a double taboo — sex between men and between brothers. Where there was a limited sanction for discussing homosexuality, there was none for homosexual incest. Certainly the institutional setting within which Edel worked was not conducive to such speculation. He taught at New York University, eventually becoming the first Henry James Professor of European and American Literature. He received several grants to help him finish his multivolume work, including two Guggenheims and a Bollingen Fellowship. The hundreds of individuals, memoirists, curators, literary executors, and members of the James family who opened their archives to him might well have demurred if in the first volume (1953) he had announced that the central relationship of Henry's life was built around a passionate love for his brother. In fact, it is quite likely that later volumes of the biography would have been squelched if he had come up with such a thesis in the first volume!

The restrictions on Edel's vision by private and public restraint are all the more disheartening in that a book of literary criticism was published in 1962 — *Henry James and the Jacobites* by Maxwell Geismar — that might have enabled Edel to see things more clearly, had he been able to dare a little more. Geismar, a critic and historian of American literature, explores with brilliant if sporadic insight the role of brotherly love in the Jamesian canon. He traces it in tales like "The Pupil" and "The Turn of the Screw," and in the novels *What Maisie Knew, The Sacred Fount*, and *The Awkward Age* — the last of which he calls "a kind of dialogue of incest." At one point Geismar notes, "there is no doubt as to the recessive, intertwined emotions of infantile and often quite incestuous sexuality which James, all so innocently, poured into these narratives."[8]

Geismar analyzes in some detail "The Pupil," a curious tale about a loving relationship between an eleven-year-old named Morgan Moreen and his tutor, Pemberton, who ultimately rejects the boy. While Edel describes the work in pederastic terms as "a delicate tale of a sensitive boy and his attachment to his tutor," Geismar sees it in a darker frame altogether, calling it "a study of [James's] familiar orphan princeling, who had the good fortune to gain an older and protective filial guardian. Perhaps this was what William James *should* have been; or what Henry himself wanted — but still how these curiously incestuous if not directly homosexual and potentially perverse relationships hovered around his unconscious!"[9]

Such hints and speculations did not provoke a response in Edel, who at the time the Geismar volume appeared was working on Volume IV of the biograph, subtitled "The Treacherous Years." He was not prepared to revise his analysis of William and Henry, an analysis that washed out the sexual love in their relationship and limited it chiefly to sibling rivalry. Edel's insights are often daring and his surmises brilliant, but he never takes the final step from repressed sexuality to active libidinal feeling. Thus, in denying Henry the freedom of his passions, Edel condescended both to his subject and to his time, and conformed to the implicit taboos of his own society and personal experience.

The gay critic of today, however, working in a more permissive cultural climate and charged with a "preunderstanding" of the facts of James's life, is in a position to make new conjectural leaps. My own continuing researches into the life and work of Henry James have yielded data and interpretations which, right or wrong, are noteworthy in that they stem from the premise that expressed sexuality was an important component in James's life, at least during his younger years. Working from this premise, I was able to pursue avenues of inquiry closed to earlier investigators. What follows is a detailed presentation of one chain of evidence. My purpose is not to show that Edel is "wrong" nor to diminish the greatness of his achievement, to which we are all indebted, but to show that his unconscious bias skewed his conclusions, thus proving the truth of Crew and Norton's statement that heterosexuals do not have "the best perspective from which to accurately view the gay experience . . . because they lack awareness of the non-erotic nuances of the daily casual life of homosexuals in a hostile society. . . ."[10]

Of Henry James's many English friends, perhaps his closest was Edmund Gosse, a linguist, poet, and literary critic who was half-American (his mother came from Boston). Gosse was married and a deeply closeted homosexual. For example, only after fifteen years of friendship, in 1890, did Gosse admit to J. A. Symonds, around the time the latter was working on *A Problem in Greek Ethics*, that indeed he was gay, thus confirming the suspicions Symonds had voiced earlier. "Years ago I wanted to write to you about all this," Gosse wrote to Symonds, "and withdrew through cowardice. I have had a very fortunate life, but there has been this obstinate twist in it!"[11]

It is highly unlikely that Gosse expressed his gay feelings to another friend, Henry James. One suspects their friendship flourished not because of what was said but because of what was left unsaid. Henry undoubtedly sensed Gosse's essential nature and was doubly reassured — both by Gosse's gayness and by his muteness on the subject. It seems unlikely that Henry would have chosen Gosse as the recipient of his disapproving views of Oscar Wilde and the court case ("the squalid gratuitousness of it all . . . this guilt of obscenity . . . this hideous human history") if he had previously heard Gosse's confession of homosexuality.

In 1920, in two consecutive issues of *The London Mercury*, four years after Henry's death, Gosse published two short memoirs of his old friend.[12] He speaks of Henry's personality at some length, describing his manner as "grave, extremely courteous, but a little formal and frightened." He says Henry was "superficially gregarious, essentially isolated." Gosse remarks that, especially during the years in London, before Henry's removal to Lamb House in Rye in 1896, "there had hung over him a sort of canopy, a mixture of reserve and deprecation, faintly darkening the fullness of communion with his character; there had always seemed to be something indefinably non-conductive between him and those in whom he had most confidence. . . ."[13]

I quote this assessment of Henry's shy and withdrawn character, even in the company of an intimate friend, in order to set in perspective the extraordinary revelation James made to Gosse one evening at Lamb House around the turn of the century. It is the atypicality of the occasion that makes it important. In another writer the expression of so much emotion would not be remarkable; in Henry James it is unusual to the highest degree. Gosse writes:

> I was staying alone with Henry James at Rye one summer, and as twilight deepened we walked together in the garden. I forget by what meanders we approached the subject, but I suddenly found that in profuse and enigmatic language he was recounting for me an experience, something that had happened, not something repeated or imagined. He spoke of standing on the pavement of a city, in the dusk, and of gazing upwards across the misty street, watching, watching for the lighting of a lamp in a window on the third storey. And the lamp blazed out, and through bursting tears he strained to see what was behind it, the unapproachable face. And for hours he stood there, wet with the rain, brushed by the phantom hurrying figures of the scene, and never from behind the lamp was for one moment visible the face. The mysterious and poignant revelation closed, and one could make no comment, ask no question, being throttled oneself by an overpowering emotion.

And for a long time Henry James shuffled beside me in the darkness, shaking the dew off the laurels, and still there was no sound
at all in the garden but what our heels made crunching the gravel,
nor was the silence broken when suddenly we entered the house
and he disappeared for an hour.[14]

Before examining this account in detail, two additional points should
be made.

First, Henry told his young friend Hugh Walpole the same story
around 1911 or 1912 — roughly a dozen years later — during a week-
end visit by Walpole to Lamb House. Walpole, who was one of three
young men cherished by the elder James (the others were Hendrik
Andersen and Jocelyn Persse) recalled the occasion almost thirty years
later:

Sexually also he had suffered some frustration. What that frustration was I never knew, but I remember him telling me how he had
once in his youth in a foreign town watched a whole night in
pouring rain for the appearance of a figure at a window. "That
was the end . . ." he said, and broke off.[15]

The second point concerns Leon Edel's treatment of this anecdote
twice-told. "I didn't use it in the biog," he wrote to me quite simply,
after I had called it to his attention. Edel dismissed the episode in his
letter to me as "the whole story about James's straining in the night
to look at someone in a window."[16] In other words, he attached no
unusual significance, psychological or biographical, to the account.

By contrast, I find the window episode very resonant for James, both
biographically and as an aid to interpretation of certain passages; but in
this conclusion I am helped immeasurably by my gay instincts. My arguments fall into three categories — but first the memory itself.

If we assume that Henry's relationship with William was the central
one of his life, then we must assume that this story, with its heavy
burden of pain, related to William — to some betrayal or rejection of
Henry. What are we to conclude from the few clues that survive? First,
that William failed to keep a promise to appear: ". . . and never from
behind the lamp was for one moment visible the face." The sight of
William's face, after the lamp was lit in the third-story window, might
have been a signal that Henry, waiting in the street below, was welcome
upstairs. On the other hand, William's nonappearance might have been
a sign that someone else was with him, someone whose presence excluded Henry in some definitive way. Could it have been a woman — a
replacement for the shy and loving introvert waiting below? Could it
have been a final choice by William, his long-dormant heterosexuality

asserting itself? We will probably never know for sure. But we do know that Henry was left, quite literally, out in the cold, the sign not given, the welcome not extended. And the rejection was final. The rendezvous not kept constituted "the end" of Henry's relationship with William as it had been. Henry was deeply hurt and never fully recovered.

1. *The Psychological Perspective.* Henry, as we know, was not given to much display of emotion. Like many of his characters, he often used conversation as a way of evading the swell of heavy but unnamed passions underneath. Yet here he is, breaking through the reserve that usually encumbered him, telling a story that "throttled" his hearer with "an overpowering emotion." After telling it, Henry must disappear for an hour, apparently too shaken to continue. A dozen years later he tells the same story to Walpole, then must break off because once again the passion threatens to break through.

It is notable that Henry could not manage either to name "the unapproachable face" at the window or even to give it a sex. This is common where homosexuality is involved, since to give the loved one a sex would reveal all. Where true emotion is concerned, the homosexual must be discreetly neuter.

Then there is the time lapse. Henry speaks of his "youth," according to Hugh Walpole. I hope to show the episode as occurring in Rome in December 1873, which would place it approximately forty years before James related the story to young Hugh. Can anyone doubt its significance when it can still render Henry incapable of speech forty years later?

In 1916, in the final days before his death, Henry's confused and emotional ramblings were noted down by his secretary, sister-in-law, and niece. At one point he said to his niece, Peggy, "I hope your father will be in soon — he is the only person in all of Rome I want to see." Later he remarked, "I should so like to have William with me." This is interesting on several counts. At the time, William had been dead six years. Yet, he had sprung to intense life for Henry, then in his heroic life-and-death struggles. And there is the choice of city. Why Rome? William and Henry had spent long periods together in New York, Boston, Cambridge, London — but only a few weeks in Rome. The best explanation is that the intensity of their sojourn in Rome, its traumatic quality for Henry, gave that city an importance in his unconscious that led to its expression during the hallucinations of his last days.

2. *The Biographical Perspective.* Walpole relates that the incident took place "in a foreign town." A chronology of the trips abroad by Henry James reveals the following:

Trip I: 1843-45
Trip II: 1855-58

Trip III: 1859
Trip IV: 1869-70
Trip V: 1872-74
Trip VI: 1875

Since William was born in 1842 and Henry in 1843, the first three trips, which included the whole family, can be dismissed as likely times for the window episode: both boys would have been too young. Trip IV, 1869-70, when Henry was twenty-six, was a grand tour made by him alone. Trip VI, also by Henry alone, led to his permanent settlement abroad, first in Paris, then in London. That leaves Trip V, a time when both young men were in Europe and spent about two months in each other's company. It was a critical time both chronologically and emotionally for the two brothers, as a look at the events before and after should make clear.

After his fifteen-month *Wanderjahr* in Europe, 1869-70, Henry returned to his parents' home in Cambridge. He was twenty-seven. The trip had been a passionate and wonderful time for him — not only his first trip abroad as an adult but his first one alone. He called it "a banquet of initiation." He visited England, Scotland, Switzerland, Italy, France, Monte Carlo. He had planned to stay longer, but in January 1870, in Rome, he was stricken with an illness that forced his return home. Edel describes Henry's ill health as "a function of intense inner malaise." It was apparently one of those ailments, so common in the James family, that always seemed to strike when someone was having a good time. The three older children — William, Henry, and Alice — were dogged by mysterious and undiagnosable illnesses for much of their lives.

The spring of 1870, when Henry returned from his "passionate pilgrimage in Europe" and settled down in Cambridge, inaugurated a frustrating time for him. His notes, diaries, and letters of the two years he spent at home reveal boredom, loneliness, tension. At this time he began to write seriously and with daily discipline, producing a series of tales, including "A Passionate Pilgrim" and "The Madonna of the Future"; a short novel, *Watch and Ward*; as well as reviews, travel pieces, and art notices. He wanted to flee Cambridge and Boston, their stifling atmosphere and provincialism, believing his future lay in Europe, but he could not summon up the will power to make the break. Some powerful need or inertia kept him at home. In later years he would write of these "deadly days" in Cambridge and the queerness of his life after returning from abroad.

The fiction written during this period, deals, under various disguises, with Henry's domestic discontent. Edel describes them as speaking of "dispossession, disinheritance, exile, usurpation." He writes: "On a deeper level they picture Henry's double exile — his sense of being an outsider at home, his fear of being an outsider in Europe." The tale "Guest's Confession" and the novel *Watch and Ward* dramatize the conflicts of fraternal pairs (brothers or male cousins). On one level they picture much fraternal animosity, as the brother-figures compete for the affection of a woman. But underneath the hostility one finds dependency. In *Watch and Ward*, for example, the two cousins, Hubert and Roger, are described as follows:

> He and Roger had been much together in early life and had formed an intimacy strangely compounded of harmony and discord. . . . Roger was constantly differing, mutely and profoundly, and Hubert frankly and sarcastically; but each, nevertheless, seemed to find in the other a welcome counterpart and complement to his own personality.[17]

In these fictions, with their mixture of rivalry and dependence, there is no escape from the relationship except through death.

It was with relief that Henry escaped from Cambridge two years after his return — in May 1872, conducting his aunt Kate and sister Alice abroad. He immediately began to feel better. A year and a half later, in fall 1873, after the two women had returned to America, his brother William joined him in Italy. Before considering their fraternal tour, however, let us briefly examine William's condition at the time.

William's life, from his twenty-third to his thirty-sixth year, when he finally married and left home, was, Edel tells us, "marked by recurrent lapses in health and spirit." He had great difficulty finding himself. His youth was marked by turmoil, chronic illness, career equivocation, despondency, and — during his medical studies at Harvard — a near-nervous breakdown. In the years 1870-72, when Henry was also at home, William suffered a series of backaches (an echo of Henry's "obscure hurt"), headaches, eye-trouble, loss of appetite, and melancholy. His status as oldest son and first-born did not seem to shield him from severe mental disequilibrium. He had decided first to be an artist, then a scientist, then a doctor (he received his M.D. in 1869, during Henry's *Wanderjahr* in Europe). But he had no intention of setting up practice and took up teaching instead.

He began teaching physiology at Harvard in 1872 and in spring of 1873 was offered a renewal of his appointment by President Eliot, with the prospects of a permanent post. William accepted, then reneged, then accepted again; then decided he might take a year off and join his brother in Europe. He debated this for several months, "amid fits of despondency and languor," and finally made up his mind in late summer 1873. He would leave Harvard and join Henry. He sailed in October and went directly to Florence, where Henry was waiting. William's letter to his sister, immediately after arriving around midnight, is revealing: "The Angel sleeps in number 39 hard by, all unwitting that I, the Demon . . . am here at last. I wouldn't for worlds disturb this his last independent slumber."[18] William, for years, had mockingly referred to Henry as "the Angel," a term that recalls not only his sweetness as a child but his contrast to William's own forthright, energetic, tempestuous nature. That he characterizes himself as "the Demon" and implies that Henry will not slumber independently soon again has interesting overtones.

The brotherly tour started off well. They went to Rome after some weeks in Florence. Henry wrote in the morning, met William for lunch. They took afternoon walks and drives, and often dined with American friends of Henry's. In this atmosphere William felt better at once. His health and spirits improved dramatically. Henry wrote his father of the "especial charm of seeing Willy thriving under it all as if he were being secretly plied with the elixir of life." He seemed to Henry "greatly contented."

At first the brothers lived in a Roman hotel, the Hôtel de Russie, near the Piazza del Popolo. Henry, however, discovered that an apartment he had rented the previous spring, on the Corso, was vacant, and moved there. William stayed on at the hotel but made use of Henry's fourth-floor sitting room and balcony.

Knowing the two brothers as we do, it is clear that this harmonious interlude cannot last. Some emotional devastation, expressed as physical illness, will occur. And that is what happens. After just one month in Rome, William comes down with a light case of malaria. It is decided that Florence will be a healthier place for his recovery, so they trek north, to the dismay of Henry, who deplores the prospect of waking up to "see the dirty ice floating down the prosy Arno and find life resolved into a sullen struggle to catch half an hour's sunshine a day on a little modern quay. . . ." A few days after writing this letter to his sister, it is Henry's turn to fall sick. This he does, with a splitting headache, a bronchial cough, and a fever. It is serious enough for William to hire a nurse. The fever ends after three nights but the headache remains. William can find no specific cause for the illness. He informs his parents that it is "an abnormal brain fever." Henry describes it himself as "a strange and mysterious visitation, but it would be hard to say just what it was."

We now have the ingredients of the window episode. The brothers are abroad together and in their youth, though not in the first flush of it. At first both are happy in each other's company. Then vexation or tension or the need for privacy decides them against living together. In Rome, Henry moves to the apartment on the fourth floor (contrasting with the "third storey" mentioned by Gosse, a discrepancy that may be explained by a memory lapse by James or Gosse, or by different numbering systems current in Italy and England). Nevertheless, their time together is idyllic and productive — until everything falls to pieces.

Edel writes: "It seemed once again, as in the time of their youth, that the Angel and his brother could not long remain in each other's company without experiencing a certain amount of physical discomfort. Henry's headaches, we may speculate, had an emotional origin. . . ."[19] Later he notes: "Put into the briefest and crudest terms, William, in Italy, could be quite simply a headache for Henry."

As we might expect, they cut short their time together. As soon as Henry was on the way to recovery, William left him in Florence and went to Venice, and then to Dresden. In March 1874 he sailed home from Bremen — all this without seeing his brother again.

If we look at the results of this trip, we find that it marks a watershed in the lives of both brothers. When Henry finally tore himself away from Europe and returned to America in 1874, he did not resume residence in Cambridge, where William was still living. Instead, he spent six months in New York, visited the parental and fraternal home only briefly, and in October 1875 turned his back on America, sailing to Europe for good. His later visits to America were in connection with deaths in the family, not reentries into American life. He never really lived in his native country again nor felt himself to be wholly American, confirming this late in life by adopting British citizenship.

After his return in March 1874, William was increasingly able to make his peace with teaching at Harvard and with himself. In 1878 he was able to marry. Five children resulted from the union, plus twenty years of stability and great achievement — until renewed ill health cut short his career.

Thus, if we set the few months in Europe in a larger biographical perspective, we see that it represented a fork in the road for the brothers. No doubt their brief time together was full of good things — intellectual adventure, sightseeing, conversation — but at the same time it clearly marked a permanent change in the relationship. They never again sought each other out so avidly nor spent so much time in each other's company. Something changed, or died, in December 1873 in Rome — chaining Henry and freeing William for the rest of their lives. It was truly "the end."

3. *The Textual Perspective.* If the "window-straining episode" is a major obsession in Henry's emotional life, then it is logical to expect it would surface, under various disguises, in his fiction, as do the relationships between various sets of brother-figures. I believe we can find several places where the theme appears, if we broaden the search to include fictional circumstances where the act of sexual exclusion or rejection, *expressed visually,* occurs.

In *Portrait of a Lady*, Isabel Archer becomes aware of the intimacy between her husband and his former mistress, Madame Merle, not because she is told about it before or after her marriage, but because one afternoon in her drawing room she detects their relationship by their relative positions and by the way they look at each other. It is a visual detection, not a verbal one. And it is not discussed or acted upon for a long time. Isabel absorbs and nourishes it — indeed, seems to feed emotionally on the fact of her sexual exclusion.

In *The Princess Casamassima*, the young, effeminate bookbinder Hyacinth Robinson is standing on the street when he glimpses Paul Muniment, the protective older-brother figure, descend from a cab with the princess and enter her house for a sexual assignation. This sexual exclusion is so devastating to Hyacinth that soon afterwards he shoots himself — ostensibly because he cannot fulfill his promise to assassinate a radical but actually because he cannot bear the evidence of his betrayal.

In *The Ambassadors*, Lambert Strether, sent to Paris to fetch Chadwick Newsome home to America, is disillusioned at the climax of the book by a glimpse of Chad and Madame de Vionnet together on the river — a glimpse that testifies to their sexual intimacy and excludes him.[20]

In *The Golden Bowl*, a critical moment occurs when Maggie, standing on the street below, sees her husband, Prince Amerigo, embracing his former mistress, Charlotte, on the balcony.

In the climactic scene of "The Turn of the Screw," it is the apparition of Peter Quint, "the hideous author of our woe," that appears at the dining room window, horrifying the governess and killing Miles — a reversal of the previous pattern in that those betrayed now are on the inside of a window looking out.

Leo Bersani, in summing up betrayal scenes in James, writes:

> . . . it would be foolish to pretend we can avoid "going behind" James's interest in these pictures. His preference for *this* technique of compositional compression makes us feel, inevitably, that composition profits here from some obsessive memory, a memory of glimpsed intimacy interpreted as both violent and treacherous. And it's perhaps an inability — or for reasons we can naturally never know, an unwillingness — to recuperate from the impact of that vision which explains the exasperating avoidance of fact and direct statement in the late fiction.[21]

Bersani goes on to state that a psycho-critical" case could be made for "a skeletal psychology of vision" in the work of James. Seeing, he points out, is both punishment and revenge for James; betrayal allows the one betrayed to continue the relationship while pretending not to. This, of course, sums up the tortured lifetime relationship between William and Henry James.

Combing through the complete works of Henry James would no doubt yield many more fictional uses of the obsessive memory, a project that some future researcher may undertake. Balconies, windows, doors, all viewed from a distance by someone excluded from the life and warmth within, are the ingredients waiting to be discovered. The haunted room or the room *as test*, as we encounter it in tales like "Owen Wingrave" or "The Jolly Corner," are suggestive also. Even the photographs by Alvin Langdon Coburn (stage-directed by Henry himself) that serve as frontispieces for the New York Edition of the complete works contain a preponderance of house facades, sometimes viewed in mist or rain. These, too, might be analyzed as derived from the obsessive memory.[22]

Obviously, there are many unanswered questions to the interpretation offered here. We have no direct statement by either William or Henry. We must rely on biographical clues and textual disguises. It is not unlikely that only critics who are predisposed to such an interpretation, who bring to the subject a "preunderstanding" of the evasions and semiotics of male love, will agree with my interpretation. Other critics are likely to see it as irrelevant or a case of special pleading or merely idiosyncratic.[23] This situation, as I pointed out earlier, stems from the personal and social experiences that govern the vision, and the freedom to speculate about the vision, of every reader. The blindness or conscious self-censorship that accompanies so much critical work of those hostile to homosexuality can only be overcome by the persistent and extraordinary efforts of gay scholars themselves, who must trust their instincts here, as in so many other areas of life.

NOTES

[1]*College English: An Official Journal of the National Council of Teachers of English*, 36, No. 3 (1974), "The Homosexual Imagination."

[2]For a complete discussion of my evidence on Henry James's attachment to his brother, see *The New Republic* (28 April and 5 May 1979) and *The Advocate* (20 Sept. 1979). The latter includes a lengthy interview with Leon Edel. The *New Republic* articles are available as a unit from Books Bohemian, Box 6246, Glendale, CA 91205.

[3]Leon Edel, Letter to Richard Hall, 21 April 1979, reprinted in the *Advocate* article.

[4]See *The Advocate*.

[5]Leon Edel, "The Figure under the Carpet," in *Telling Lives: The Biographer's Art*, ed. Marc Pachter (Washington: New Republic Books, 1979), p. 25.

[6]See *The Advocate*.

[7]Edel's attitude toward homosexuality in James apparently changed over the years. Byrne R. S. Fone, now a professor at City College of New York, reports that in a graduate course with Edel at New York University in 1961, he proposed a term paper to discuss the effect of Henry James's homosexuality or hidden homosexuality in his writings but was turned down by Edel with the statement that homosexuality in James was "irrelevant or unprovable or both."

[8]Maxwell Geismar, *Henry James and the Jacobites* (New York: Houghton Mifflin, 1962), p. 167.

[9]Geismar, p. 115.

[10]Louie Crew and Rictor Norton, "The Homophobic Imagination: An Editorial," in *College English*, p. 285.

[11]Phyllis Grosskurth, *The Woeful Victorian: A Biography of John Addington Symonds* (New York: Holt, Rinehart and Winston, 1964), p. 280. Interestingly, Edel in IV, 123-24 of *Henry James* declares that this Gosse letter to Symonds has been "grossly misinterpreted as an admission by him of his own homosexuality." Edel believes it actually testifies to "Gosse's need to ingratiate himself with his fellow-writers rather than to cultivate the confessional mode." Grosskurth, however, believes that the letter did constitute a confession of homosexuality.

[12]Edmund Gosse, "Henry James," *The London Mercury*, 1, No. 6 (April 1920) and 2, No. 7 (May 1920).

[13]Gosse, *The London Mercury*, 1 No. 6, 680, and 2, No. 7, 29.

[14]Gosse, *The London Mercury*, 2, No. 7, 33.

[15]Sir Hugh Walpole, "Henry James: A Reminiscence," in *Horizon*, 1, No. 2 (1940), 76; cited in H. Montgomery Hyde, *Henry James at Home* (New York: Farrar, Straus & Giroux, 1969), p. 228.

[16]Leon Edel, Letter to Richard Hall, 3 Oct. 1979.

[17]Henry James, *Watch and Ward* (New York: Grove Press, 1960; rpt. New York: Grove Press, 1979), p. 47.

[18]Leon Edel, *Henry James: The Conquest of London, 1870-1881* (New York: Discus Avon, 1978), p. 144.

[19]Edel, *Henry James: The Conquest of London*, pp. 154-155.

[20]It is interesting to note that Strether first becomes aware of Chadwick's residence by standing in the street below and observing a figure on the balcony. This turns out to be Chad's friend John Little Bilham. A similar balcony setting occurs when Strether finally meets Chad, this time in a box at the theater. Strether describes it as "quite one of the sensations that count in life."

[21]Leo Bersani, *A Future for Astyanax: Character and Desire in Literature* (Boston: Little, Brown and Company, 1976), p. 134.

[22]For this suggestion about the photographs of Alvin Langdon Coburn, I am indebted to Andrew Rubenfeld.

[23]After my two articles on the James brothers appeared in *The New Republic*, I was the target of an attack, essentially political, in a Birchite newsletter called "The Cultural Watchdog."

William Faulkner's *Absalom, Absalom!*: An Exegesis of the Homoerotic Configurations in the Novel

Don Merrick Liles, M.A.

I

From 1951, when *Absalom, Absalom!* was reissued and the novel began to be studied in the college and university classes, students of the novel have been regularly and insistently perceiving possible homoerotic configurations in some of the principal events and characters.[1] Clearly the novel deals with the taboos against incest and miscegenation, but the purpose of this study is to demonstrate an additional taboo that is likewise central to an understanding of the thematic unity of the novel: the proscription of homoeroticism. One's understanding of *Absalom, Absalom!*, which Albert J. Guerard concludes is "perhaps the greatest American novel,"[2] is diminished without a full awareness of the homoerotic components in many of the major events and characters in the conjectural reconstructions made by Mr. Compson, Quentin, and Shreve. (In "Divorce in Naples," 1931, Faulkner wrote a short story centered on an explicit homoerotic relationship, but in no major novel does Faulkner utilize homoeroticism more significantly than in *Absalom, Absalom!* Because of critical neglect of this component and because of the importance of this novel in modern fiction, this study shall be restricted exclusively to *Absalom, Absalom!*)

The published criticism of the novel has generally ignored the homoerotic component of *Absalom, Absalom!*; the first mention of the theme occurred in 1955 when Ilse Dusoir Lind wrote:

> Shreve, whose youthful curiosity and romanticism make him a suitable collaborator in the Bon-Henry legend, projects the fraternal affection, mildly homosexual in basis, which exists between his roommate and himself.[3]

Don Merrick Liles teaches English and Classics at City College of San Francisco, San Francisco, CA 94112. He is the translator/editor of the American English volume of the *Lexikon of Ancient Greek Eroticisms Translated into Modern Languages*.

This perceptive but fleeting observation concerning the Shreve-Quentin relationship is inadequate because it does not explore the importance of Quentin and Shreve's projection of themselves into their joint creation of the Henry-Bon relationship.

Then, in 1968, Richard Adams wrote:

> At this stage of the process, as the author's voice breaks in once more to specify, "all that had gone before" is "just so much that had to be overpassed"; and it is "not the talking alone which did it, performed and accomplished the overpassing, but some happy marriage of speaking and hearing wherein each before the demand, the requirement, forgave condoned and forgot the faulting of the other — faultings both in the creation of this shade whom they discussed (rather, existed in) and in the hearing and sifting and discarding the false and conserving what seemed true, or fit the preconceived — in order to overpass the love, where there might be paradox and inconsistency but nothing fault nor false" (p. 316). What is meant here, as the context of the word "marriage" suggests and as the larger context in which the passage occurs clearly shows, is partly the homosexual attraction between Bon and Henry, which is paralleled if not created by that between Quentin and Shreve, and out of which, by their account, the attraction between Bon and Judith develops. This emotional complex contributes a good deal of energy and conviction to the sense which the author is building up of an understanding by the narrators and the reader of what must "really" have happened.[4]

Adams, quoting from Chapter viii of the novel, goes further than Lind and identifies the homoerotic attraction between Henry and Bon *and* between Quentin and Shreve. Adams states that this attraction "contributed a good deal of energy and conviction," but he scarcely explores that energy and conviction.

In 1975, John T. Irwin briefly commented:

> We should note that the relationship between Bon and Henry, as it is imagined in the narrative, possesses homoerotic overtones, so that, for example, Bon's intended marriage to Judith is portrayed as a vicarious consummation of the love between Bon and Henry, a love that is in fact consummated in a *liebestod* when Henry kills Bon. The same latent homoeroticism is present in the relationship of the two narrators Quentin and Shreve, as is evidenced in Quentin's obsessive sensitivity in *The Sound and the Fury* when his classmates at Harvard refer to Shreve as Quentin's husband. . . . Indeed, the latent homoerotic content in the story

of Bon and Henry may well be simply the projection of Quentin's state made in the act of narration.[5]

Many Faulkner students may deplore Irwin's blurring of the boundaries between *The Sound and the Fury* and *Absalom, Absalom!*, and many may likewise deplore the blurring of the conjectures of Mr. Compson and of Quentin and Shreve. However, Irwin labeled his study a "speculative reading," and his purpose is to treat the novels as an unbroken flow of psychological material, not as distinct literary entities. Although Irwin identifies the "latent" homoeroticism in the relationships of Henry and Bon, Quentin and Shreve, nowhere does he examine the significance of the homoeroticism. Nor need he turn to *The Sound and the Fury* for evidence of the homoerotic relationship between Quentin and Shreve.

The following year, in 1976, Albert J. Guerard mentioned

> an exceedingly interesting triangular pattern, one that fascinates the speculative Mr. Compson and significantly disturbs Quentin. . . . The supposition is that Bon effortlessly "seduced the country brother and sister," though we know little of Judith's response. Henry is attracted ("with the knowledge of the insurmountable barrier which the similarity of gender hopelessly intervened") to a figure of idealized (and feminized) urbanity. In time he gives that "complete and abnegant devotion which only a youth, never a woman, gives to another youth or man." But as Henry may share his sister through his devoted identification with Bon, so at least wishfully he could share the brother-in-law through that fancied union with her. Bisexual incest (which would later be seen as doubly incestuous, with Bon known as blood brother) thus combines with a familiar homosexual or homoerotic maneuver.[6]

Guerard recognizes the homoerotic and incestuous triangular tangle, but he does not mention the possibility of a homoerotic projection on the part of Quentin and Shreve, and he deals exclusively with Mr. Compson's hypotheses in Chapter iv, reducing the scope and importance of the homoeroticism in the novel.

These four critics, while acknowledging the plausibility of some homoerotic components, have left the topic essentially unexplored.

The purpose of this study is to examine the thematic relevance of the homoeroticism in the novel generally, and specifically in the two sections where it is most apparent: the first in Chapter iv, in Mr. Compson's account of the Henry-Bon-Judith triangle; and the second in Chapters viii and ix, in Shreve and Quentin's joint creation of the Henry-Bon relationship. We shall first consider Mr. Compson's conjectures in Chapter iv.

II

One of Faulkner's major stylistic devices in *Absalom, Absalom!* is the recurring short, emphatic sentence or phrase that signally interrupts the sweeping flow of long, involuted, richly embedded, and multilayered sentences. These short sentences or phrases are usually repeated with echoic variations throughout a section of the novel and in diction that expresses seemingly obvious meaning. In fact, however, the meanings are of sufficient complexity that much critical study has been devoted to the explanation of their difficulties. A celebrated example is Sutpen's "innocence."

In the opening paragraphs of Chapter iv Mr. Compson says bluntly to Quentin, "Because Henry loved Bon" (p. 89). And in the ensuing eight pages this clause is reiterated with variations: "Because he loved Bon" (p. 90); "Yes, he loved Bon who seduced him as surely as he seduced Judith" (p. 96); and ". . . he loved grieved and killed, still grieving and, I believe, still loving Bon" (p. 97). Simultaneously Mr. Compson emphasizes the erotically charged word *seduced*: the first use occurs on page 92 and then recurs in variations seven times, finally culminating in Mr. Compson's conjecture that

> . . . it was not Judith who was the object of Bon's love or of Henry's solicitude. She was just the blank shape, the empty vessel in which each of them strove to preserve . . . what each conceived the other to believe him [Bon] to be — the man and the youth, seducer and seduced, who had known one another, seduced and been seduced . . . before Judith came into their joint lives even by so much as girlname. (pp. 119-120)

Mr. Compson, therefore, not only postulates the plausibility of homoerotic attraction between Henry and Bon, he also considers in his detached, almost cynical and nihilistic way that the homoerotic component in the Henry-Bon-Judith triangle is the strongest force in that triangle. Although Mr. Compson is detached, he persistently sees the incestuous and homoerotic configurations in conventionally heterosexual terms:

> . . . this is the pure and perfect incest: the brother realizing that the sister's virginity must be destroyed in order to have existed at all, taking that virginity in the person of the brother-in-law, the man whom he [Henry] would be if he could become, metamorphose into, the lover, the husband; by whom he would be despoiled, choose for despoiler, if he could become, metamorphose into the sister, the mistress, the bride. Perhaps that is what went on, not in Henry's mind but in his soul. (p. 96)

Mr. Compson's word choice here (e.g., husband, mistress, bride) is analogous to the choice of words he uses to characterize Bon. The recurrent use of *feminine* (pp. 95, 96) and its variants to describe Bon produces a Bon who is almost a *fin de siecle* aesthete. One can reasonably infer that Mr. Compson correlates male homosexuality with effeminacy; in other words, he is assuming conventional heterosexual attitudes toward the patterns of male homoerotic relationships.

This conventional perception of the Henry-Bon homoerotic attraction is not nearly so important in the novel as is Mr. Compson's failure to explore the ramifications of the homoeroticism in the Henry-Bon tragedy. His failure is a direct result of his fixated heterosexual viewpoint. He suggests that Henry was paralyzed "with the knowledge of the insurmountable barrier which the similarity of gender hopelessly intervened" (p. 95), although Mr. Compson does recognize a difference in the attraction between Henry and Bon and between Judith and Bon. Mr. Compson observes that:

> "Bon, who for a year and a half now had been watching Henry ape his clothing and speech, who for a year and a half now had seen himself as the object of that complete and abnegant devotion which only a youth, never a woman, gives to another youth or a man. . . ." (p. 107)

Even with such marked awareness of the homoerotic element in the Henry-Bon relationship, when Mr. Compson comes to explain why Henry killed Bon after the four years of "durance, waiting," he reveals the shortcomings of a perspective that includes no understanding of the variety and pervasiveness of emotions in homoerotic attraction. Mr. Compson can imagine that Henry's frequent demands that Bon "renounce" are a command to give up the New Orleans octoroon mistress or even Judith, but he fails to imagine that Henry's motive in making these demands might be to cease being a "sort of junior partner in a harem" (p. 119) and to have Bon exclusively for himself. Instead, Mr. Compson believes that the "harem" includes only the octoroon mistress and Judith. Here we can clearly see the limitations in Mr. Compson's imaginative capacity. If he were able to postulate that Henry felt himself a concubine in Bon's harem, then Mr. Compson could partially understand Henry's motivations for killing Bon. Mr. Compson reiterates "Henry loved Bon," but he cannot make the simple connection that Henry *does* truly love Bon for all that love may mean. Granted, Mr. Compson has only an imperfect knowledge of the situation in Chapter iv (e.g., he does not know at the time that Bon is a half-brother of Henry and Judith, and he does not know that Bon is part Negro), but these limitations in his knowledge should not impair his insight into the power of homoerotic emotions, should not prevent his understanding that Henry may have killed Charles Bon out of anger that Bon was deserting Henry to marry someone else. And "marry someone else" is the appropriate phraseology here because Mr. Compson approaches the triangle heterosexually: he postulates that Henry wants to become "the sister, the mistress, the bride" (p. 96). (We shall later see in the Quentin-Shreve sections of the novel that Henry's motivations for killing Bon are in fact much more complex.)

Possibly seeking a nihilistic summation, Mr. Compson says to Quentin:

> "It's just incredible. It just does not explain. Or perhaps that's it: they don't explain and we are not supposed to know. . . . against that turgid background of a horrible and bloody mischancing of human affairs." (pp. 100-101)

Thus, even though Mr. Compson can hypothesize a homoerotic attraction between Henry and Bon, his failure to identify imaginatively with the homoeroticism and follow its profound influence on subsequent events is entirely characteristic of his fixated heterosexual outlook and of his cynical detachment from life. He is partially portrayed in the novel by this failure, and a reader can find significant evidence for an understanding of Mr. Compson when the reader fully understands this failure.

III

Before the collation of Faulkner's manuscript and the published text of *Absalom, Absalom!* appeared in 1971, many readers had assumed that the novel was "primarily about Sutpen."[7] After the publication of the collation, readers could clearly see that principal themes of the immensely complex work converge in the crises of Quentin Compson. In the course of several revisions, Faulkner pushed Quentin forward into the vortex of the motifs of the novel. Thus, an exegetic interpretation of Quentin and Shreve's joint creation of the Henry-Bon relationship becomes crucial to a reader's understanding of Quentin's role in the novel.

In Chapter viii, the penultimate and climactic chapter, Quentin and Shreve create a far more elaborate homoerotic configuration than Mr. Compson's. They become completely identified with the relationship between Henry and Bon.

> . . . Quentin and Shreve, the two the four the two still talking — the one who did not yet know what he was going to do, the other

who knew what he would have to do yet could not reconcile himself — Henry citing himself authority for incest, talking about his
Duke John of Lorraine as if he hoped possibly to evoke that con-
demned and excommunicated shade to tell him in person that it
was all right. . . . the two the four the two facing one another
in the tomblike room. . . . (p. 346)

So complete becomes Quentin and Shreve's projection into the other
couple that the chapter culminates in their living inside Henry and Bon
while the final, tragic events of their last months are not merely re-
enacted but imaginatively created. Quentin and Shreve's conjoined act
of creating frequently provokes one or the other to interrupt the hypotheses, and occasionally their shared silences indicate their mutual searching for plausible actions and motivations.

Quentin and Shreve stared at one another — glared rather —
their quiet regular breathing vaporizing faintly and steadily in the
now tomblike air. There was something curious and quiet and pro-
foundly intent, not at all as two young men might look at each
other but almost as a youth and a very young girl might out of
virginity itself — a sort of hushed and naked searching. . . .
(p. 299)

Another significant characteristic of this chapter is Faulkner's use of
auctorial intrusions that validate what Shreve and Quentin imagine,
e.g., "that drawing room of baroque and fusty magnificence which
Shreve had invented and *which was probably true enough*" (p. 355,
italics added); "whom Shreve and Quentin had likewise invented and
which was likewise probably true enough" (p. 355); "Quentin took that
in stride without even hearing it just as Shreve would have, since both
he and Shreve believed — *and were probably right in this too* —
(p. 336). The author's intrusions in Chapter viii are exceptionally important because they are the only auctorial validations for any of the
narrators' conjectures in the novel. For a reader looking for sanction
for an understanding of the events and human relationships in the novel,
therefore, the Quentin-Shreve hypotheses are the most valuable of all.

Early in the chapter, Shreve creates a vengeance-driven Eulalia Bon
and her greedy lawyer, both of whom are exploiting Charles Bon in
order to achieve their goals. At midpoint in the chapter, however, the
focus of the novel shifts radically.

"And now," Shreve said, "we're going to talk about love." But he
didn't need to say that either, any more than he had needed to
specify which he meant by he, since neither of them had been

thinking about anything else; all that had gone before just so much that had to be overpassed and none else present to overpass it. . . . That was why it did not matter to either of them which one did the talking, since it was not the talking alone which did it, performed and accomplished the overpassing, but some happy marriage of speaking and hearing . . . — in order to overpass to love, where there might be paradox and inconsistency but nothing fault nor false. "And now, love. . . ." (p. 316)

After the fully developed loveless monomania of Sutpen in the preceding chapters, such a shift to love as the motivating force is a major modulation in the novel, a modulation that no published criticism has emphasized. Bon will now save a wounded Henry (not the reverse, as Mr. Compson believes). Bon will now seek merely tacit recognition from Sutpen, not vengeance. Bon is willing to renounce marriage with Judith, etc. When Quentin interrupts Shreve by saying, "But it's not love" (p. 322), Quentin is correcting Shreve who has momentarily lapsed and created a Bon who indifferently considers taking Judith as a "cup of lemon sherbet" rather than a whiskey (p. 322). In their insistence that love be the cornerstone for measuring the plausibility of the actions and thoughts of Henry and Bon, Shreve and Quentin are attempting to understand the events in the novel from a radically different point of view than the perspectives of Miss Rosa and Mr. Compson. And from this moment to the end of the chapter, when Henry shoots Bon at the gate of Sutpen's Hundred, Shreve and Quentin adhere to this perspective.

They also create a Henry who is motivated by love. Henry repudiates his family and home, not to champion the marriage between Bon and Judith, as Mr. Compson imagines (p. 100), but because Henry loves Bon enough to follow him anywhere and because he wants to learn if Bon is truly his brother. Shreve even makes a Henry who vows complete and total surrender of his being to the man he loves:

> . . . Henry . . . maybe one morning during that spring waked up and lay right still in the bed and took stock, added the figures and drew the balance and told himself, *All right. I am trying to make myself into what I think he wants me to be; he can do anything he wants to with me; he has only to tell me what to do and I will do it; even though what he asked me to do looked to me like dishonor. I would still do it.* (pp. 329-330)

In creating the Christmas Eve 1860 library scene, Shreve hypothesizes that Sutpen told Henry that Bon was Henry's brother. While that encounter occurs, Bon and Judith are walking in the garden, but Bon's attention is not directed at Judith. He says to her, "Go. I wish to be alone to think about love" (p. 333). At this moment Bon hopes that Sutpen is preparing to call for him so that Sutpen can say that Bon is his son. After Sutpen dispassionately fails to send for Bon, however, Shreve is unable to cope with the juxtaposition of such lovelessness with Bon's and Henry's searching needs.

> Shreve ceased. . . . So that now it was not two but four of them riding the two horses through the dark over the frozen December ruts of that Christmas Eve: four of them and then just two — Charles-Shreve and Quentin-Henry, the two of them both believing that Henry was thinking *He* (meaning his father) *has destroyed us all,* not for one moment thinking *He* (meaning Bon) *must have known or at least suspected this all the time; that's why he has acted as he has, why he did not answer my letters last summer nor write to Judith, why he has never asked her to marry him*; believing that that must have occurred to Henry, certainly during that moment after Henry emerged from the house and he and Bon looked at one another for a while without a word then walked down to the stable and saddled the horses. . . . because he must have now understood with complete despair the secret of his whole attitude toward Bon from that first instinctive moment when he had seen him a year and a quarter ago; he knew, yet he did not, had to refuse to, believe. (pp. 333-334)

If Henry at this moment does understand "with complete despair the secret of his whole attitude toward Bon," we should examine carefully what this understanding includes. In the Quentin-Shreve invention there are two types of knowing, not only for Henry at this moment in 1860 but for him and Bon throughout the remainder of the novel. There is conscious knowledge, but more often and more importantly there is intuitive knowledge, or "instinctive" knowledge, as the auctorial voice labels it (p. 334).

First, Henry intuitively knows that he has been erotically drawn to Bon from their original encounter (p. 330); and because of the homoerotic taboo, Henry feels despair. Then, Henry intuitively wants Bon to be his brother (p. 316), but because of the incest taboo, Henry again feels despair. Henry generously wants to offer Judith to Bon (p. 325), thus relieving his own anxiety stemming from the homoerotic and incest taboos, but this produces despair because he would be losing Bon and because he would then be condoning incest between his own brother and sister. Finally, Henry knows he can offer Judith, but this would mean losing both Judith and Bon.

At this point in the Shreve-Quentin narrative, Henry is in a vortex of emotional currents that buffet him, causing him to respond violently and bewilderingly. When he kills Bon at the gate of Sutpen's Hundred four years later, he is still wrestling with these and other terrifying difficulties. In the Shreve-Quentin invention Henry comes to a torturous acceptance of incest and even the prospect of Bon's desertion of him for Judith; but recoil occurs at the gate and contributes to Henry's killing of his lover/brother/rival. After Bon's death Henry's life within the novel is a void.

We must also examine what Bon knows on Christmas Eve 1860. He knows intuitively that Sutpen is his father, and he knows that for some unfathomable reason Sutpen refuses to acknowledge him as a son. He also knows that Henry is surrendering his life to him, and he wants that love to be a positive bedrock in his life. Apparently Bon, like Shreve, is never troubled by the homoerotic and incest taboos. Although he vacillates in his attitude toward marrying Judith, Bon believes that if Sutpen were to acknowledge him, he would renounce Judith (p. 327). So devoted is he to his quest for paternal recognition that he even considers giving up Henry and Judith if his father would send even "*a lock of his hair or a paring from his finger nail*" (p. 326). At last, however, after Sutpen's final rejection in the winter of 1864 (p. 329), Bon turns desperately and searchingly to Henry for acknowledgment and acceptance.

With these preconditions in the forefront of their understanding of the Henry-Bon relationship, Shreve-Quentin jointly construct an unspoken, hypothetical scene that emphasizes the crucial themes of the novel — the scene in the Confederate Army bivouac in the winter of 1864, when defeat pervades the cold air. After meeting with Sutpen in the army tent, Henry does not tell Bon that he has just learned that Bon is part Negro. But Bon intuits that Henry now knows, and Bon quietly asserts, "*So it's the miscegenation, not the incest, which you cant bear*" (p. 356). In considering Henry's excruciating dilemma at this moment, we must recognize that Henry does accept miscegenation. All his life he has mutely accepted Clytie as his half-black half sister. Unlike the Henry in Mr. Compson's conjectures, Henry in the Shreve-Quentin narrative has accepted the octoroon mistress in New Orleans as "something else about Bon to be, not envied but aped if that had been possible" (p. 336). Nevertheless, the reader must also recognize the limited conditions under which Henry accepts miscegenation.

Both Clytie and the octoroon mistress are acceptable to Henry because in the Southern caste system they live their lives openly as second-class human beings: one as a "house nigger" and the other as a mistress carefully bred for sexual pleasure.

When Bon asks, "Who will stop me, Henry?" (from marrying Judith), it signals the last opportunity that Bon will ever have for acceptance and acknowledgment from someone whom he loves. Within the novel this test is not only Bon's final attempt for human validation; it is even more importantly Henry's last chance to prove to himself and to Bon that he fully loves Bon. Henry can reply only, *"No. . . — No. No. No"* (p. 357). Henry's taboo-crammed conscience in those negatives is the conscience of a Southern gentleman in 1864 — a man struggling with a Gordian knot of love and revulsion for a longstanding male lover, recently revealed as part Negro, now threatening to leave him for their sister.

But Henry has progressed to the point where he can proffer some acceptance to Charles Bon. Henry says, *"You are my brother"* (p. 357), but Bon — who knows that Clytie exists — realizes that such an acknowledgment is partial at best in the Southern caste system. He replies, injecting sex explicitly into Henry's turmoil, *"No I'm not. I'm the nigger that's going to sleep with your sister. Unless you stop me, Henry"* (p. 358). At this point the vortex of emotion is most turbulent. Bon offers Henry a choice: he can respond according to the social conventions, or he can achieve human greatness by "overpassing to love" (p. 316). Henry, after all, is a white Southern youth who has sacrificed all for Bon, and they have been sleeping near or beside each other from university days and through four years in the army. But Bon has been living skin-close to Henry as a white, idolized, idealized gentleman. Even if Bon has suspected intuitively that Sutpen rejected Eulalia Bon because she was partially black, the mores of the South demand that Bon be subservient to all whites. Henry, who loves Bon more than any one person in his life and has devoted all his adult years to him, simply cannot accept a black man masquerading as a white man in the roles of his lover, brother, commanding officer, and prospective brother-in-law.

So when Bon says, "Unless you stop me, Henry," Henry is offered a choice, and he fails. Henry cannot say, "I love you — man, black, brother — I love you." The inextricably tangled taboos overwhelm him, effecting a course of action that ends in the love/hate murder and leaves the remainder of his long, long life a vacuous nothingness: he kills the man he loves, the man who threatens to desert him, the man who threatens to seduce his sister, the man who is a black impostor.

In the following and final chapter the novel focuses on the struggle within Quentin, who, in 1910, is being forced to relive Henry's tragedy long after the love-death at the gate of Sutpen's Hundred in 1865. Significantly, Faulkner places Quentin and Shreve in bed in the Harvard dormitory room; we can infer that Faulkner intends to emphasize even further the homoerotic parallels between Henry-Bon and Quentin-Shreve. Shreve's function as a Bon surrogate is absolute in his statements and actions in the final chapter. His differentness from Quentin is never more apparent, despite the "geological umbilical" (p. 258) of the Mississippi River connecting them as near twins. Shreve, feeling and hearing Quentin's shivering, hammers hard: "Do you understand it?" (p. 362). Yet he has just offered Quentin the overcoats as a source of warmth (p. 361), and his action exactly repeats Bon's offer of his overcoat to Henry (p. 356). This act of love is important because Shreve is never troubled by a conscience proscribing homoeroticism, incest, and interracial love. Quentin's statement, "You cant understand it. You would have to be born there" (p. 361), is a defensive assertion that an outsider, a Canadian, cannot understand the relentless power of traditional Southern taboos. However, Shreve certainly does understand, and he proves his understanding by posing for Quentin the same dilemma that Bon posed for Henry. On the last page of the novel, Shreve says:

> I think that in time the Jim Bonds [racially mixed human beings] are going to conquer the western hemisphere. Of course it won't be quite in our time and of course as they spread toward the poles they will bleach out again like the rabbits and the birds do, so they won't show up so sharply against the snow. But it will still be Jim Bond; and so in a few thousand years, I who regard you will also have sprung from the loins of African kings. Now I want you to tell me just one thing more. Why do you hate the South? (p. 378)

Because of demoralizing, socially engendered obstructions, Quentin, like Henry, cannot "overpass to love." Shreve — male, almost brother, lying in bed and feeling the shudders of Quentin — accepts with no anxiety the future probability that he will have black blood. Essentially, Shreve has confronted Quentin with a choice: "Regard me — apparently white — as a black man sleeping in this room beside you. Do you understand why you cannot accept this situation?"

The novel may present a hierarchy of the taboos, and if so, the taboo that is apparently most powerful is the one forbidding interracial love. Certainly it compels Henry and Quentin to respond most violently. The incest taboo causes anguish in Henry and Quentin, and we know that Faulkner used and explored the incest taboo not only in this novel but also in several other major novels, including *The Sound and the Fury*. The homoerotic taboo apparently does not have equivalent power in Southern white men, if Henry and Quentin can be regarded as typical of that group. Faulkner's purpose, nevertheless, is *not* to disentangle the three; on the contrary, he has consciously and inextricably ensnarled them as motivating forces in the emotional struggles of Henry and Quentin. Whatever resemblance the taboos may have lies in their all being taboos, needlessly leading to tragedy: the consequences whenever the channels of love between human beings are blocked.

IV

When Faulkner was at the University of Virginia during the last years of his life, he told a student discussing *Absalom, Absalom!*:

> It was, as you say, thirteen ways of looking at a blackbird. But the truth, I would like to think, comes out, that when the reader has read all these thirteen different ways of looking at the blackbird, the reader has his own fourteenth image of that blackbird which I would like to think is the truth.[8]

A fourteenth image of the novel can be one without any perception of the homoerotic configurations, thus reducing the scope of the work, but a fifteenth image with an understanding of the full range of the potentialities of human love provides a far richer appreciation of Faulkner's awesome achievement in *Absalom, Absalom!*

NOTES

[1]All page references in this paper to Faulkner's *Absalom, Absalom!* will be to the Random House Modern Library edition (New York, 1951).

[2]*The Triumph of the Novel: Dickens, Dostoyevsky, Faulkner* (New York: Oxford Univ. Press, 1976), p. 339.

[3]"The Design and Meaning of *Absalom, Absalom!*" in *William Faulkner: Four Decades of Criticism*, ed. Lind Wilshimer Wagner (Lansing: Michigan State Univ. Press, 1973), p. 277. Originally published in *PMLA* (Dec. 1955), pp. 887-912.

[4]*Faulkner: Myth and Motion* (Princeton, N.J.: Princeton Univ. Press, 1968), pp. 195-196.

[5]*Doubling & Incest/ Repetition & Revenge: A Speculative Reading of Faulkner* (Baltimore: The Johns Hopkins Univ. Press, 1975), pp. 77-78.

[6]Guerard, pp. 309-310.

[7]Gerald Langford, *Faulkner's Revision of* Absalom, Absalom!: *A Collation of the Manuscript and the Published Book* (Austin: Univ. of Texas Press, 1971), p. 3.

[8]Frederick L. Gwynn and Joseph L. Blotner, eds., *Faulkner in the University* (New York: Vintage Books, 1965), pp. 273-274. Originally published in Charlottesville: The Univ. of Virginia Press, 1959).

The Merchant of Venice:
The Homosexual as Anti-Semite
in Nascent Capitalism

Seymour Kleinberg, Ph.D.

When I first read *The Merchant of Venice*, I was dismayed by the anti-Semitism and the materialism of the Venetian world. The play held no charm for me, and I decided that it was simply not very available for someone like myself. Twenty years later, in 1978, after a summer as an NEH fellow at Berkeley, researching the subject of sodomy in the Renaissance, I reread the play. I still found it to be about anti-Semitism under mercantile capitalism, but now just as clearly it was also about homosexual eroticism in conflict with heterosexual marriage, about the rivalry of romantic male friendship with the claims of conventional marriage. This paper explores the relationship of these themes — money, ethnic hatred, sexual rivalry — and argues that they are analogous to one another; they are the matter and the feelings that define the merchant of the title.

Literally, that merchant is Antonio, though in the popular mind the title always invokes Shylock. Part of my argument is that the popular response is also the literal one: Shylock is Antonio. They are psychological counterparts. Antonio is a virulently anti-Semitic homosexual and is melancholic to the point of despair because his lover, Bassanio, wishes to marry an immensely rich aristocratic beauty, to leave the diversions of the Rialto to return to his own class and to sexual conventionality. Antonio is also in despair because he despises himself for his homosexuality, which is romantic, obsessive, and exclusive, and fills him with sexual shame.

For decades now, scholars and critics have noted Antonio's peculiarities. Most see an innocent infatuation in a lugubrious melancholiac, a type Shakespeare was fond of exploiting and an infatuation that was time-honored, dating back to the blood brotherhood of the Germanic tribes on one hand and to the classical Greeks on the other.[1] But in the

---

Seymour Kleinberg is Professor of English at the Brooklyn Center of Long Island University. He is the author of *Alienated Affections: Being Gay in America* and the editor of *The Other Persuasion: Short Fiction about Gay Men and Women*.

113

1950s, literary critics came under the influence of psychoanalytic thought, and the wholesome nature of Antonio's feelings was questioned. His passivity was the hallmark of neurosis, a defensive pose against "strong homosexual inclination."[2] It was further argued that Antonio's latent homosexuality was really a defense of Shakespeare's, as was the anti-Semitism of the play: Antonio and Shylock were two defenses of the poet against the anxiety he had portrayed in the sonnets, where homoeroticism and usury were complicated metaphors for each other.[3]

In the next decade, the reading of the plays and the sonnets as emotional biography was dismissed as naive. But too much discussion had taken place to dismiss Antonio as unimportant to *The Merchant of Venice*. Typically, a scholar decided that "there is, of course, no need to suggest an active homosexuality between the two men."[4] Some critics admitted that perhaps on Antonio's part, but never Bassanio's, the love bordered on the passionate, an "incipient homosexual relationship . . . less innocent than conventional Renaissance friendship."[5]

This is still the dominant reading today: Antonio may be repressed and perverse, but Bassanio is innocent. And it is consistent with contemporary attitudes toward Shylock, which sentimentalize the play by seeing Shylock as the victim rather than the villain. Such distortions enervate all the readings of character and relationship. Antonio and Bassanio are just the dearest friends; Portia is completely noble when she isn't being delightfully playful. Of course, the play then is a failure, a mishmash of contradictions, inconsistent about character and confused in its moral vision.

Despite the discomfort of affirming Shylock's villainy after the fate of European Jewry during World War II, critics are once again insisting on describing him with the accurate harshness he deserves. But once Shylock's unattractiveness is restored, it is possible to reconsider Antonio and, finally, Portia herself. It is possible to play Shylock with sympathy without ruining the play entirely, as Laurence Olivier did some years ago for an English televised version, in which Shylock's final "speech" is off-stage and off-camera, his true response to his enforced conversion to Christianity at the end of the trial scene: a terrifying scream so shocking that the play dissolves into prophecies of Auschwitz. At that moment, even if we do not hate Portia and condemn all of Venice, they are permanently outside our sympathy. That is an interesting play, but not the one Shakespeare wrote. It may even be a better play, more suitable to modern ideas of justice, but I doubt it. It is a less complex drama, simpler, flatter. The play Shakespeare wrote does look to the future rather than back to the work that preceded it, but it is the future ambiguities of *Twelfth Night*, the enigma of *Measure for Measure*, the despair of *Troilus and Cressida*, perhaps even the cynicism of *All's Well That Ends Well*.

If one wishes to see the plays refracted in the sonnets, assuming the lyric poetry is less masked, then the erotic triangle of the sonnets and the ambiguous sexual character of the speaker's feelings for the young man can serve as a mirror of *The Merchant of Venice*.

It is unmistakable that Antonio and Bassanio are "lovers"; a number of characters, especially Lorenzo, say so. The question is whether Lorenzo and the others, including Antonio, are using the word in its rarer sense of intimate but platonic friends, or whether they use it to denote that friendship while slyly suggesting the erotic nature of the true relationship.

In the canon, of the nearly 150 times Shakespeare uses the words *lover, lover's, lovers,* and *lovers',* only nine of those instances can be argued as sexually innocent, and four of them are in the play under discussion. Three others occur in *Julius Caesar,* one in *Coriolanus,* and one in *Love's Labors Lost.*[6] In these three plays there is no evidence of sexual suggestion. The term carries the meaning given it by Malone when he glossed it in his edition: "In Shakespeare's time this was applied to those of the same sex who had an esteem for each other."[7] Malone cites Ben Jonson's letter to John Donne in which he signs himself, "Your true lover."

The lexicons, however, note that the overwhelming meaning of *lover* is the modern one, and examples of Shakespeare's lack of reticence about homoeroticism are everywhere in the sonnets and the plays. Even the casual line by the fool in *King Lear,* "He's mad that trusts in the tameness of a wolf, a horse's health, a boy's love or a whore's oath" (III, vi, 19),[8] acknowledges the ordinariness of pederastic infatuation in a society that seemed to tolerate homosexuality or bisexuality for men who had already done their service to society and posterity in marriage and paternity.

Until recently, scholars have been so diffident or so evasive about the subject that their speculations often seem senseless. The modern line is articulated by J. W. Lever: intense male friendship at the end of the sixteenth century in England emerged as a major literary theme; the new seriousness about friendship owed much to Italian Platonism, to the idea of a new kind of love marked by an "absence of physical homosexuality," *Amor Razionale.*[9] Platonic homosexuality belonged to an Italianate culture that was casual about bisexuality, but the new love was not a euphemism for erotic homosexuality. This has been the basis for the standard reading of the sonnets: he loves him but sleeps with her; or he loves him but does not want to sleep with him because the beloved's sex is an odd, unlucky accident, so he sleeps with her in frustration or guilt or lust, but without much affection. That is a valid reading of the ambiguity surrounding the bond between the men in the triangle of the sonnets, but the drama tells another story of the triangle of Antonio, Bassanio, and Portia. Here the conflict is between an assertion of sexuality that is shameful or dangerous and the institution of marriage, between the anarchy of sterile romantic passion and the lawfulness of wedlock.

Critics like Lever presume the friendship must be platonic because the penalties for sodomy were so severe that no poet could venture such sentiments as those in Shakespeare's plays and poems without enormous risk unless the behavior of those involved was innocent, regardless of their inclinations. *Sodomy* by the late sixteenth century always meant "buggery," and sometimes the terms were used interchangeably, as in the English Act of 1533, reissued in 1563, whereby sodomy/buggery was again made a capital offense. *Buggery* is a corruption of *bougrerie*, a reference to the Albigensians, whose religious heresies were supposed to have come from Bulgaria. Thus, sodomy as buggery has its roots in heresy. This is why it was held as so abhorrent, worse even than incest, with which it was compared.[10]

How then are we to account for the openness of Marlowe, both in the life and in the drama, no less James's court and Buckingham's career ("Elizabeth was king; now James is queen")?[11] Nor was this exclusively the vice *anglais*. Pope Julius III (1500-55) was notorious, and the story of Henry III of France, who escaped from Poland dressed as a woman to claim the French throne on the death of his brother, was widely known. There is a mysterious schism between the law of the land, with its penalty of burning at the stake (reserved for heretics, witches, and sodomites) and the evidence of pederasty and bisexuality among Elizabethan aristocrats, for example, the circle centering around the Earl of Southampton and the Jacobean court. Southampton, one of the likeliest candidates for the young man of the sonnets and Shakespeare's sometime sponsor, was a patron of homoerotic and pornographic verse as well.[12] Perhaps he and his circle escaped censure and danger because they married. All upper-class men married. Their duties to property, propriety, and posterity demanded an heir. After that, their romantic predilections were less important socially as long as they were reasonably discreet. Even Richard Barnfield (1574-1627), whose life and career span both reigns and who wrote the most blatant pederastic poetry of the period, *The Affectionate Shepherd* (1594), married and retired to the country to rear a family.

It is on this subject that *The Merchant of Venice* begins: the need to marry. The immediate opening involves Antonio and his friends, who are trying to discern the cause of his melancholia, which Antonio confesses even he is bored with. The temperament Shakespeare and the Elizabethans called melancholia we would paraphrase as depression or neurosis. It is suggested that his sadness is caused by love, the conventional cause, and Antonio does not absolutely deny it when he says, "Fie, fie" (I, i, 46).[13] As soon as he is alone with Bassanio, they investigate a plan by which Bassanio can repay his enormous debts, the largest of which he owes Antonio — if only Antonio will lend him still more money. The yoking of money and love is made explicitly and immediately in the first scene; Bassanio says he owes Antonio "the most in money and in love." Antonio, more frankly, replies that "My purse, my person, my extremest means lie all unlocked to your occasions." In the sonnets, such a line with so much innuendo would be the moment of complicated ironies, and of much scholarly comment: for example, of Shakespeare's fondness for using debt and usury as metaphors for sexual longing. Here in the play, the line elicits no comment; its boldness is so literal it may need none. Plainly, everything is available: Antonio's purse and his person are interchangeable.

When the solution to Bassanio's debts is revealed to be Portia, the heiress of Belmont, Bassanio presents her first as wealthy, then as fair and good; he adds casually that she already seems disposed toward him. Tactfully, he does not elaborate, nor does he mention his feelings, if any, for her. He merely states that she rivals the Golden Fleece, and many Jasons, that emblem of constancy, come to woo her. On these conditions, Antonio is satisfied. Bassanio is a proper young aristocrat: spendthrift, flighty, charming, and beautiful, and he must marry sometime. Only merchants like Antonio can afford to remain single.

Antonio is not married, nor is there ever any hint of such a possibility. Knowing how difficult they are to live with, Shakespeare rarely marries off his melancholiacs. Coincidentally, while there is no clear evidence that these melancholiacs share an aversion to women, they are often more comfortable in exclusively male company, preferably that of a beloved friend (see Jacques in *As You Like It*, Antonio in *Twelfth Night*, Hamlet and Horatio).

Antonio's first characteristic is his melancholia and singularity. His second characteristic is that he hates Jews, notably Shylock. True, all of Venice is casually anti-Semitic, as it is racist in *Othello*, but Shylock tells us that Antonio is special, particularly vicious toward him, spitting on him in public while calling him a misbeliever and a cutthroat dog. Indeed, "Jewish dog" is Antonio's favorite curse for Shylock. Even when he is asking for desperately needed money for his beloved Bassanio, he cannot control his contempt for Shylock. Antonio promises him that even with a loan he is just as likely to spit on him, call him names in public, and worse, undercut Shylock's usury by lending money interest-free — when he has it again. He combines bravura and tactlessness.

This web of money and love, homoeroticism and anti-Semitism, is established as the context of the play before the first scenes are finished. Love exists only on the condition of money, a case made more than once in the play. When Shylock's daughter, Jessica, elopes with her gentile lover, Lorenzo, she not only takes full caskets with her, she jokes as she climbs out her window, "I will . . . gild myself/ With some moe ducats, and be with you straight" (II, vi, 49-50), to which Lorenzo replies that he loves her heartily. Later, when Shylock is told of the elopement, his confusion of his love for Jessica and his passion for his money is intended to be comic. We are told, not shown, that he does not know which grieves him more, the loss of the daughter or the ducats. Our reporters, Salerio and Salanio, find such confusion of money and feeling absurd because Shylock is so coarse about it, apparently so vulgar in his failure to make the distinction. Later in the play, when he refuses to translate feelings into cash, when his grief has turned into hatred and no amount of money can buy that from him, he is no longer amusing. Then, depending on one's sentiments, he is nearer to monstrousness or tragedy. Certainly, he is no longer vulgar.

In the third act, when Shylock has his grand moment of rhetoric about Jewish humanity, presumably falling on the deaf ears of the two Jew-baiters he is speaking to, he makes his feelings very clear. All that he has left of his dignity is his hatred of Christians, especially Antonio. This is interesting but not a subject for compassion. When Tubal enters to tell Shylock of Jessica's profligacy, her spending spree in Genoa where she threw money to the winds to celebrate her honeymoon, we also learn of her contempt for her father, her mother, and her past. She swapped a ring for a monkey on a chain. Shylock cries, "Out upon her! — thou torturest me, Tubal! — it was my turquoise, I had it of Leah when I was a bachelor: I would not have given it for a wilderness of monkeys" (III, i, 125-28). More than one reader has agreed that this is Shylock's really redeeming moment of humanity, his memory of himself as a man in love, who solemnized that love in the symbol of a ring.

The next scene is Bassanio and the three caskets; he chooses correctly. Freud's essay on this scene is one of the masterpieces of psychoanalytic criticism. His thesis is that this choice is simply love over death, that in fact death is transformed into love in the universal wish of mankind to find immortality in the denial of mortality.[14] In simpler terms, it is the choice of marriage and generation, which is also the choice of life and is perhaps the only life eternal.

In Venice, gold and silver are currency; but in Belmont, a world of love and music, they seem to have no meaning except as ornament. Yet at the moment Bassanio chooses the lead casket, Portia has an aside in which she prays that her love for him will be moderate, within the bounds of reason and not subject to the passions of jealousy or despair:

O love be moderate, allay thy ecstasy,
In measure rain thy joy, scant this excess!
I feel too much thy blessing. Make it less,
For fear I forfeit! (III, ii, 111-114)

This anxiety is odd, since she is in love with Bassanio and helpless to change her situation. Why does she want the ecstasy of love, "this excess," to be *scanted*, a term borrowed from the idiom of usury?

The moment is swept away with the joyous discovery that Bassanio has guessed correctly; he is now engaged and a millionaire. The two swear oaths of loving loyalty symbolized by the exchange of rings. One assumes that the destiny of engagement rings in Belmont will be different from that of turquoises in Venice, but the fate of Leah's ring casts a shadow on this emblem of love exchanged in the presence of Jessica and Lorenzo. Then comes news that Antonio is forfeit to Shylock, and Portia, immersed in her feelings, manages to make an extraordinarily vulgar quip that eclipses Shylock's confounding of daughters and ducats. When she learns the background of Bassanio's debt to Antonio and of the odd security Shylock demanded, Portia tells Bassanio that after they are married he can have all the gold he needs to ransom his friend, even twenty times the original "petty debt" of 3,000 ducats. Then she puns, "Since you are dear bought, I will love you dear." So much for Jewish monopolies on vulgarity or confusions of feelings and money.

As the act ends, we learn that Antonio is helpless because Venetian law must honor all issues connected with money, otherwise the justice of the state will be "impeached." The honor of mercantile capitalism is spelled out: it demands the compulsive adherence to the letter of the law, regardless of how unjust the consequences may be. If money has already been deeply confused with feeling, it has now locked into the issue of honor.

In Bassanio's absence, Lorenzo tries to cheer Portia up, saying that "if you knew to whom you show this honor/ How true a gentleman you send relief" (i.e., Antonio), "how dear a lover of my lord your husband," then she'd not mind the separation though it occurred before their wedding night. Again, the pun on *dear* is raised: beloved, expensive, rare. Portia is now inspired; she must save this man herself. She announces that she is going into retreat for a few days, assuring Lorenzo that "this Antonio/ Being the bosom lover of my lord,/ Must needs be like my lord" (III, iv, 16-18). But she will see for herself. Lorenzo's description of so "dear a lover" resonates with suggestion for her. This triangle is best completed in person. It is not that Portia suspects her husband of sodomy; such suspicion is too vile for the delicate air of Belmont, though Portia is neither naive nor prudish. But she is ignorant; the mysteries of male affection, with its remarkable loyalty and apparent selflessness, are as foreign to her as the mysteries of marriage. She has heard of both and experienced neither.

At the trial scene in Act IV, all the themes of the play are brought together. Antonio reiterates his hatred of Jews in a line that even the most apologetic of Shakespeare's critics cannot ignore. He tells the court it is wasting its time trying to dissuade Shylock: "You may as well do anything most hard/ As seek to soften that — than which what's harder? —/ His Jewish heart" (IV, i, 78-80). When Shylock is told by the Duke that he cannot expect mercy in heaven if he renders none here, Shylock replies that he has done nothing that will require mercy. He goes on to argue by analogy: would the Venetians treat their slaves as their children? would they marry them to their heirs? Of course not. And now Shylock "owns" Antonio, to do with as he wishes, for this pound of flesh is "dearly bought" — an eerie, exact echo of Portia's pun and a poetic linking together of Shylock, Antonio, and Portia in some dim emotional bond for which the complications of the plot merely serve as metaphors.

When Bassanio gallantly if meaninglessly offers to lay down his life for his imperiled friend, Antonio answers the gesture with "I am a tainted wether of the flock,/ Meetest for death — the weakest kind of fruit/ Drops earliest to the ground, and so let me" (IV, i, 114-116). A "wether" is a sterile male sheep. Why has Antonio abandoned his stoicism? Why does he regard himself as sterile and sick, "tainted," weak, deserving of death? Why is he in despair and self-loathing?

His sense that he is sick and therefore deserves death is his confession of sin, of sexual shame, his veiled admission that he deserves to die because he is a sodomite. It is irrelevant what Bassanio and Antonio have actually done under the guise of their publicly admired courtly friendship. It is entirely relevant that Antonio thinks himself disgusting.

Portia saves Antonio by finding the law pertaining to aliens who threaten the lives of Venetian citizens: those aliens automatically forfeit all their wealth and their lives. A law that presumed alien criminals would be wealthy surely had Jews in mind. If Shylock had been a Venetian citizen, nothing could have saved Antonio. But Jews are not citizens. Shylock forgot that he is at best a guest, and none too welcome. As long as he is Jewish, he is alien and vulnerable.

Antonio hates Shylock not because he is a more fervent Christian than others, but because he recognizes his own alter ego in this despised Jew who, because he is a heretic, can never belong to the state. He hates Shylock, rather than himself, in a classic pattern of psychological scapegoating. What Antonio hates in Shylock is not Jewishness, which, like all Venetians he merely holds in contempt. He hates himself in Shylock: the homosexual self that Antonio has come to identify symbolically as the Jew. It is the earliest portrait of the homophobic homosexual. The basis for that identification between Antonio and Shylock is complex. They are both merchants of Venice, both lend money, both are involved with Bassanio, and both indirectly and painfully become involved with Belmont. Most of all, they have in common that they are heretics. Shakespeare equates the sodomite and the Jew symbolically and psychologically, as they were already equated under Elizabethan law, which allotted the common fate of burning to witches, heretics, and sodomites.

But another, older, more crucial connection between sodomites and Jews was available to the Elizabethan mind. Prior to the Renaissance, sodomy had meanings other than buggery; it was once used to include the sin of bestiality, *bestialitas*, which had the same sexual meaning it does in modern usage, but which had special theological meanings as well.[15] There were cases of men tried and burnt for bestiality. In an obscure work of the turn of this century, Professor E. P. Evans in *The Criminal Prosecution and Capital Punishment of Animals* remarks:

> It seems rather odd that the Christian lawgivers should have adopted the Jewish code against sexual intercourse with beasts, and then enlarged it so as to include the Jews themselves. The question was gravely discussed by jurists whether cohabitation of a Christian with a Jewess, or vice versa, constitutes sodomy. Damhouder (Prax., res. crim. c.96 n.48) is of the opinion that it does, and Nicholas Boer (Decis., 136, n.5) cites the case of a certain Johannes Alardus, or Jean Alard, who kept a Jewess in his house in Paris and had several children by her: he was convicted of sodomy on account of this relation and burned, together with his paramour, "since coition with a Jewess is precisely the same as if a man should copulate with a dog (Dope. Theat. ii, p. 157)." Damhouder includes Turks and Saracens in the same category.[16]

Shylock, the Jewish dog, already a heretic, is also symbol for the sodomite; conversely, Antonio the sodomite with his heretical desires is linked to the other alien in Venice, the not quite human Jew.

At the same moment that Antonio confesses his guilt and desire to die, converting his despair into a martyrdom of love, Portia is faced with a struggle for her husband. She must rescue him from this infatuation with Antonio, so steeped in noble sentiment, romanticism, and perhaps erotic power, so that he can be fully free to enter marriage. She listens carefully while Antonio says farewell to Bassanio:

> Commend me to your honorable wife.
> Tell her the process of Antonio's end,
> Say how I loved you, speak me fair in death,
> And when the tale is told, bid her be judge
> Whether Bassanio had not once a love. (IV, i, 273-77)

Antonio is confident that Portia will be able to judge, since both of them feel alike; he does not say that Bassanio had a friend beyond compare: he had a love beyond compare. Perhaps he puns when he says "honorable" wife, inferring he was the dishonorable one. What is really important is his resurgent bravura, his assurance that she will never be able to do for *their* beloved what he has, despite her fabled wealth. His request to Bassanio demands that all the parties concerned acknowledge that there has indeed been a triangle of emotional power, which only decorum has prevented from being fully understood. It is not Portia, but Antonio who has made Bassanio rich, and therefore happy.

Bassanio is so deeply moved that he offers to sacrifice everything he owns: his fortune, his life. He even throws in his wife's life, "sacrifice them all to this devil to deliver you." Both Shylock and Portia are astonished by this extravagance. Shylock mutters in contempt and aside, "These be the Christian husbands!" thinking of Jessica and her fate; for such as this she betrayed her father, mother, past. Portia, as the young lawyer, interjects, "Your wife would give you little thanks for that/ If she were by to hear you make the offer." She came to Venice to find out what was between her husband and his friend, who she suspected may have been "alike"; well, now she knows.

It will be even trickier to rescue Bassanio than it was to free Antonio. Portia is struggling for mastery now, and it is far more than the conventional mastery of reason over passion, the passion she feared would reduce her to the same abject dependence that her father and his will had placed her in before. Is she always to be a chattel? Is she never to be her own mistress? If she must be married without choice or consent, if she must love her beautiful husband even if his past is shadowed in sexual secrecy, she will at least have a husband all her own, one whose loyalty is exclusively hers: he is to remember whose millions he now has access to, and he is to reevaluate that extravagance which would fling everything, her and her money, to the Jews.

In this charged atmosphere of ethnic hatred, sexual mystery and jealousy, self-loathing, and revenge, Portia succumbs. Despite the lovely rhetoric about mercy that is the most famous speech in the play, when Shylock is vanquished, forced to convert to what he has always hated, she adds the most sadistic line in the scene: "Art thou contented, Jew?" She turns her anger at Antonio on Shylock, expressing it as contempt, and expressing it with a cruelty she does not have to mask. In one stroke she confirms for us Shylock's view of Christians and their society: wretched as he is, what should one expect of Jews if Christians behave this way? It is not that Shakespeare is for Shylock; it is that he is contemptuous of all Venice.

When Portia, still in disguise, demands the ring as payment for her lifesaving work, it is no trivial prank. She wants back the ring she gave Bassanio and that he swore would never leave his finger while he was her husband. She also wants him to refuse. She wants the ring because she no longer trusts her happiness to him, but she wants him to refuse it so that she can forget his extravagance, dismiss it as hyperbole. It is her crucial moment. If he refuses to give her the ring, it means he remembers his vow, and that both she and he can enter the institution of marriage in true conformity. If he gives her the ring, his broken vow annuls her own. For a moment Bassanio resists, but he surrenders to Antonio's persuasion in the play's most overt moment of sexual competition: "My lord Bassanio, let him have the ring,/ Let his deservings and my lord withal/ Be valued 'gainst your wife's commandment" (IV, i, 449-451). Bassanio yields the ring to one "man" at the behest of another, the ring that linked him to the world of women and marriage. His loyalty to Portia is remiss compared to what he feels for Antonio. Bassanio has many assets; he is beautiful and generous and sincere, but he is also shallow. Out of sight, out of mind. When he was at Belmont, he forgot about Antonio until he was arrested. Now he is with Antonio in Venice, and Portia seems very far away.

For Portia, Bassanio's failure is her victory; the terms of the marriage are void. She has lived up to the agreement of her father and society, and until now has agreed to be dispensed as men saw fit. Her husband replaced her father as her legal master, but he has broken faith, her faith in his word. She is free to negotiate for her freedom. In the fifth act, the issue of sexual competition is mirrored in the agon between men and women and in the conspiratorial bonding between men, the real subject of the squabbling. The ring is now more than a symbol; it is a key. Who has the ring is master of the bedroom. Portia makes that plain; she will yield herself only to the man who has the ring. Since she herself has it, she means to yield to no man ever again. Instead, she will show that she is free to bestow herself as she wishes.

When Bassanio and Antonio arrive, Bassanio introduces his lover to his wife: "This is the man, this is Antonio,/ To whom I am so infinitely bound" (V, i, 134-135). Portia observes wryly, "You should in all sense be much bound to him,/ For (as I hear) he was much bound to you." Emotional loyalty is identified with the money that has passed between Shylock and Antonio. With that money borrowed from one merchant by another, Antonio has given Bassanio away in marriage only to keep him bound to himself as firmly as ever, perhaps even more. Without Shylock, it could never have been accomplished. Bonding, senses, money are punned upon as issues of loyalty and honor, erotic preference, and emotional commitment rise to the surface of the scene.

Portia pretends to quarrel; Antonio ruefully observes it and remarks, "I am the unhappy subject of these quarrels." Portia agrees with him but says, "You are welcome notwithstanding." That is, despite the fact that you are a guest in my house, that you are alive entirely because of my intervention, you have come between a lawful husband and wife:

what further claims can you now have? While Bassanio swears that he will never again be careless about his promises to her, submitting entirely to her ("Pardon this fault and by my soul I swear/ I never more will break an oath with thee"), she is not satisfied — not until Antonio offers security for Bassanio's promise, as he did once before:

> I once did lend my body for his wealth,
> Which, but for him that had your husband's ring,
> Had quite miscarried. I dare be bound again,
> My soul upon the forfeit, that your lord
> Will never more break faith advisedly. (V, i, 249-253)

It is what she has been waiting to hear; if he once offered his body to Jews, it is only fair that he now offer his soul.

The happy ending of the play is the triumph of heterosexual marriage and the promise of generation over the romantic but sterile infatuation of homoeroticism. In this competition, Shakespeare as ever is conservative. Portia must rescue her beloved and guarantee that as corrupt as the world is, with its translation of every feeling into cash, at least she and Bassanio will live to perpetuate it. Though Belmont appears to be different from Venice, it is really the same world, but here Jews like Jessica are welcome converts and sodomites like Antonio brief guests.

If *The Merchant of Venice* is filled with mitigated resolutions for its lovers and villains and fools, that is the way of the world. Antonio of Venice is the symbol of the corruption of erotic feeling under nascent mercantile capitalism, a world where melancholia is romance and sexual guilt is translated into ethnic hatred.

What difference does such a reading of this play make? Is it better because it concerns a homosexual Jew-hater, rather than a monstrous Jew who is practically a butcher? (To be sure, either view is more cogent than one that sees the play as being about a pompous young woman who quotes Scripture about Christian mercy and never understands the subject, that is, the conventional reading, which makes the play a sentimental failure, a thematic mess unable to link together the Rialto and the moonlit terraces of Belmont.) Here is a reading without sentiment. The play is filled with ambiguities about sexuality and money, love and hatred. Nothing is simple, least of all who we are or what we are. What links us to both the Rialto and Belmont is our recognition of our painful complexities and our terrible vulnerabilities before the coldness of the world.

NOTES

[1]M. R. Ridley, *Shakespeare's Plays* (New York: E. P. Dutton and Co., 1938) is typical: "Antonio does little but wander lugubriously across the stage, an embodiment of the humor of

melancholy, enjoying poor health and indulging an enfeebling infatuation for Bassanio" (p. 91).
E. K. Chambers in *Shakespeare: A Survey* (London: Sidgwick and Jackson, 1925) hints at a connection between Antonio and the sonnets, an "echo" (p. 117).

For a full scholarly but entirely unpsychological view of the subject of male bonding, two useful works are Laurens J. Mills, *One Soul in Bodies Twain: Friendship in Tudor Literature and Stuart Drama* (Bloomington: Indiana Univ. Press, 1937) and Lu Emily Pearson, *Elizabethan Love Conventions* (Berkeley: Univ. of California Press, 1933). For a discussion of the psychological and social implications of the subject, see C. S. Lewis, *The Allegory of Love* (London: Oxford Univ. Press, 1936): "The deepest of worldly emotions in this period is the love of man for man, the mutual love of warriors who die together fighting against odds, and the affection between vassal and lord" (p. 9). Lewis' discussion refers to *The Song of Roland*, the work that exemplifies the tradition of male bonding. Alistair Sutherland and Patrick Anderson, eds., *Eros: An Anthology of Friendship* (London: Anthony Blond, 1961) define their subject as "any friendship between men strong enough to deserve one of the more serious senses of the word 'love'" (p. 8). Thorkil Vanggaard, *Phallos: A Symbol and Its History in the Male World* (New York: International Universities Press, 1972) has a lengthy and definitive discussion of male bonding in Norse culture, which he claims included "a genital aspect, based on mutuality and equality between the partners" (p. 119), but which precluded buggery. Most recently, John Boswell, *Christianity, Social Tolerance and Homosexuality* (Chicago: Univ. of Chicago Press, 1980) discusses the subject of Platonic love: "only love between persons of the same gender could transcend sex" (p. 27). Boswell adds, however, that there was a definite but not necessarily conscious sexual nature to the many intense male friendships he documents (p. 134).

[2]E. E. Krapf, "Shylock and Antonio: A Psychoanalytic Study on Shakespeare and Antisemitism," *The Psychoanalytic Review*, 42 (April 1955), 118. See K. B. Danks, "The Case of Antonio's Melancholy," *N & Q, NS*, 1 (1954), 111. Earlier, Arthur Acheson tried to connect the play and the sonnets with the life of the author in *Shakespeare's Sonnet Story* (London: B. Quaritch, 1933), pp. 342-83. For an early Freudian view of the subject, see T. A. Ross, "A Note on *The Merchant of Venice*," *British Journal of Medical Psychology*, 14 (1934), 303f.

[3]While biographical readings of the sonnets are increasingly unfashionable or uninteresting to scholars and critics, the lyrical poetry and the drama have been used to enlighten each other since the eighteenth century; usually the sonnets are used to discuss the plays. The latest scholarly edition of the sonnets, edited by Stephen Booth (New Haven and London: Yale Univ. Press, 1977), continues to see all of the canon as one continuous work but disdains biographical inquiry as naive.

The use of usury as an elaborate metaphor for sexuality has long been noted. Leslie A. Fiedler, *The Stranger in Shakespeare* (New York: Stein and Day, 1972) was the first to write extensively of usury as both moneylending and copulation in the sonnets and the play. John Boswell has an interesting comment on the mutual unnaturalness of usury, heresy, and sodomy (p. 331). The most articulate and thorough discussion of this subject is Marc Shell, "The Wether and the Ewe: Verbal Usury in *The Merchant of Venice*," *Kenyon Review*, 1 (1979), 65-92.

[4]J. D. Hurrell, "Love and Friendship in *The Merchant of Venice*," *Texas Studies of Literature and Language*, 3 (1961), 332.

[5]Hurrell, p. 340. See also Graham Midgley, "*The Merchant of Venice*: A Reconsideration," *Essays in Criticism*, 10 (1960), 119-33.

[6]Alexander Schmidt, *A Shakespeare Lexicon*, 3rd ed., rev. and enl. Gregor Sarrazin (New York: B. Blom, 1968). Also Marvin Spevack, *A Complete and Systematic Concordance to the Works of Shakespeare* (Hildesheim, Germany: Georg Olms, 1970).

[7]In William Shakespeare, *Complete Works*, ed. with notes by Malone et al. (London: J. Rivington and Sons, 1790), III, 67n.

[8]William Shakespeare, *King Lear*, ed. Kenneth Muir, The Arden Edition of the Works (London: Methuen, 1952).

[9]*The Elizabethan Love Sonnet* (London: Methuen, 1956, 1966), p. 204n. Lever seems to understand the issue but is too decorous or timid to pursue it. See the discussion on p. 103 f. and p. 164 f. The subject of erotic friendship was usually referred to as an issue of "bisexuality," first by Lu Emily Pearson, p. 254 f., and later by G. Wilson Knight, *The Mutual Flame* (London: Methuen, 1955), p. 35 f. Fiedler is the first to have taken up the subject succinctly and lucidly. He puts the homosexual Antonio in a context of aliens like Jews and women, and gives a brilliant reading of the play, particularly of the last act. He also notes that there are two homosexual lovers called Antonio in Shakespeare and concludes that the later character in *Twelfth*

Night is the same psychological person as the merchant. Fiedler sees the relationship as platonic and Antonio as an "advocate of an austere Uranian love for whose sake the older lover educates to manliness the boy he adores, and in whose name he is prepared to die, though he knows he cannot ask as much in return, since that boy must rather die to him by marriage" (p. 132).

[10]Laurence Stone, *The Crisis of the Aristocracy, 1558-1641* (London: Oxford Univ. Press, 1965), p. 491 f. See also Ivan Bloch, *Sexual Life in England, Past and Present*, tr. William H. Fostern (London: F. Aldor, 1938); Vanggaard, p. 153; Vern L. Bullough, *Homosexuality, A History* (New York: New American Library, 1979), pp. 34-35, 170-71; and Derrick Sherwin Bailey, *Homosexuality and the Western Christian Tradition* (New York: Longmans, Green, 1955).

John Boswell argues that in the thirteenth century *bougrerie* would not have meant "sodomy," though it could have meant "usury" (usurers were cited as "bougres") and may generally have meant "heretic," p. 290.

[11]G. P. V. Akrigg, *Jacobean Pageant or The Court of King James I* (New York: Atheneum, 1967). See also Gordon Rattray Taylor, "Historical and Mythological Aspects of Homosexuality," in *Sexual Inversion: The Multiple Roots of Homosexuality*, ed. Judd Marmor (New York: Basic Books, 1965), p. 145.

[12]G. P. V. Akrigg, *Shakespeare and the Earl of Southampton* (Cambridge, Mass.: Harvard Univ. Press, 1968). See also H. Montgomery Hyde, *The Other Love: An Historical and Contemporary Survey of Homosexuality in Britain* (London: Mayflower, 1972). A number of writers cite the work of William Lithgow, "Rare Adventures and Painful Peregrinations" (Glasgow, 1906), which was first written between 1609 and 1622 and describes his travels. Lithgow praises the Venetians for their anti-Jewish attitudes and remarks on the "unfortunate rifeness of sodomy" in the city; cited by Taylor, p. 141, and by Sutherland, p. 144. See also John J. McNeill, S.J., *The Church and the Homosexual* (Kansas City, Kan.: Sheed Andrews and McMeel, 1976).

[13]William Shakespeare, *The Merchant of Venice*, ed. John Russell Brown, The Arden Edition of the Works (London: Methuen, 1955). All citations are from this edition of the play.

[14]Sigmund Freud, "The Theme of the Three Caskets," *Imago* (1913).

[15]Montague Summers, *The History of Witchcraft and Demonology* (New York: Alfred Knopf, 1926). I am indebted to the Summers work for the information on Evans that follows.

[16](London: W. Heinemann, 1906), p. 152. Cited in Summers, note 43, Chapter iii, "Demons and Familiars."

The Lesbian Hero Bound: Radclyffe Hall's Portrait of Sapphic Daughters and Their Mothers

Inez Martinez, Ph.D.

Radclyffe Hall wrote her first novel, *The Unlit Lamp* (1924), about lesbian love but did not become famous for defending the infamous until she published *The Well of Loneliness* in 1928. This novel was banned in England, translated into eleven languages, and became "the one novel that every literate lesbian in the four decades between 1928 and the late 1960s would certainly have read."[1]

Contemporary feminist critics find piety toward Radclyffe Hall difficult and appear relieved that they can at least applaud her courage in risking sapphic subject matter. They are embarrassed by her writing style, by the suffering she portrays, and by what they deem her misogyny. Lillian Faderman and Ann Williams in "Radclyffe Hall and the Lesbian Image," Dolores Klaich in *Woman + Woman*, and Blanche Cook in "'Women Alone Stir My Imagination': Lesbianism and the Cultural Tradition" all deplore the self-pity and self-loathing" in Hall's lesbian heroes.[2] Jane Rule in *Lesbian Images* frankly accuses Hall of believing men superior to women and of worshiping patriarchy.[3] All these critics imply that the alleged poverty of Hall's psychological vision is justly mirrored in her ineptitude as a writer, in her "turgid and maudlin" style.[4] Both Rule and Cook ascribe this poverty of vision to Hall's reading Karl Heinrich Ulrichs and Krafft-Ebing.[5]

The disapproval of these critics, even though tightly reined, leaves them stymied by the continuing impact of Hall's novels. As Klaich says: "It's difficult to imagine a liberated lesbian of today relating to *The Well of Loneliness* except as an historical curio, and it comes as a surprise to hear the totally hip young woman in Kate Millet's 1971 film *Three Lives* tell of how she read it 'digging' it."[6] Apparently, that young

Inez Martinez is Associate Professor at Kingsborough Community College, where she teaches a course on women and literature. She has her Ph.D. in American Literature. Among her publications is an article, "Women Artists: Key to the Female Psyche," in *Quadrant*, Summer 1979. She is now writing a novel of her own.

woman's enthusiasm is not freakish, since, according to Rule, *The Well of Loneliness* "remains the lesbian novel" against which others continue to be compared.[7]

I believe that Hall's rendering of the psyche in her two lesbian novels has little to do with what she read or what she had her characters read, and I believe the power of her portrait of the lesbian hero in love with the beautiful woman accounts for the continued meaningfulness of the novels, even to "hip" readers. Modern readers persist through her prose (written appropriately enough in the mode of heroic elaboration rather than, say, ironic or elliptical terseness) because Hall wrote of the failure of hero-beauty eros, and because she grounded this failure in the hero's worship of a consuming mother.

Eros based on opposition involves an attempt to unite with what one is not. The hero-beauty opposition poses strength or feats at one pole and beauty or being at the other. Historically, of course, strength and doing have been associated with the male hero, and beauty and being with the adored female. The terms in which Hall rendered the basic emotional dynamic between these two poles are conventional enough: her heroes have to struggle against fear, draw upon personal resources, and be endlessly protective in order to offer feats to the worshiped woman; the female is charged with so valuing her beautiful being that she is willing to be worshiped, gratefully accept protection from her hero, and bestow on her hero approval, admiration, and her self. The hero does not consciously identify as the beautiful flower who needs protection and whose life purpose is fulfilled simply through being — even if to be so serves her. In turn, the worshiped female — even if controlling events herself — does not identify with the competitor triumphing through personal strength and gaining life's purpose by winning a flower to protect.

Hall departed from convention by simply removing the sex-linking from these two poles. In Joan Ogden, hero of *The Unlit Lamp*, and in Stephen Gordon, hero of *The Well of Loneliness*, but particularly in Stephen, Hall created female protagonists who naturally and utterly identify with the heroic position. These characterizations imply that the hero-beauty dynamic is archetypal, i.e., a way of manifesting a human potential (in this case erotic attraction) inherent in the human psyche.

Although Hall created lovers for her heroes, lovers who identify with the worshiped female, the women who possess the power of approval for Joan and Stephen are their mothers. In most respects no two women could be more different than Mrs. Ogden and Anna Gordon, but the two of them are identical in refusing to affirm the maturation of their daughters and in assuming that absolute service from them is their due. Ultimately, it is in the struggle against the values of their mothers that

Joan and Stephen must choose between self-affirmation and self-sacrifice.

This dilemma led Hall to an uncharacteristic critique of self-sacrifice. In her other novels Hall idealized characters capable of total self-abnegation in the service of others. In Maddalena of *Adam's Breed*, in Hannah of *The Sixth Beatitude*, and in Christopher of *Master of the House* Hall seemed to think the Christian cross, the nailing together of love and death, a vindication of human suffering.[8] Because Hall's attitude in these novels is passionately orthodox, her description of the destructiveness of self-sacrifice in her lesbian heroes is particularly arresting. As she has plotted their lives, maturation demands self-affirmation at the cost of pain to the beloved.

At this point a wary reader might think I am writing in support of the commonplace idea that lesbian love is a substitute mother-daughter relationship. Charlotte Wolff, M.D., in her theory about lesbianism, gave this idea the status of professional opinion: "Lesbians expect from one another nothing less than the wish-fulfillment of an incestuous mother-daughter relationship."[9] According to Wolff's theory, the biological mother proves unloving and the daughter develops a desire for a compensatory dependence.[10] This idea is not unknown in literature before Hall wrote or since. Ethel Sidgwick, in 1914 in *A Lady of Leisure*, Valerie Taylor in 1959 in *Whisper Their Love*, and Sybille Bedford in 1969 in *A Compass Error* wrote of self-absorbed mothers having daughters who fall in love with women.

Until recently, the paucity of study and of uncensored material written by lesbians themselves gave the "surrogate mother" theory about the genesis and nature of lesbian love almost sole possession of the field of inquiry. The improbability of that uniqueness would be enough to lead me to imagine that lesbian love, like heterosexual love, is in fact quite various in its motives, purposes, and expressions, and that the relationships of lesbian daughters and their mothers will, upon study, prove to be as diverse and complicated as those of heterosexual daughters and theirs. Fortunately, literature bears me out. For example, the excellence of a mother-daughter relationship is the inspiration for lesbian love in Colette's "Night without Sleep" and in Naomi Mitchison's "A Delicate Fire," while the women who love women in Elisabeth Thorneycroft Fowler's *The Farringdons* and in Rita Mae Brown's *Rubyfruit Jungle* are orphans.

The pattern in Hall's novels at once resembles the commonplace idea about lesbian love and differs essentially from it. In Hall's rendering, both heroes have mothers who are intensely selfish and do not want their daughters to be themselves. But the solution for the daughters does not lie in a substitute mother-daughter relationship; rather, Joan and Stephen are tasked to wrest the affirming power from their mothers and assume it themselves. In Hall's novels, such self-affirmation is a condition for successful lesbian love; unfortunately, it is by definition inaccessible to the heroic attitude.

In *The Unlit Lamp*, Hall focused on the paralysis experienced by the hero through fear of guilt and through excessive desire to protect the beloved from pain. The weak beloved in this novel is the mother herself, Mrs. Ogden, a beautiful woman whose husband fails her by becoming ill. The years she spends nursing Colonel Ogden cause her beauty to fade and lead her to an obsessive need to be taken care of, "to break down utterly, to become bedridden, to be waited upon hand and foot";[11] in short, simply to be and be served. Mrs. Ogden's neediness is exacerbated by unrelieved sexual frustration. Instead of having an affair with the one man she has ever felt physically attracted to, she focuses her love energy on her daughter, Joan, and expects her to make up for her frustrations.

Both mother and daughter are aware of this situation. By the time Joan is twelve, Mrs. Ogden actively fantasizes keeping her in a lifelong, perfect relationship and manipulates her for sympathy and affection:

> She would listen for Joan's footsteps on the stairs, and then assume an attitude, her head back against the couch, hand pressed to eyes. . . .
> Then Joan's strong, young arms would comfort and soothe, and her firm lips grope until they found her mother's; and Mrs. Ogden would feel mean and ashamed but guiltily happy, as if a lover held her. (p.6)

As Joan grows older, she realizes she represents "a substitute for all that Mrs. Ogden had been defrauded of" (p. 107). Joan does not know, however, that Mrs. Ogden intends never to let her go.

Joan as hero conceives of herself as a protector, is moved by helplessness, and is angered by injustice. Joan's heroic strength charms two people besides her mother. Richard Benson is a heroic type like herself, but one who understands that the doers of the world have to be careful not to get "bottled" by those they love. Joan's other admirer is her tutor, Elizabeth Rodney. Elizabeth, even more than Richard, perceives the danger stirred by Joan's strength in relation to Mrs. Ogden. Looking at Joan, she admires and worries about her:

> Joan was so quiet, so reserved, so strong. . . . She loved stray cats and starving dogs and fledgelings that had tumbled out of their nests . . . and Mrs. Ogden. . . . Mrs. Ogden was so exactly like a

lost fledgeling. . . . Poor woman, poor woman, poor Joan. . . ."
(p. 16)

Elizabeth soon comes to love Joan as passionately as Mrs. Ogden does,
and the two of them fight over her bitterly.

Mrs. Ogden and Elizabeth realize their rivalry quite early. When Joan
is fourteen, Mrs. Ogden wonders if the girl will take from her "almost
bankrupt mother" the "golden coin of love" and give it to the woman
helping her discover knowledge (p. 58). At about the same time Elizabeth begins scheming to get Joan to attend Cambridge and directly challenges Mrs. Ogden to let her daughter go: "Don't let her worry about
you . . . don't let her *spend* herself on you!" (p. 79). War is thus
officially declared, and Mrs. Ogden refrains from banishing her enemy
only because she is afraid Joan will go away with her.

Both women know Joan believes her self-respect depends upon her
protecting the needy. Accordingly, they both proclaim their needs, pro-
voking Joan's guilt in order to bind her to them. For example, after
Elizabeth burns her hands rescuing a burning woman, Joan is thrilled
to take care of her. Mrs. Ogden immediately develops horrible headaches that require Joan's constant attention. Elizabeth, too, consciously
manipulates Joan, as when she tells her that she refused an offer of
marriage from Richard Benson's brother, Lawrence, because she was
"too busy thinking of someone I cared for very much and of how
they could get free and make a life of their own. . . . So you see,
Joan, you mustn't fail me" (p. 146).

Compared to Mrs. Ogden, Elizabeth is an immensely sympathetic
character. She truly wants Joan to mature into herself; indeed, she sacrifices her own life to Joan's self-actualization. Educated and talented,
she abandoned her ambitions to take care of her brother. Now hoping to
live a realized life vicariously through Joan's escape and career, she
relinquishes her freedom and becomes totally dependent upon Joan's
decisions.

The hub of Joan's choices is her attitude toward inflicting pain. The
first time the subject of her own independence arises, she warns Elizabeth: "I hate being hurt and hurting, and I think you have to do that
if you're really ambitious" (p. 85). For six years, Joan extends her
protection to her parents and in the process breaks her promise to Elizabeth to join her in London to study. Elizabeth accuses her of preferring
to their friendship the martyred virtue of protecting her mother.

Elizabeth leaves, but she can no more live life for herself than Joan
can. She returns to tend Joan while Joan tends her now-widowed mother
and her tubercular sister. Not until Joan's sister dies does Joan pull
her courage together to hurt her mother and serve herself: "'Good God!'
she thought bitterly, 'can there be no development of individuality in

this world without hurting oneself or someone else?' She clenched her fists. 'I don't care, I don't care! I've a right to my own life'" (p. 296).

Mrs. Ogden responds by using every trick of submissive martyrdom she knows, calling up "all the chivalry and protectiveness of which Joan's nature was capable" (p. 299). At the moment of truth, Joan cannot leave her. This second betrayal brings a confessional letter from Elizabeth, her last communication before leaving Joan for good. Elizabeth writes that she has missed "experiences" and consequently has been "hungry for her birthright." Her repressed energy "flowed away from its natural course . . . to you, Joan. Thus it was that my desire to help forward a brilliant pupil grew, little by little, into an absorbing passion. . . . I lived for you, for your work, your success; I lived in you, in your present, in your future, which I told myself would be my future too" (p. 312). Both Mrs. Ogden and Elizabeth have staked their erotic lives on Joan, and Elizabeth loses. She loses because she herself was prone to self-sacrifice and permitted Joan to try to leech off her in turn.

When she first fails to keep her promise to live with Elizabeth, Joan begs her tutor not to leave, using terms that literally echo Mrs. Ogden: "Joan faced her with bright, desperate eyes. 'Elizabeth, you can't go away, I need you too much'" (p. 197). After Elizabeth returns Joan continues to drink up her affection while postponing giving her her desire. Many years after their final separation, Joan is tending her crotchety and possessive mother at a summer resort. There Dr. Richard Benson recognizes her as a "virgin daughter withering on her stem" in attendance on a "gentle, tyrant mother" (p. 341), and he tries to bring Joan back to herself. Part of his attempted cure is a frank analysis of how she once tried to do to Elizabeth what her mother has succeeded in doing to her. He tells Joan: "There was one tentacle more tenacious than all the rest; it clung . . . until she cut it through, and that was *you*, who were trying unconsciously to make her a victim of your own circumstances" (p. 360).

Elizabeth proves herself more worthy of life by doing what Joan cannot do: by inflicting pain, cutting the tentacle of need. She finally marries Lawrence Benson, emigrates with him to South Africa, and becomes a social force in Capetown. What life she has left, she takes.

Fate is equally just to Joan; what life she has left, she gives. Hall records the end of Joan's life with the exactness of a scientist marking cause and effect. Joan, emotionally timid, suffering the neuralgias of advanced middle age, watches her mother grow indifferent to the whims the daughter has spent her life vainly trying to satisfy. One morning she finds that her mother has quietly died in her sleep. Now Joan has nothing to do but support herself, but the only way she knows how to do that is to nurse those who can't take care of themselves. Her aunt finds her a job caring for an old man, mentally retarded, arrested in emotional development at age six. The novel ends with Joan learning to appease him.

When Hall presents her protagonist with the possibility of lesbian love, it is hardly as a substitute for Joan's relationship with her mother. In fact, Joan cannot live out that love until her relationship with her mother has ceased being more important to her than her own self. In other words, Hall presents as a condition of fulfilled lesbian love the surrender of heroic martyrdom. Joan would have to give up her virtuous identification as the self-sacrificing strong one; she would have to affirm her own life and possibilities above all. Then she might escape the values of her mother; then she might live with and love Elizabeth Rodney. Instead, she worships protectiveness and self-sacrifice, and becomes herself an unfulfilled leech capable of supporting herself only through the abject helplessness of others.

Bitter as Joan's fate is in *The Unlit Lamp*, Stephen's in *The Well of Loneliness* is even more so. At least Joan enjoys the ambivalent pleasure of her mother's approval of her sacrifice. Stephen's mother, Anna Gordon, while accepting Stephen's sacrifices and service as her due, withholds all approval from the beginning.

The mother Stephen has to contend with is — according to customary lights — a fully realized woman. She grew up in Ireland as the "lovely, lovely Anna Molloy, much admired, much loved and constantly courted";[12] married the rich, handsome, and honorable Sir Philip Gordon; shared with him his magnificent Morton estate; and bore him a child. If this daughter, Stephen, had reminded Anna of herself instead of Sir Philip, Anna's life would have been a female-role paradise, replete with beauty, love, marriage, child, wealth, respect, protection.

Stephen, in contrast to Anna, is not beautiful, nor much admired, loved, or courted. Their differences are not merely those of appearance. As a young child, to Anna's frustration, Stephen insists on riding astride and becomes a brilliant rider, fearless at the hunt. Stephen is a student and a writer, whereas Anna knows "little or nothing" of the classics because "her poetry lay in her husband" (p. 80). Anna is repelled by the adventure of the new, such as Sir Philip's motorcar, while the challenge of novelty attracts Stephen. In short, Anna identifies with being beautiful, Stephen with being heroic and adoring beauty in other women — beginning with Anna.

Unquestionably, the most divisive difference between Anna and Stephen is their experience of love. Stephen loves gallantly; that is, she identifies with the strong and extends protection to those whom she loves for their beauty. At seven years old, she accompanies her mother to town and conceives of herself as her mother's "escort," offering Anna her arm while crossing streets. From the root of such protective love grows Stephen's erotic life — and her capacity for self-sacrifice.

As a young adult Stephen extends her protection to the socially despised Angela Crossby, an American actress who has married a newly wealthy vulgarian. Stephen first meets Angela by reaching into the middle of a dogfight to save Angela's terrier. Her love for Angela reaches its deepest point the night Angela is most vulnerable, the night Angela confesses having prostituted herself during her acting career and, indeed, by marrying. Stephen is stirred by this revelation and gives Angela the pearl she chose for her earlier because of its extraordinary purity. Stephen's identification with heroic strength not only enables but demands of her that she embrace weakness.

Angela feels no reciprocal protectiveness. In fact, when she fears Stephen will expose Angela's affair with the homophobe Roger Antrim, Angela turns Stephen's letter of protest over to her husband, who then sends a copy to Anna. Anna uses the letter to defend herself for always having felt physically repelled by her daughter: "Now I know that my instinct was right; it is you who are unnatural, not I" (p. 220).

The difference between the mother's and the daughter's experiences of love is here made explicit. Anna says: "And you presumed to use the word love in connection with . . . these unnatural cravings. . . . I have loved your father, and your father loved me. That was *love*" (p. 201). Stephen defends herself: "As my father loved you, I loved. . . . It made me feel terribly strong . . . and gentle. . . . I gave all and asked nothing in return — I just went on hopelessly loving" (p. 201).

The reward for Stephen's hopeless loving is betrayal by Angela, rejection by Anna. She is directly asked to choose between her own welfare and her mother's when Anna announces they cannot both live at Morton. Stephen loves nature with her whole strength and first came to love it through the beauty of Morton. But faced with Anna's ultimatum, she chooses for Anna — and leaves Morton.

Stephen seems to need a woman who represents beauty-being yet can love her without wanting Stephen to deny herself. This dream is untested until Stephen reaches her thirties and meets Mary Llewellyn — in World War I at the French front in an all-women ambulance corps. Characteristically, Stephen resists acting on her passion until Mary protests that that restraint is making her unhappy. At last Stephen can please the beloved by pleasing herself. All should be well.

But then Anna writes to Stephen in Paris (where she lives in exile with Mary), invites Stephen to visit Morton, and excludes Mary from the invitation. Stephen imagines herself with Mary at Morton, imagines denying Mary in order to avoid incensing Anna. She envisions Anna rejecting Mary as once she rejected Stephen: "I would rather see you dead at my feet. . ." (p. 333). To protect Mary, therefore, Stephen makes light of the exclusion and goes to Morton by herself, but the problem of getting Mary into English society is now clear.

Stephen has a friend who understands her dilemma. And Puddle, Stephen's old governess, herself a repressed lesbian, has a strategy: Stephen must become a famous writer and protect her beloved through her prestige as an artist. Stephen responds by returning to Paris and shutting herself up in her study to write her heart out.

Stephen's effort leaves Mary to entertain herself — a difficult task because living as the beautiful one demands the presence of the hero. Not only does Mary not have Stephen's presence; she has no one's, for they have no society. Worse still, Puddle's strategy fails. Stephen does write a marvelous book, and the couple receive an invitation to visit the home of English gentry, but as soon as the hostess understands Stephen and Mary are lesbians, she disinvites them. Mary turns to the society of unhappy fellow "inverts." She begins to drink and to become bitter.

Into this grim situation comes Stephen's one childhood friend, Martin Hallam. To his dismay, Martin falls in love with Mary, and she, in spite of herself, comes to care for him. Stephen faces the knowledge that Mary is "deeply unhappy" and then begins systematically to weaken the tie of love between them. She rejects Mary sexually and whets Mary's jealousy of Stephen's friend Valérie Seymour.

When Stephen visits Valérie and asks her to back up her assertion that they have slept together, Valérie agrees but angrily, and expresses horror at choosing suffering: "Aren't you being absurdly self-sacrificing? . . . Protection! Protection! I'm sick of the word. Let her do without it; aren't you enough for her? . . . it seems mad to me. For God's sake keep the girl, and get what happiness you can out of life." Stephen answers, "No, I can't do that" (p. 434).

After a night's absence from home, Stephen sends word to Martin to wait outside her house and then proceeds to complete the drama of her mock affair. She lies to Mary, resists Mary's grief and sense of betrayal, watches her lose faith in their love. Mary runs from the house and meets Martin; Stephen has accomplished her final self-immolation.

Following her betrayal of herself and her love, Stephen's womb is "possessed" by "legions" of inverts, and as their spiritual mother she addresses a Job-like prayer to God: "We have not denied You, then rise up and defend us. Acknowledge us, oh God, before the whole world. Give us also the right to existence!" (p. 437).

In the antiheroic speech she gave Valérie earlier, Hall shows her understanding of the hollowness of Stephen's prayer. Although she presents Stephen as a worthy hero in an unworthy world, Hall exposes her heroism as inherently self-defeating. Stephen ultimately denies herself everything she cares for: home, England, friends, mate — even truthfulness and honor. In the end Stephen chooses not to acknowledge herself. Thus her prayer to God to acknowledge her seems a transparent shirking — a projecting — of responsibility.

The plot of *The Well of Loneliness* shows the double-edgedness of the heroic attitude toward the beloved. On the one hand, Stephen's identifying with the heroic stance results in overwhelming generosity and purity of motives. On the other hand, inherent in the idea of the beloved as a needy flower lies a dehumanizing arrogance. Stephen denies Mary's responsibility for, or participation in, selecting her life's mate. Mary, of course, is thereby infantalized. The heroes, Stephen and Martin, fight over Mary — and deliver and receive her — as if she belonged to them. Stephen's self-sacrifice, in other words, because she in no way questions her heroic stance, not only degrades herself and her love, but also Mary, the beloved.

The figure whose values triumph completely is Anna. She rules Morton unopposed. Puddle lives with Anna, serving her to the end. Anna recognizes only heterosexual love and marriage, and Stephen finally capitulates through the person of her own beloved. Anna basically wants Stephen to repudiate herself, and through the purposeful destruction of her relationship with Mary, Stephen does as Anna wishes. Anna, beauty-being incarnate, demands all of her heroic daughter, and she gets it.

Stephen's compulsive drive to protect those she loves makes any other outcome impossible. She would have to be willing to let Mary live through whatever pain sharing love with her would involve, and as hero Stephen cannot do that. She would have to challenge Anna for possession of Morton, and as protector she cannot. Finally, Stephen would have to integrate into herself the essential function of the worshiped woman — that of affirming the hero. She would have to acknowledge herself and lay her own claims on the world, abandoning her total identification as hero, before she could keep her lover.

The trap Hall's lesbian heroes cannot escape, then, is twofold: belief in the virtue of self-denial through service to those they love, and dependence on their mothers to want them to become their whole selves. The only ones who want them to grow are their lesbian lovers. Stephen and Joan, however, fail to take from their lovers a sense of being entitled to fulfillment; they remain servants of heroic virtue awaiting entitlement from their mothers. In the tension between self and other they lack the courage to choose self, and although Hall does not condemn them, she does not spare them the consequent loss of personality and love.

NOTES

[1]Lillian Faderman and Ann Williams, "Radclyffe Hall and the Lesbian Image," *Conditions*, 1 (April 1977), 32.

[2]Faderman and Williams, p. 38; Dolores Klaich, *Woman + Woman: Attitudes toward Lesbianism* (New York: Morrow Quill Paperbacks, 1979), p. 209; Blanche Wiesen Cook, "'Women Alone Stir My Imagination': Lesbianism and the Cultural Tradition," *Signs*, 4 (Summer 1979), 721, 731.

[3]Jane Rule, *Lesbian Images* (New York: Pocket Books, 1976), pp. 62, 64.

[4]Cook, p. 731.

[5]Rule, p. 56; Cook, p. 733.

[6]Klaich, p. 195.

[7]Rule, p. 52.

[8]An essential aspect of the heroic experience is willingness to confront death. Hall's version of this experience is markedly Christian in her insistence on self-sacrifice.

[9]Charlotte Wolff, *Love between Women* (New York: Harper Colophon Books, 1971), p. 110.

[10]Wolff, pp. 148-49.

[11]Radclyffe Hall, *The Unlit Lamp* (London, 1924; rpt. New York: Jonathan Cape and Harrison Smith, 1929), p. 8. Page numbers of quotations taken from this work will be placed in the body of the text.

[12]Radclyffe Hall, *The Well of Loneliness* (New York: Pocket Books, 1950), p. 85. Page numbers of quotations taken from this work will be placed in the body of the text.

An Essay in Sexual Liberation, Victorian Style: Walter Pater's "Two Early French Stories"

Richard Dellamora, Ph.D.

The following essay challenges a common view of the career of Walter Pater: that he criticized Victorian religious beliefs and social mores in his first book, *Studies in the History of the Renaissance* (1873), then spent the rest of his life backing down.[1] Such a retreat appears to be evident in his decision to delete the notorious Conclusion from the second edition, now retitled *The Renaissance* (1877).[2] Nevertheless, I will argue that his decision was made in order to avoid entangling himself in further arguments with his critics at Oxford, critics who had already shown an ability to damage his academic career. At the same time, he added to the opening chapter an attack on religious and moral bigotry that refers to his own difficulties at Oxford. Writers on Pater have scarcely noticed another major change in the second edition, the addition to the first chapter of passages discussing *The Friendship of Amis and Amile*, a thirteenth-century French romance centered on male friendship.[3] Analysis of the romance and of Pater's interpretation indicates that in adding this discussion, he made both more explicit and more nuanced his view of the value of the body in human relationships and of the importance of libidinal elements in Christianity and in medieval culture. His historical analysis parallels a theoretical analysis whereby Pater argues the necessity and worth of the libidinal aspects of culture generally.[4] The rapprochement with Christianity that a critic like David DeLaura sees in Pater's revision exists, but alongside his continuing opposition to organized religion.

Richard Dellamora is Associate Professor of English and Cultural Studies at Trent University in Peterborough, Ontario, where he has taught since completing doctoral work at Yale University in 1971. Besides publishing on literature, the visual arts, and sexuality in nineteenth-century writers, he also writes about modern and contemporary art in the United States and Canada.

139

I

In this section I will analyze both the original version of the first chapter of Pater's book and its revision in the second edition. This analysis, though detailed, is necessary to show both the humanist polemic with which Pater began and its extension, in the second edition, to include the claims of male love. Because he offers his analysis as historical, I have also referred to the medieval texts on which he bases his arguments. Pater sees in the texts esteem for the body. In *The Friendship of Amis and Amile* in particular, he sees a rapprochement between eroticism and Christianity, as well as a positive individual and cultural narcissism. My own consideration of the medieval texts further bears out Pater's interpretation.

While critics always remember the suppression of the Conclusion in the 1877 edition of *The Renaissance*, much less attention is paid to the other major change in the edition, the revision of the opening chapter. In the first edition the opening chapter had been entitled "Aucassin and Nicolette." It is well known for Pater's suggestion in it that the Renaissance had already begun in the twelfth century in France.[5] Pater associates this "great outbreak" of the human spirit both with philosophic rationalism and with aberrant sexual behavior.[6] He instances the romance of the philosopher Abelard with his young niece Heloïse to exemplify both: "the name of Abelard, the great clerk and the great lover, connects the expression of this liberty of heart with the free play of human intelligence round all subjects presented to it" (*SHR*, p. 4). Pater associates Heloïse and Abelard both with the courtly-love poetry of Provence and with a thirteenth-century prose and verse romance, *Aucassin and Nicolette,* which he proceeds to discuss, emphasizing its delight in detail and expression for their own sake and its "faint air of overwrought delicacy, almost of wantonness" (*SHR*, p. 10). Particularly, he notes "this rebellious element, this sinister claim for liberty of heart and thought" (*SHR*, p. 16). He ends the chapter by quoting the hero Aucassin saying (naturally, in French) that he would rather be in hell with Nicolette than in heaven with monks (*SHR*, p. 17). In the course of the chapter Pater speaks of the rebirth of Venus as well as of the return of the god Amor in the guise of Aucassin (*SHR*, pp. 15, 14). This erotic renewal signals the "medieval Renaissance" (*SHR*, p. 15).

In the 1877 revision of the chapter, now called "Two Early French Stories," Pater has added a new element, *The Friendship of Amis and Amile.* While he describes this work as a thirteenth-century romance, the story exists in one version as early as the late eleventh century; and the version that Pater uses is in form a saints' legend. The essence of the story is "the testing of the fidelity of two friends."[7] In *Christianity, Social Tolerance, and Homosexuality*, John Boswell observes that "there is no hint of sexual interest between the knights, but their love for each other explicitly takes precedence over every other commitment."[8] Pater regards this latter aspect as the antinomian element of the story. In retelling the tale, he emphasizes as well the specifically bodily aspect of the friendship, an aspect that suggests that Boswell may be overly cautious in not noting a "sexual interest" below the religious surface of the legend. Pater observes that in it "that free play of human affection, of the claims of which Abelard's story is an assertion, makes itself felt in the incidents of a great friendship, a friendship pure and generous, pushed to a sort of passionate exaltation."[9] Pater quotes from the romance a long section in which the angel Raphael appears to Amis while he and Amile are sleeping alone together in Amis' sick chamber. The angel informs Amis that his "body shall be made whole" (*R* 1877, p. 13) only if Amile kills his own children and bathes Amis in their blood. With anguish, Amile does so; and Amis is healed. At the end of the story, after the death of the two men, the body of one miraculously moves to the church in which the body of the other is being kept. Pater uses this passage to end the revised essay. (In the romance there are other mentions of the body, too. Friends from childhood, "the two children fell to loving one another so sorely that one would not eat without the other, they lived of one victual, and lay in one bed."[10] Later, they embrace and kiss when they meet as adults. Though these contacts are not sexual, they are physical. Body is important in their friendship.)

The Friendship of Amis and Amile may be read as a text in which the figure of Christ as supreme Knight is assimilated to a cult of friendship that is almost Greek.[11] Both protagonists are antitypes of Christ in his double aspect of loving and sacrificial friend of whom it may be said, "Greater love than this no man has, that one lay down his life for his friends" (John 15 : 13-14). At one point in the romance Amis lays down his life for Amile by agreeing to fight in single combat in his place; Amile in turn lays down his life by proxy by slaying his children so that Amis may be healed. Generally, the knighthood or "chivalry" of the two friends is closely associated with Christ (Morris, pp. 296, 306-07).

In the tale, Christian love, sacrifice, and male friendship are conflated. The writer also stresses the importance of chastity. Though Amis warns Amile not to yield to the daughter of the French king, he does, thereby occasioning the need for Amis to rescue him by combat with a knight who has challenged Amile before the king. Amis then tests Amile a second time by sending him to stay with Amis' own wife. Again he advises Amile not to sleep with the woman. Since the two friends are doubles, Amis' wife mistakes Amile for her husband, nor does he undeceive her. But "a night-time whenas they lay in one bed, then Amile laid his sword betwixt the two of them, and said to the woman: 'Take heed that thou touch me in no manner wise, else diest thou straightway by this sword.' And in likewise did he the other nights, until Amis betook him in disguise to his house to wot if Amile kept faith with him of his wife" (Morris, p. 301).[12] Only after this test does Amis fight and slay Amile's accuser. Later, after Amile's children have been first killed and then miraculously restored to life, Amile and his wife "even unto their death . . . held chastity" (Morris, p. 308). The emphasis on chastity carries a hint of the superiority of male friendship to hetero-sexual love, even to married love. As well there is a suggestion that Amis and Amile fall short of one another in at times preferring women to each other. I have already mentioned that Amile fails Amis (and Christ) by going to bed with the daughter of the French king. Earlier, Amis had set out to search for Amile; but after meeting and marrying a wife, Amis forgets his quest for a year and a half before remember-ing and telling his men: "We have done amiss in that we have left seeking of Amile" (Morris, p. 298). This lapse indicates uxoriousness on Amis' part, a shortcoming his wife pays for when he sends Amile to her in disguise and for which he himself pays when, after he has become a leper, his wife "had him in sore hate, and many a time strove to strangle him" (Morris, p. 303).

In the 1877 edition, Pater deploys his quotations from *The Friendship of Amis and Amile* on either side of his discussion of *Aucassin and Nicolette*. Doing so, he suggests sexual connotation in the friendship of Amis and Amile. Pater paraphrases the description in the romance of the golden-haired Aucassin's beauty. Aucassin, "the very image of the Provençal love-god" represents the "ideal intensity of passion" (*R* 1877, p. 25).[13] At the center of the romance are the secrets of sexual intimacy, imaged in "the little hut of flowers which Nicolette constructs in the forest, whither she has escaped from her enemies" (*R* 1877, p. 21). The hut is a test of Aucassin's love:

> So she gathered white lilies,
> Oak-leaf, that in green wood is,
> Leaves of many a branch I wis,
> Therewith built a lodge of green,
> Goodlier was never seen,
> Swore by God who may not lie,
> "If my love the lodge should spy,
> He will rest awhile thereby
> If he love me loyally." (p. 46)[14]

When Aucassin and Nicolette meet in the lodge, "either kissed and clipped the other, and fair joy was between them" (p. 57). It is there too that Nicolette heals Aucassin's shoulder, injured when he fell from his horse.

The attractiveness and intimacy of the two lovers add the element of sexual interest about which the story of Amis and Amile is silent. By associating the works, Pater revives not just Amor but specifically the homoerotic Amor of Greek tradition. The "antinomian" elements of *Aucassin and Nicolette* — Aucassin's rejection of an asexual Christian paradise, his rejection of knightly duty in preference for love (p. 20), his sexual contact with Nicolette before marriage (pp. 63, 72) — indicate nonconformity with the norms of courtly love and suggest that nonconformity underlies *The Friendship of Amis and Amile* as well. Pater also indicates his preference for the intensity of a tale of male friendship by the fact that he has juxtaposed it with a heterosexual romance that parodies "the love theme" of serious romance.[15] At one point, for instance, Aucassin intervenes in a fight in which the only weapons are baked apples, eggs, and fresh cheeses. After he slays many men, he is begged to desist, since "it is nowise our custom to slay each other" (p. 62). Pater has chosen a parodic instance of heterosexual romance to compare with what he calls the "strength" of the tale of Amis and Amile, a strength not only of sworn friendship but also, in the version of the story that Pater is following, of feudal obligations and Christian faith.

Pater makes it clear that he is aware that the rival claims of friendship and love may be claims between two kinds of love. Seeing this conflict also in the later thirteenth-century romance of Chaucer, *The Knight's Tale*, Pater says: "Such comradeship, though instances of it are to be found everywhere, is still especially a classical motive, Chaucer expressing the sentiment of it so strongly in an antique tale, that one knows not whether the love of both Palamon and Arcite for Emelya, or of those two for each other, is the chiefer subject of the *Knight's Tale*" (*R* 1877, p. 9). His further reference to the "sweet . . . daily offices" of Palamon and Arcite in prison is a coded reference to sexual intimacy. In finding male love in an "antique" tale by a medieval writer, Pater connects medieval, Christian culture with the tradition of homosexual friendship in Greek culture.

II

The ideal of male love that Pater specifically introduces with reference to *The Knight's Tale* is androgynous in character, combining strength with sweetness.[16] The masculine connotation of *strength* is already evident in Pater's application of the term to *The Friendship of Amis and Amile*. *Sweetness*, his term for *Aucassin and Nicolette*, suggests artistic playfulness, beauty, and sensuality. It also suggests femininity. Pater had borrowed the term *sweetness* from his Oxford contemporary Matthew Arnold; but the addition of a sexual charge is his own. DeLaura notes that Abelard was one of Arnold's heroes too; nevertheless, the "'worship of the body'" with which Pater later inflects and infects Arnold's critical terminology is "emphatically no part of Arnold's proposed pattern of human life" (p. 243).[17]

In infusing the strength of *The Friendship of Amis and Amile* with the sweetness of *Aucassin and Nicolette*, Pater achieves a cultural and erotic synthesis that he identifies with the Renaissance both in its classic sixteenth-century phase and in its earlier manifestation during the Middle Ages (*R* 1877, pp. 16-17). The medieval Renaissance does not merely juxtapose these terms; they are dialectical, and Pater discovers sweetness within *The Friendship of Amis and Amile* itself.[18] Besides being an act of literary interpretation, this discovery enables Pater to divine the structure of personal relations in a much earlier period. Further, the interpretation is cultural. He regards eros as crucial in an integrated culture. The love of Amis and Amile adds a necessary sweetness to the severe and patriarchal order imaged in the legend. In this way, Pater provides what one might call a model of cultural narcissism. The love of Amis and Amile figures a libidinal aspect of medieval culture without which it would be rigid, brutal, and hysterical. Finally, the synthesis of sweetness and strength in *The Friendship of Amis and Amile* and in the medieval Renaissance itself reaffirms a permanent tendency in human action and culture towards androgyny, a conciliation of "masculine" and "feminine" values. Accordingly, the Christ who stands above and is typified by events in the story of Amis and Amile is feminized in their mutual love.[19]

In referring above to "cultural narcissism," I have in mind Freud's view of the place of narcissism in the mature self. In Freud, opposed terms ultimately include each other in dynamic relations. For instance, in the lecture "The Libido Theory and Narcissism" (1917), he describes narcissism as the libidinal element of the ego and as "the source of the Ego Ideal" though earlier he had opposed the terms *ego* and *libido*.[20] In other words, the "*ideal ego*" or "conscience" derives from libido and has as its object the restoration to the self of primal bliss.[21] When, however, the external object of the libido and this "ego-censor" (p. 429) contradict each other, neurosis may ensue. In the lecture Freud focuses on neuroses that occur precisely when the attraction towards someone of the same sex conflicts with the demands of conscience. Writing forty years before him and with great suppleness, Pater observes the same need for conciliating the object of libido with moral choice. In "Two Early French Stories," he considers the need not only as it affects Amis and Amile individually but as it is fulfilled in their love. In this context, moreover, he goes a step further in seeing androgyny as crucial to the development of a sound culture. Such cultures seldom occur, and Victorian England is not among them; but in his writing Pater repeatedly celebrates their advent. He sees the urge to achieve "the harmony of human interests" (*R* 1877, p. 29) as a primary impulse in Western culture.

III

Pater's handling of medieval materials as discussed above might be considered wholly profane in spirit, with Christ and Christianity being valued only as both become expressive of androgynous values. Further, Pater's analysis is in a line of nineteenth-century argument, both French and English, that tends to reduce religion to sexuality.[22] In this section, I will discuss the rationalizing, scientific aspect of Pater's approach. In Section IV, however, I will try to explain how Pater's presentation of Christianity combines erotic and religious elements without reducing one to the other.

At the time of Pater, it was commonplace to reduce religious meaning to psychological. For instance, in *Idylls of the King* Tennyson "treats the quest for the Holy Grail as an example of mass hysteria. The whole thing originated, he makes perfectly clear, in the frustrated sexual desires of a young woman who had been disappointed in love and gone into a nunnery."[23] In *Madame Bovary*, Flaubert portrays Madame Bovary's schoolgirl religiosity as a displacement of sentimental erotic yearnings.[24] In "Two Early French Stories" Pater cites Victor Hugo's *Notre Dame de Paris* as exemplifying the "rebellious" tendency of medieval culture (*R* 1877, p. 27). In that novel the scholarly, devout, and dutiful Archdeacon Claude Frollo pursues his studies into the profane arcana of alchemy and thereafter falls into a wholly destructive passion for the virginal Esmerelda. Pater had plotted a similar trajectory in his early review of William Morris' *The Defence of Guenevere* (1858). Concluding a discussion of the transformation of medieval religion into the "rival religion" of courtly love, Pater observes: "That whole religion of the middle age was but a beautiful disease of [sic] disorder of the senses. . . . Reverie, illusion, delirium; they are the three stages of a fatal descent both in the religion and the loves of the middle age. Nowhere has the impression of this delirium been conveyed as by Victor Hugo."[25] Mariolatry is reduced to the worship of the courtly lady, the idolization of Christ to the idolization of the knight. By the same logic, pious edification is transformed by the clerical author of *The Friendship of Amis and Amile* into homoerotic reverie. "This low descendental view" echoes in turn Pater's biography.[26] A devout adolescent intent on becoming a clergyman, Pater lost his faith while a student at Oxford (1858-62), probably at the same time that he became conscious of his homosexual orientation.

IV

The interpretation of culture proposed here goes beyond the rationalizing aspect of Pater's analysis at the same time that it makes the point that a revisionary view of sexual relations has implications for the understanding and transformation of culture itself. By 1877 Pater had eschewed a positivist approach that offered to explain religion as an epiphenomenon of psychology. Rather, he was now ready to attempt a rapprochement between Christianity and eros that is very much his own. When DeLaura observes a "new welcome extended to Christianity" (p. 261) in "Two Early French Stories," he is referring to passages like the following added in 1877: in "the Renaissance . . . the human mind wins for itself a new kingdom of feeling and sensation and thought, not opposed to, but only beyond and independent of the spiritual system then actually realised" (*R* 1877, p. 7). Such statements, however, are conciliatory in a highly qualified way. Pater's refusal to oppose Christianity is a refusal to engage in dogmatic disputes, which falsify his sense of "the more sincere and generous play of the forces of human mind and character, which I noted as the secret of Abelard's struggle" (*R* 1877, p. 28). In the sentence quoted by DeLaura, Pater asserts the independence of culture from the demands of religious orthodoxy. His most positive comment about Christianity is one in which he describes Abelard or, more generally, the humanist as "reaching out to and attaining modes of ideal living, beyond the prescribed limits of that system, though possibly contained in essential germ within it" (*R* 1877, p. 8). The "essential germ" of humanism may be contained within Christianity. This claim, however, grants little to orthodox belief at the same time as it concedes to humanism, with its "reason and heart and senses quick" (*R* 1877, p. 8), a basis of Christian authority.

Pater's comments on the Christian "system" have a context in contemporary liberal writing. For instance, at the same time as Pater was writing the essays that would later appear in *Studies in the History of the Renaissance*, John Stuart Mill also criticized conventional sexual norms in *On the Subjection of Women* (1869). And in *On Liberty* (1859) he too had contrasted custom, conventional Christianity, and public opinion to individual liberty and growth:

> The creed remains as it were outside the mind, incrusting and petrifying it against all other influences addressed to the higher parts of our nature; manifesting its power by not suffering any fresh and living conviction to get in, but itself doing nothing for the mind or heart, except standing sentinel over them to keep them vacant. To what an extent doctrines intrinsically fitted to make the deepest impression upon the mind may remain in it as dead beliefs, without

being ever realised in the imagination, the feelings, or the understanding, is exemplified by the manner in which the majority of
believers hold the doctrines of Christianity.[27]

Both Mill and Pater contrast an inert dogmatic Christianity to the life
of the individual.

When critics discuss Pater's move toward Christianity in 1877 and
later in *Marius the Epicurean* (1885), they need to emphasize his understanding of Christianity as valorizing the body, including the homoerotic
body. In this regard, the story of Heloïse and Abelard, with which Pater
introduces the two romances, provides an instructive point of contact
with Pater and suggests that in conflating eros and Christianity he spoke
with an understanding of medieval Christianity. The degree to which
Heloïse, who eventually became head of a religious house, internally
assented to the "system" that she served so well is open to debate.
Peter Dronke, however, demonstrates that the intensity of her love for
Abelard, and the esteem accorded it by her contemporaries, are not in
doubt. In a letter that Pater would have appreciated for its conciliation
of religious and erotic feeling, Peter the Venerable, Abbot of Cluny and
prince of the Church, wrote to Heloïse at Abelard's death:

> My illustrious and dearest sister in God: this man to whom you
> cleaved, after the sexual oneness, with the stronger and finer bond
> of divine love, he with whom and under whom you have long
> served God — I tell you, God is now cherishing him in his lap,
> in place of you, or like a replica of you. And at the second
> coming, at the sound of the archangel and the trumpet heralding
> God descending from the heavens, God will restore him to you
> through his grace, having preserved him for you.[28]

It is further worth observing that Abelard himself "explored with great
sensitivity and feeling the nature of the love between . . . two men"
in his *planctus* of David for Jonathan.[29]

Pater's positive remarks about Christianity occur in a passage in
which he sees contemporary opposition to Abelard in the Church as
one between "the mere professional, official, hireling ministers of that
system, with their ignorant worship of system for its own sake, and the
true child of light, the humanist" (*R* 1877, pp. 7-8). This dichotomy is
Pater's riposte to his critics at Oxford, including the bishop there, after
publication of *Studies in the History of the Renaissance*. The book had
also prompted an attack on Pater by a colleague and former student at
his Oxford college, John Wordsworth, grandnephew of the poet. As a
result, Pater missed a routine promotion that instead went to Wordsworth. The setback was a shock that would in itself adequately account

for Pater's decision to withdraw the Conclusion from the second edition (1877). He had additional reason, however, in that the Conclusion
had been parodied by "the horrid undergraduate" W. H. Mallock in his
successful satirical novel of 1876, *The New Republic* (Brake, p. 50).
By deleting the Conclusion and rewriting Chapter i, Pater for the moment
regained control of his meaning.

He made his decision to delete that Conclusion no later than Novem-
ber 1876 (*Letters*, p. 17). That same year, he decided to stand for
Professor of Poetry at Oxford. Though he was aware that he would be
strongly opposed, he knew that he merited the position. Nonetheless,
opposition took an unexpected turn when Benjamin Jowett, Master of
Balliol College and chief political power in Oxford at the time, black-
mailed Pater by threatening to disclose some incriminating letters. According to rumor, it was Mallock who gave the letters to Jowett (Brake,
p. 48). While no evidence for the specific date of Jowett's showdown
with Pater has yet been discovered, it likely occurred between February
1877, when a student publication opposed Pater's candidacy, and April,
when he withdrew his name (Brake, p. 48; Small, pp. 314-315).[30] In
the meantime, Pater was also attacked in an article in the March issue
of *The Contemporary Review* (Small, p. 315).

In the same month that saw his humiliation, the second edition of *The
Renaissance* was being bound (Small, p. 314). In suppressing the original Conclusion, Pater had tried to avoid "well-recognised controversy,
with rigidly defined opposites, exhausting the intelligence and limiting
one's sympathies" (*R* 1877, p. 28); but he added a polemic against
what his biographer would later refer to as "vile little opportunists"
(Brake, p. 48). As well, he also now took the opportunity to celebrate
male friendship, a celebration that elaborates his view of the libidinal
element of culture and at the same time extends the claims for "liberty
of the heart" to male love. Doing so, he was willing to reconsider
Christianity so as to include homosexuality within it, a process he continued in *Marius the Epicurean*.

Writing the essay was an act of courage that also illuminated homoeroticism in Western culture. On these grounds, Pater was an important
originator of homosexual criticism. He saw homoerotic interpretation as
a means of affiliation whereby homosexuals in different times and places
may confirm their experience and use it as a means of access to alien
cultures. A century before John Boswell wrote of "The Triumph of
Ganymede" in the literature of 1050 to 1150, Pater had already divined
and written about it in "Two Early French Stories," though he did not
write about the specifically homosexual texts that Boswell adduces.[31] It
is worth keeping in mind, moreover, that Pater's homosexual polemic
coincided with a general polemic in praise of the diversity of erotic and

other experience. As well, he was always concerned to see eros and personal freedom in relation to cultural formation and change. This plurality of concerns in Pater recommends itself well to critics today.

NOTES

[1]U.C. Knoepflmacher, *Religious Humanism and the Victorian Novel: George Eliot, Walter Pater, and Samuel Butler* (Princeton: Princeton Univ. Press, 1965), pp. 7-8, 153-55. Geoffrey Tillotson, "Pater, Mr. Rose and the 'Conclusion' of *The Renaissance*," in *Criticism and the Nineteenth Century* (London, 1951; rpt. Hamden, Conn.: Archon Books, 1967), pp. 124-46.

[2]For Pater and Oxford politics, see Laurel Brake, "Judas and the Widow: Thomas Wright and A. C. Benson as Biographers of Walter Pater: The Widow," *PSt*, 4 (May 1981), 39-54. See also Walter Pater, *Letters*, ed. Lawrence Evans (Oxford: The Clarendon Press, 1970), pp. xxi-xxii, but see also p. 13n; hereafter cited in text as *Letters*. For a debate on Pater's reasons for deleting the Conclusion, see Lawrence F. Schuetz, "The Suppressed 'Conclusion' to *The Renaissance* and Pater's Modern Image," *ELT*, 17 (1974), 251-59; and "Pater and the Suppressed 'Conclusion' to *The Renaissance:* Comment and Reply," *ELT*, 19 (1976), 313-21. See also Michael Levey, *The Case of Walter Pater* (London: Thames and Hudson, 1978), pp. 141-44.

[3]For an exception, see Richard L. Stein, "The Private Themes of Pater's *Renaissance*," *Psychoanalysis and Literary Process*, ed. Frederick Crews (Cambridge, Mass.: Winthrop, 1970), pp. 175-177.

[4]See, for instance, Robert L. Caserio, *Plot, Story, and the Novel: From Dickens and Poe to the Modern Period* (Princeton: Princeton Univ. Press, 1979), pp. 50-56.

[5]He drew the suggestion from French writers. See Walter Pater, *The Renaissance: Studies in Art and Poetry: The 1893 Text*, ed. Donald L. Hill (Berkeley: Univ. of California Press, 1980), pp. 304-05; hereafter cited in notes as *R 1893*.

[6]Walter Pater, *Studies in the History of the Renaissance* (London: Macmillan, 1873), p. 2; hereafter cited in text as *SHR*.

[7]MacEdward Leach, ed., *Amis and Amiloun*, Early English Text Society, O.S. no. 203 (1937; rpt. London: Oxford Univ. Press, 1960), p. xx. See also Ojars Kratins, "The Middle English *Amis and Amiloun*: Chivalric Romance or Secular Hagiography?" *PMLA*, 81 (1966), 347-54; Dale Kramer, "Structural Artistry in *Amis and Amiloun*," *Annuale Mediaevale*, 9 (1968), 103-22; Kathryn Hume, "Structure and Perspective: Romance and Hagiographic Features in the Amicus and Amelius Story," *JEGP*, 69 (1970), 89-107; Kathryn Hume, "*Amis and Amiloun* and the Aesthetics of Middle English Romance," *SP*, 70 (1973), 19-41; and Diana T. Childress, "Between Romance and Legend: 'Secular Hagiography' in Middle English Literature," *PQ*, 57 (1978), 311-22, esp. 318-19.

[8]John Boswell, *Christianity, Social Tolerance, and Homosexuality: Gay People in Western Europe from the Beginning of the Christian Era to the Fourteenth Century* (Chicago: Univ. of Chicago Press, 1980), p. 240.

[9]Walter Pater, *The Renaissance: Studies in Art and Poetry*, 2nd ed. (London: Macmillan, 1877), p. 9; hereafter cited in text as *R 1877*.

[10]I quote from the translation of William Morris, *The Friendship of Amis and Amile*, in *The Collected Works*, introd. May Morris (New York: Russell and Russell, 1966), XVII, 295.

[11]For sexuality in Greek male friendship, see Richard J. Hoffman, "Some Cultural Aspects of Greek Male Sexuality," *Journal of Homosexuality*, 5 (1980), 217-25; K. J. Dover, *Greek Homosexuality* (London: Duckworth, 1978), p. 170 et passim; Boswell, chs. i and ii passim; John Addington Symonds, *Studies in Sexual Inversion* (n.p.: privately printed, 1928), p. 19. Gervase Mathew touches on the relation of sexuality to medieval friendship though he makes no use of the gay literature that John Boswell discusses ("Ideals of Friendship," in *Patterns of Love and Courtesy*, ed. John Lawlor [London: Edward Arnold, 1966], pp. 46, 49).

[12]Leach, discussing *Amis and Amiloun*, an English version of the tale, remarks: "The motivation of the incident is the common one used throughout the story: it is as much a test of Amis' friendship for Amiloun as the judicial combat is a test of Amiloun's friendship for Amis" (pp. xlvi-xlvii).

[13]The appeal of this figure to homoerotic sensibility is indicated as well in that the poem attributed to Pierre Vidal which Pater refers to at this point is one that he knew from John Ad-

dington Symonds' *An Introduction to Dante* (1872). Symonds, a bisexual, rhapsodizes over the image of "Chivalrous Love" (*R* 1893, pp. 316-17).

[14]References to *Aucassin and Nicolette* in the text are to Andrew Lang, *Aucassin and Nicolette* (New York: Barse and Hopkins, n.d.).

[15]D. H. Green, *Irony in the Medieval Romance* (Cambridge: Cambridge Univ. Pess, 1979), p. 99.

[16]For a discussion of the importance of these terms in Pater's critical vocabulary, see Billie Andrew Inman, "Pater's Conception of the Renaissance: From Sources to Personal Ideal," *VN*, 47 (Spring 1975), 22-24.

[17]References to DeLaura in the text are to David J. DeLaura, *Hebrew and Hellene in Victorian England: Newman, Arnold, and Pater* (Austin: Univ. of Texas Press, 1969). For a discussion of the relation of Arnold and Pater, see pp. 165-91, 202-22, 240-44 et passim. Michelet also uses the term *sweetness* to characterize Abelard (*R* 1893, p. 308).

[18]As well he might. Taking *Amis and Amiloun* as "the medieval English classic on . . . friendship," Mathew notes that the first known Anglo-Norman version (c. 1200) "begins by promising that it will be a song of love, of loyalty, and of great sweetness ('d'amour, de leaute, et de grand doucour')" (p. 45). I have already mentioned the "sweet . . . daily offices" of Palamon and Arcite.

[19]For the feminization of Christ in Pater's writing see my essay "Pater's Modernism: The Leonardo Essay," *UTQ*, 47 (Winter 1977/78), 137, 145. I also discuss this process in my current study of *Marius the Epicurean*.

[20]Marthe Robert, *The Psychoanalytic Revolution: Sigmund Freud's Life and Achievement*, trans. Kenneth Morgan (New York: Harcourt, 1966), p. 312.

[21]Sigmund Freud, *The Standard Edition of the Complete Psychological Works*, trans. James Strachey (London: The Hogarth Press, 1971), XVI, 429.

[22]*R* 1893, pp. 308, 317-18. Pater's reading of medieval culture shares attributes with what Herbert Sussman calls "second-generation Pre-Raphaelitism," a phenomenon that he associates with A. C. Swinburne, D. G. Rossetti, and William Morris. Sussman says that the work of these writers "deals openly with wholly non-respectable forms of sexuality, employs a style that often moves toward the evocative and *symboliste*, and is presented as the expression of an adversary culture." See Herbert Sussman, "The Pre-Raphaelite Brotherhood and Their Circle: The Formation of the Victorian Avant-Garde," *VN*, no. 57 (Spring 1980), p. 7. In particular, Swinburne in his *William Blake* (1868) gave Pater the passage from *Aucassin and Nicolette* with which he ends the chapter in the first edition as well as the general idea of "the old Albigensian 'Aucassin' and all its paganism." See Algernon Charles Swinburne, *The Complete Works*, ed. Sir Edmund Gosse and Thomas James Wise (London, 1925; rpt. New York: Russell and Russell, 1968), XVI, 135, 136n. Cf. *R* 1893, p. 303.

[23]A Dwight Culler, *The Poetry of Tennyson* (New Haven: Yale Univ. Press, 1977), p. 228.

[24]Gustave Flaubert, *Madame Bovary: A Story of Provincial Life*, trans. Alan Russell (Harmondsworth: Penguin, 1967), pp. 48-49, 50-53. See Gerald Monsman, *Walter Pater* (Boston: Twayne, 1977), p. 21.

[25]James Sambrook, ed., *Pre-Raphaelitism: A Collection of Critical Essays* (Chicago: Univ. of Chicago Press, 1974), p. 107. In the passage, "of" is an obvious misprint of "or."

[26]Culler, p. 229.

[27]John Stuart Mill, *On Liberty*, ed. David Spitz (New York: Norton, 1975), p. 40.

[28]Peter Dronke, *Abelard and Heloise in Medieval Testimonies* (Glasgow: Univ. of Glasgow Press, 1976), p. 23.

[29]Boswell, p. 238. See Peter Dronke, *Poetic Individuality in the Middle Ages: New Departures in Poetry 1000-1150* (Oxford: The Clarendon Press, 1970), p. 116.

[30]Although Brake implies that the meeting occurred before Pater decided to delete the Conclusion (p. 51), for the reasons that I adduce in the preceding paragraph, I believe that Pater reached this decision on his own. It is more likely that Jowett would have intervened in 1877 when controversy about Pater was spilling over into the press. I realize, however, the limited worth of inference when a date is in question, and I look forward to more biographical information becoming available.

[31]Boswell, pp. 243-266.

To Love a Medieval Boy

Thomas Stehling, Ph.D.

The great cultural renaissance during the twelfth century in Western Europe included a sudden flourishing of homosexual poetry.[1] Just as men were laying the foundations for universities, reviving interest in law and science, developing the tools of scholastic philosophy, and learning again to appreciate classical literature, so too were men writing poems of love and seduction among men or between older men and boys, as well as poetic defenses and condemnations of homosexuality. Thus in the century before the great shift in attitude toward homosexuality, from tolerance to intolerance — a shift John Boswell has described in *Christianity, Social Tolerance, and Homosexuality* — we find the culmination of a long if sparse tradition of medieval homosexual poetry, a tradition that reaches back through the Carolingian poets of the ninth century, the North African poets of the sixth, to the late classical poet Ausonius.[2]

But despite this long tradition and the large number of homosexual poems produced in the twelfth century, medieval heterosexual poetry is much more familiar to modern readers than its homosexual counterpart. The twelfth century is particularly well known for the achievements of heterosexual poets. This is the period when poets were discovering the delights of nature; when goliards were singing the praises of wine, women, and dice; when troubadors and minnesingers were inventing courtly love.

In some ways the neglect of homosexual poetry is understandable: it resembles heterosexual poetry in so many ways as to seem only a minor subcategory of it. Medieval poetry in general was highly conventional in form and ideals; it is not surprising, therefore, that homosexual verse conforms to models familiar from heterosexual verse. Poets did not strike out to create homosexual poetry different in kind from heterosexual verse. In fact, medieval poets often seem to have thought of the two kinds of love as equivalent. For example, Marbod of Rennes, a late eleventh-, early twelfth-century poet, shows no preference for one sex

---

Thomas Stehling teaches medieval literature in the Wellesley College English Department. He has also written about Chaucer, Middle English lyric poetry, and the act of reading in the Middle Ages.

over the other in his "Repentance for Lecherous Love" ("Poenitudo lascivi amoris"):

> Quid quod pupilla mihi charior ille, vel illa,
> vix vellet fari dum se sentiret amari.
> . . .
> Displicet amplexus utriusque quidem mihi sexus.

(Marbod, col. 1656)

(Why do those dearer to me than my eye, either he or she,
Scarcely want to talk as long as they feel they are loved?
. . .
The embraces of both sexes now displease me.)[3]

His contemporary Baudri of Bourgueil similarly confesses an early interest in both boys and girls:

> Obiciunt etiam juvenum cur more loquutus
> virginibus scripsi nec minus et pueris.
> Nam scripsi quaedam quae complectuntur amorem,
> carminibus meis sexus uterque placet.

(Baudri, no. 161, lines 183-86, p. 156)

(They reproached me too: why did I, speaking in the
customary way of young men,
Write to maidens and no less to boys?
For I wrote certain things which treat of love
And both sexes are pleased with my songs.)

This casual indifference to female/male distinctions contrasts strongly with the weight our own culture places on sexual preference. It also helps to explain the great similarities between homosexual and heterosexual poetry in the Middle Ages.

These resemblances, however, go only so far; subtle and significant differences between homosexual and heterosexual poetry distinguish them and can help us understand homosexual experience and poetic practice in the Middle Ages. Three poets, Marbod, Baudri, and Hilary the Englishman, give us convenient material for measuring the homosexual and heterosexual poetry of the High Middle Ages against each other. Both Marbod and Baudri wrote descriptions of ideal masculine and feminine beauty, and Hilary wrote two remarkably similar love poems, one to a boy and one to a woman.

DESCRIPTIONS OF IDEAL BEAUTY:
INSISTENCE ON THE NORM

Marbod of Rennes (c. 1035-1123) was born and educated in Angers. He was appointed master of the cathedral school there around 1067 and in 1097 became bishop of Rennes in Britanny. In one of his poems he describes a beautiful girl, in another a beautiful boy. The rhetorical structures of the two poems suggest that both descriptions are ideal, and to compare them is to see that these two ideal descriptions are virtually indistinguishable from each other. First the girl:

> Egregium vultum modica pinguedine fultum.
> Plus nive candentem, plusquam rosa verna rubentem,
> sidereum visum, spondentem mollia risum,
> flammea labrorum libamina subtumidorum,
> dentes candentes modicos seriemque tenentes,
> membraque cum succo, moresque bonos sine fuco
> illa puella gerit quae se mihi jungere quaerit.

> (Marbod, col. 1655)

> (An extraordinary face enhanced by a slight plumpness,
> Shining whiter than snow, blushing redder than the spring rose;
> A starlike gaze, a smile promising tenderness,
> Slightly swollen lips like fiery offerings;
> Good straight teeth, shining white,
> Strong limbs, guileless good manners —
> All these has the girl who wants to unite herself to me.)

After this opening the speaker surprisingly reports that despite her beauty he does not love this girl but a suitor of hers, a boy she scorns. The force of this opening description and of the turn that follows it depends on the reader responding to the lines as a picture of ideal feminine beauty.

Marbod's description of a boy is similarly a portrait of ideal beauty:

> De puero quodam composuit Horatius odam,
> qui facile bella possit satis esse puella.
> Undabant illi per eburnea colla capilli,
> plus auro flavi, quales ego semper amavi.
> Candida frons ut nix, et lumina nigra velut pix,
> implumesque genae grata dulcedine plenae,
> cum in candoris vernabant luce ruboris.
> Nasus erat justus, labra flammea, densque venustus.

Effigies menti modulo formata decenti.
Qui corpus quaeret quod tectum veste lateret,
tale coaptet ei quod conveniat faciei.

(Marbod, cols. 1717-18; translated in Boswell, p. 370-71)

(Horace composed an ode about a certain boy
Who could easily enough have been a pretty girl.
Over his ivory neck flowed hair
Brighter than yellow gold, the kind I have always loved.
His brow was white as snow, his luminous eyes black as pitch;
His unfledged cheeks full of pleasing sweetness
When they flushed bright white and red.
His nose was straight, lips blazing, teeth lovely,
Chin shaped after an appropriate model.
Anyone wondering about the body which lay hidden under his
      clothes
Would be gratified, for the boy's body matched his face.)[4]

After this opening, Marbod reminds the boy that his good looks will
fade and that he should yield to his suitors while he is still young.

The two ideals show marked similarities. Both descriptions emphasize
proportion and measure: her face has moderate-sized teeth ("dentes . . .
modicos"), while his nose is "justus" and his chin is shaped after an
appropriate or "decent" model ("modulo formata decenti"). More strik-
ingly, Marbod uses the same terms to describe the same features in
both the boy and the girl. Both have blazing lips ("labra flammea,"
"flammea labrorum libamina"), and both have complexions mixed of
red and white. The boy's forehead is as white as, and the girl's face
is whiter than, snow ("candida . . . ut nix," "plus nive candentem").
His cheeks flush with rosy light; her face blushes redder than the rose.

Baudri of Bourgueil (1046-1130) sees the same similarities in beautiful boys and girls. Born in Meung-sur-Loire, he studied under Marbod
at the cathedral school in Angers. Having become a Benedictine monk,
he was made abbot of the monastery Bourgueil-en-Vallée in 1089 and in
1107 was elected archbishop of Dol in Brittany. Baudri's poems show
that he clearly delighted more in boys than in girls. Of his 255 poems
most are written to men and frequently profess love.[5] By contrast, he
wrote only fifteen poems to women, and only one of these is anything
like a love poem. Here is Baudri's description of a young man:

Forma placet, quia forma decet, quia forma venusta est:
mala tenella placet, flavum caput osque modestum;
vox tua demulcet nostras et mitigat aures,
quae tam dulce sonat, quam dulce sonat Filomela.

Incertum an pueri sit vox tua, sive puellae;
Orpheus alter eris, nisi vocem sauciet aetas,
aetas a pueris quae dat differre puellas,
cum gena vestitur juvenum lanugine prima,
et pandae nares faciem speciemque venustant.
Cor pectusque meum tua vitrea lumina tangunt
sidus enim geminum cristallina lumina credo
his bene respondet caro lactea, pectus eburnum.
Alludit manibus niveo de corpore tactus.

(Baudri, no. 38, lines 7-19, pp. 23-24)[6]

(Your appearance is pleasing because it is proper and handsome;
So too your delicate cheek, your blond hair, and modest mouth.
Your voice, sounding as sweetly as the nightingale's,
Caresses and soothes our ears.
It could be a boy's or a girl's;
You will be another Orpheus, unless age injures it —
Age which distinguishes girls from boys
When young men's cheeks are first clothed with down
And a strong nose enhances their faces and looks.
Your bright, clear eyes touch my breast and heart,
For I believe those crystalline lights truly are a double star.
Your milky flesh and ivory chest match them;
The touch of hands plays over your snowy body.)

And here is Baudri's description of a beautiful woman named Constance, for whom he protests chaste love:

Non rutilat Veneris tam clara binomia stella,
    quam rutilant ambo lumina clara tibi.
Crinibus inspectis fulvam minus arbitror aurum,
    colla nitent plusquam lilia, nixve recens,
dentes plus ebore, Pario plus marmore candent,
    spirat et in labiis gratia viva tuis.
Labra tument modicum calor et calor igneus illis,
    quae tamen ambo decens temperies foveat.
Jure rosis malas praeponi dico tenellas,
    quas rubor et candor vestit et omne decus.
Corporis ut breviter complectar composituram,
    est corpus talem quod deceat faciem.

(Baudri, no. 238, lines 55-66, p. 339)

(The clear double-named star of Venus has not so rosy a glow
As those two clear, luminous eyes of yours.

When I look at your hair I think that gold has a less tawny sheen.
Your neck shines brighter than lilies or new fallen snow.
Your teeth shine whiter than ivory or Parian marble.
Lively charm breathes on your lips.
Your lips swell a little and I am warmed, set afire by them,
Though only a decent warmth heats them.
I say your tender cheeks should by rights be preferred to roses
Since red and white and all beauty clothe them.
To treat the composition of your body briefly:
It is the kind of body to fit such a face.)

If we allow for the obvious difference here — the poet's attention to
the young man's sweet voice — we again see striking parallels between
male and female beauty. And if we refer to Marbod's portraits as we
compare Baudri's two descriptions, we are reminded how easily an
ideal feature can be attributed indifferently to a boy or a woman. Like
Marbod's, Baudri's two descriptions emphasize that both the young
man's and the woman's features are modest and decent. Moreover, both
the young man and the woman have blond hair and tender cheeks (features of Marbod's boy), eyes that are compared to a double star (a feature of Marbod's girl), and bodies to match their faces (a feature of
Marbod's boy). White and rosy cheeks are shared by Baudri's girl with
Marbod's boy and girl. The ivory teeth and neck whiter than snow of
Baudri's girl recall the white, shining teeth of Marbod's girl and the
ivory neck of his boy.

Marbod and Baudri are typical in attributing so many qualities in
common to male and female beauty, for most medieval descriptions of
ideal beauty use the same details regardless of sex. Hair is almost
always golden; eyes almost always starlike; lips flaming or rosy; nose,
chin, and mouth well proportioned; and everything else (I exaggerate
only slightly) like snow, ivory, or a mix of lilies and roses. These cliches
consistently define a luminous, delicate beauty that prevails across sex
lines. It is easy to imagine the type: fine-featured blonds with bright,
clear eyes and porcelain skin quick to show color. This consistency does
more than equate male and female beauty, however; it makes male
beauty a category of female beauty. Nobody here is tall, dark, and
handsome; instead we find only fair, pretty boys. No strong, silent
types, either: descriptions prefer delicacy to strength and frequently
number a sweet voice, as we have seen in Baudri, and clever conversation among a boy's special charms.[7]

Both Marbod and Baudri emphasize the femininity in male beauty by
comparing their boys to girls. Marbod's boy "could easily enough have
been a pretty girl"; Baudri's has a voice that "could be a boy's or a
girl's." Similarly Ausonius, memorializing a beautiful boy who had died,

describes him as just past the point where he could be taken for a boy
or a girl (Ausonius, epigram 62, p. 325). And echoing another poem
attributed to Ausonius (Ausonius, uncertain work 6, p. 417), Hilary the
Englishman speculates that in the case of a beautiful English boy Nature
must have wavered when deciding whether to create a boy or a girl
(Hilary, no. 9, pp. 20-21). Nowhere, however, do we find the reverse,
poems praising an ideally beautiful girl or woman as boylike.

Constant and feminine, this ideal of beauty visited girls, women, and
boys indifferently, but not men. Though poets could call ideally beautiful females "puella," "amica," and "domina" (girl, female friend, and
lady), they call ideally beautiful males only "puer" or "juvenis" (boy or
young man), never "amicus" or "dominus" (friend or lord). In his late
twelfth-century *Ars versificatoria*, an influential poetic manual, Matthew
of Vendome says simply:

> In praising a woman one should stress heavily her physical beauty.
> This is not the proper way to praise a man. . . . Of course, some-
> times a poet, to strengthen his case, describes the splendor of a
> young man's beauty as Statius in his *Thebaid*.

> (Matthew, pp. 46-47)

Men are properly described and praised for their virtues, not for their
beauty, and both Marbod's and Baudri's poems explicitly warn that a
boy's fleeting beauty will fade as he becomes a man. This is not to
say that love poems between men did not exist (or even that men did
not find each other beautiful). Love poems between men elaborated
other poetic conventions; most frequently they infused the heat of passion into conventional expressions of friendship.[8] But they never used
idealized physical description; by convention, ideal beauty in poetry was
always boyish beauty.

The Middle Ages did not prize originality, and literary conventions
tended to perpetuate themselves. Looking for ways to describe male
beauty, medieval poets relied on models at hand. And what they found
were descriptions of women, or descriptions of boys that had been influenced by descriptions of women. We can see the bias of literary convention toward female beauty later in the century in Matthew of Vendome's *Ars versificatoria* and early in the next century in Geoffrey of
Vinsauf's even more influential *Poetria nova*, both of which provided
model descriptions only of women.[9] While an androgynous boy could
share in the beauty defined by such models, a man could not.

We can speculate further about why poets were content with such
conventions. Throughout the Middle Ages, poems railing against homosexuals accused them of making women of themselves.[10] In describing

ideal male beauty, poets may simply have been internalizing this attack, accepting and transforming it: "Yes, the boys we love are women, and see how beautiful they are." Moreover, because religion reserved its grudging approval of sex to sexual acts between a man and woman, poets may have manipulated description and made boys almost women out of a desire to bend deviation back towards the norm.

BODIES AND MANNERS: ROOM FOR DIFFERENCES

If we return to Marbod's and Baudri's poems, we see in addition to similarities significant differences in their descriptions of boys and girls. When Marbod compares the boy's and girl's features to snow and roses, his comparisons vary in degree. In what are already hyperbolic similes, the boy's coloring resembles natural models while hers exceeds them. This difference is reinforced by a second one.[11] Twice in six lines Marbod attributes to the girl's face a physical fullness absent from the boy's: her face is enhanced by a slight plumpness ("vultum modica pinguedine fultum"), and her lips are slightly swollen ("labrorum . . . subtumidorum"). As she exceeds nature in the white of her face and red of her lips, the girl here seems to expand physically. As Marbod presents it, the look of her face ("vultum") preexists the slight plumpness that enhances it, just as her lips implicitly have a proper shape, which they swell slightly beyond. This Rubenesque fullness suggests excess, fertility, and perhaps a sensuality absent from the boy's face.

Though the boy's cheeks are metaphorically full of pleasing sweetness ("genae grata dulcedine plenae"), his features exhibit no plumpness or swelling. The fact that his chin is formed after an appropriate model ("effigies menti modulo formata decenti") suggests instead that his face conforms to some Platonic ideal. Similarly, his body matches his face, and this further suggests that the boy does not exceed models but conforms to them precisely.

Differences in Baudri's portraits echo those in Marbod's. Like Marbod's girl, Baudri's Constance exceeds Nature: she has a rosier glow, a tawnier sheen; she shines brighter and whiter; her cheeks outdo roses. For Baudri, too, the ideal woman's lips swell a little. His rendering of her face is slightly overrich. By contrast, the boy fits rather than exceeds models: his voice sounds as sweetly as the nightingale's, and he will "be another Orpheus," not better than Orpheus. Like Marbod, Baudri describes the boy's face more coolly than the woman's (literally more coolly: his lips are not warm).

Though their boys' faces lack the physical swelling exhibited by the faces of their girls, neither Marbod nor Baudri fails to appreciate boys sensually; each merely reserves sensual description for the boy's body. The phrase with which Marbod describes the girl's body, "limbs with strength" ("membraque cum succo"), does not engage the visual imagination as strongly as does the invitation to wonder (literally, to seek: "quaeret") what lies under the boy's clothes. Later on in his poem about the boy, Marbod swoons with this obsessive litany: "This flesh so smooth, so milky, so unblemished, so good, so pretty, so slippery, so tender" ("haec caro tam levis, tam lactea, tam sine naevis,/ tam bona, tam bella, tam lubrica, tamque tenella"). For Marbod a girl's beauty is focused in a luscious face; the boy's face, made of the same elements more coolly invoked, is enhanced by a sexually perceived body. Like Marbod, Baudri completes his boy's description with a vividly imagined body. Baudri does more than specify a milky flesh (echoing Marbod) and ivory chest; without preparation he suddenly imagines hands playing over them. Marbod's mention of "slippery" flesh also implies touching: each poet imagines feeling the boy's body but not the girl's.

The differences here — a girl's swelling face, a boy's sexy body — are not typical of medieval descriptions generally. Medieval poets sometimes make a woman's beauty exceed nature, swelling her face or lips, or neglect her body, but sometimes they do not.[12] As for homosexual poems, it is true that some do give special attention to boys' bodies. A twelfth-century model letter from a French *ars dictaminis* (art of letter writing) shows an older man attempting to seduce a boy and writing, "If I wanted to develop this theme of boys' honor, I would certainly begin with the delightful matter of their bodies" ("Puerorum honorem si vellem prosequi, primum certe a corpore quam jocunda materia me relinquat") (Delisle, p. 200). Hilary the Englishman appreciates the body of an English boy in one of his poems: "Your dear flesh shines white as the lily" ("nitet caro cara, candens uti lilium") (Hilary, p. 20). And at least one other description of a boy fixes on his body: "His flesh shines, his thighs are delicate, his groin tender" ("candet caro, crura tenella/ sunt, inguem tenerum") (Dümmler, "Briefe," p. 360). But these examples notwithstanding, poets did not always describe the bodies of beautiful boys heatedly.

The differences in Marbod's and Baudri's descriptions are significant, therefore, not because they are generalizable to all medieval poetry but because they represent the differences between male and female beauty as perceived by a single poet. In the cases of Marbod and Baudri we can see that when each described both a boy and a girl, he transferred to the boy's body the sensuality he found in the woman's face. Each, therefore, seems to imagine boys in more overtly sexual ways. In the second half of his poem to the boy, Baudri insists that he hates the necks of bulls and oxen because they swell up, and that he hates the inflexible oak and prefers the pliant tree. These are metaphors Baudri uses to reprove the boy's haughtiness, but they are at the same time sexually suggestive. The heightened sexuality of the poems to boys suggests that the boys were more fully realized in the poet's imagination.

As if to confirm this, both Marbod and Baudri give fuller personalities to their boys than to their girls. They do so, interestingly, with a negative trait. Just as Baudri reproaches his boy for haughtiness, Marbod reproaches his boy for resisting suitors arrogantly. Ill-mannered aloofness, which neither poet finds in beautiful women, in Marbod and Baudri is characteristically associated with boyish beauty. In another poem, "Ad amicum absentem," Marbod takes on the voice of a boy writing to an absent lover (Marbod, col. 1717; translated in Boswell, p. 370). Here he does not express love-longing but instead teases his lover with threats of infidelity. In "Propter eum qui non redibat," Baudri frets because a boy he loves has broken his promise to return quickly (Baudri, no. 177, p. 169). Baudri, who has heard nothing from the boy, complains, "All youth is inconstant" ("inconstans quaeque juventus"). For Marbod and Baudri lovable boys were not loving. The accusation of haughtiness may have been a weapon of seduction, just as the pose of haughtiness may have been a boy's defense against older men. But to associate haughtiness with beauty can also enhance that beauty by making it less available or less reliable.

It is true that in some medieval Latin poems boys offer no resistance at all to seducers. One poem, for example, praises a boy like this: "His body was ready to submit to anything the sport required" ("corpusque paratum,/ omne pati quicquid iocus his cupit") (Dümmler, "Briefe," p. 360). Furthermore, we generally associate haughtiness not with boys but with the beautiful unyielding mistresses of courtly love, most familiar from twelfth-century vernacular poetry. But in this, medieval Latin poetry differs from the vernacular. Latin poetry claims less frequently that a beautiful woman's resistance to seduction makes her unfeeling and cruel; instead it usually presents its ladies without strong negative traits.

In contrast, many medieval Latin poems about boys present them as callous and supercilious. Hilary complains of the "great want of feeling" ("tanta duricia") in a boy of Angers whom he loves (Hilary, p. 18). The anonymous "Invectio in mordacem cinaedum" ("An Invective against an Irritating Catamite") accuses a young man of rejoicing at the sadness of others (Werner, no. 6, p. 5). This poem and many others, moreover, indicate clearly that boys commonly slept with men not out of any feeling for them but to earn money. The most prominent example of haughtiness, however, is the boy Ganymede as he appears in two twelfth- or thirteenth-century debate poems, "Post aquile raptus" (Boswell, pp. 392-98) and "Altercatio Ganimedis et Helene" (Lenzen; also translated in Boswell, pp. 381-89). Injured pride in one poem and a ready contempt for both women and older men in the other give these beautiful Ganymedes vivid personalities, which their more modest opponents Hebe and Helen lack.

In Marbod's and Baudri's poems haughtiness is not so important for itself as for the opportunity it gives the poets to dwell on the characters and conduct of their subjects. Marbod reports:

Asper et ingratus, tanquam de tigride natus,
ridebat tantum mollissima verba precantum,
ridebat curas effectum non habituras,
et suspirantis lacrymas ridebat amantis.

(Rough and ungrateful, like a tiger cub,
He only laughed at the gentlest words of a suitor,
Laughed at attentions doomed to have no effect,
And laughed at a sighing lover's tears.)

Similarly, when Baudri considers his young man's disdain for others, he
can describe specific details of conduct:

Vix aliquando aliquem summo tenus ore salutes,
dum tamen et salve tibi primus dixerit ipse.

(Sometimes you greet a man with barely the corners of your mouth,
Even when he has said hello to you first.)

By contrast, Marbod's and Baudri's females remain shadowy figures.
General hyperbolic praise without details of conduct keep them at a
distance. Though Marbod and Baudri appreciate both boys and girls,
their poems bring the personalities of boys to life more successfully.

LOVE POEMS: SEARCHING FOR A VEHICLE

About Hilary the Englishman we know little other than that he was a
student of Abelard's in the twelfth century at an abbey called the Para-
clete, Abelard's hermitage east of Paris. Of Hilary's fourteen surviving
poems, five are amorous: four addressed to boys and one to a woman.
Two of these love poems, "Ad Guillelmum de Anfonia" ("To William
of Anfonia") and "Ad Rosea" ("To Rosea"), resemble each other remarkably in vocabulary and structure. The first four lines from each
poem suggest the similarities:

Ave splendor telluris Anglice,
decus summum et decor unice,
de te fama testatur publice,
largitatis quam sis inmodice!

(Hilary, no. 10, pp. 21-23)

(Hail splendor of England,
Highest honor, unique beauty!
Rumor testifies publicly
How extravagantly generous you are!)

Ave sidus occidentis, sidus lucis unice,
summum decus tue gentis et telluris Anglice.

Fama multis argumentis protestatur publice
quis sit status tue mentis, quam largus inmodice.

(Hilary, no. 5, pp. 13-14)

(Hail star of the west, star of unique light,
Highest honor of your family and of England:
With many proofs Rumor testifies publicly
What the condition of your mind is, how extravagantly
    generous it is!)

The first passage is addressed to the boy, the second to the woman, but it scarcely matters which opening refers to whom. Both poems flatter their addressees in the same way. William and Rosea are almost identically beautiful, strong of mind, handsome of face, and modest. Moreover, in order to praise their subjects, the two poems use the same conceits in parallel positions. The first stanza of each introduces Rumor, a personification borrowed from Virgil, to praise the loved one. The third stanza of each poem asserts that Nature paid special attention to the creation of the beloved. Then the fifth stanza of each reintroduces Rumor to say that notwithstanding its usual tendency to inflate, Rumor cannot measure up to the truth about so wonderful a person. The similarities in the poems suggest that Hilary was like an itinerant painter ready to put anyone's face on a body he had painted in his studio.

But not quite, for there are significant differences between the poems. "To Rosea" ends with a petition that the lady command Hilary to her service, followed by an assertion of confidence now that Hilary is in her protection:

Jam securus ego vivam, ad cuncta tentamina
tutus ero, cum te divam habeam pro domina.
Sume mea, virgo decens, benigne precamina,
ut te laudet forma recens mea semper pagina.

(Now I will live secure; I will be safe
From all temptation, since I have you, goddess, for my lady.
O good virgin, receive my entreaties with indulgence
That my fresh-made page may always praise you.)

Flattery has led to confident petition and graceful compliment.

Though similarly flattering, "To William" ends in despair. The conclusion of the poem surprisingly loses sight of William and focuses instead on the speaker: he burns miserably with a malignant flame and — apparently despairing of the boy — blames fortune for his current unhappiness:

Dum spem talem haberem credulus,
dum instarem amori sedulus,
ecce venit malorum cumulus,
casus gravis et letis emulus.
Me fortune rota superior
diu tulit, sed nunc experior
quia status quanto suavior,
tanto casus est factus gravior.

(While I confidently held such hope [that fortune could not wound
    me]
And diligently pursued love,
See, a heap of troubles fell on me,
Heavy misfortunes, envious of my happiness.
The wheel of fortune lifted me higher
For a long time, but now I know from experience
The sweeter a state,
The harder the fall from it.)

This unexpected conclusion does not grow out of the poem as the conclusion of "To Rosea" does, and its abruptness seems typical of "To William" as a whole. In "To Rosea" Hilary clearly uses Rumor as a means of praising the lady. In "To William" the idea takes on a distracting life of its own: the poem pauses for eight of its fifty-six lines to ask whether Rumor is a good thing or a bad.

All through "To Rosea" each idea seems to emerge from the preceding one; "To William" seems continually to get sidetracked. Hilary's use of Nature in the two poems is a further example. In "To Rosea" Hilary first lists the lady's good qualities and then asserts that Nature paid special attention to her creation. As a result, Nature's care seems to explain Rosea's good qualities. He next focuses on her birth, a new idea but one that seems to follow logically from her creation by Nature. By contrast, "To William" introduces Nature abruptly after the question of Rumor's worth. Hilary then follows Nature's special creation of William with a new topic that has no particular connection to it: Jupiter would forsake Ganymede for such a boy. "To William" as a whole contains a greater number of poetic ideas that follow one another with neither preparation nor connection; and its conclusion, far from embracing what has gone before, introduces yet another new topic, fortune.

These differences between "To Rosea" and "To William" appear typical of Hilary. Besides "To Rosea," Hilary wrote three other poems to women, poems of courtesy and friendship, and though all of them use a variety of conceits and metaphors to sing their ladies' praises, they nonetheless all move steadily toward a closing petition or compliment (Hilary, nos. 2-4, pp. 8-13). The poems to boys, on the other hand, are all filled with sudden shifts, ideas picked up and dropped. Hilary's poem "Ad puerum Andegavensem" ("To a Boy of Angers"), for example, reads for most of its length like a search for a metaphor: Hilary is speechless in the boy's presence, he is a suitor, he is sick, he is a prisoner (Hilary, no. 7, pp. 16-18; translated in Boswell, pp. 372-73). Then, suddenly, the conclusion rings in like a teacher's threat: the boy should heed the lessons of Hippolytus and Joseph whose unswerving chastity imperiled them. Is this ironic? witty? Far from giving the reader a sense that the poem's metaphors are now tied together, this conclusion goes off on a new tangent and leaves the poem open-ended.

Hilary's two poems each entitled "Ad puerum Anglicum" ("To an English Boy") in comparison with the poems to women are similarly disjointed (Hilary, no. 9, pp. 20-21; no. 13, pp. 40-41; both translated in Boswell, pp. 373-74). In the first of them Hilary becomes openly impatient with what seems to be an inadequate convention:

> Crinis flavus, os decorum cervisque candidula,
> sermo blandus et suavis; sed quid laudem singula?
> Totus pulcher et decorus, nec est in te macula;
> sed vaccare castitati talis nequid formula.

> (Golden hair, beautiful face, and white neck,
> Winning and sweet conversation — but why praise these things
>   one by one?
> You are completely handsome; there is no flaw in you —
> Except this worthless decision to devote yourself to chastity.)

Look at the rhythm of ideas in this stanza. First, Hilary abandons description impatiently. Then, as soon as he gets to his generalization that the boy is handsome, Hilary flies off to reproach him for chastity. By the next line of the poem, the beginning of a new stanza, Hilary will have dropped the topic of chastity.

Since this restlessness can suggest Hilary's lack of control over his material or the heat of passionate composition, critics in the past have discussed the quality or sincerity of his poems to boys (Allen, Part II, p. 23; Fuller, pp. 15-16; Raby, II, 117-118; Dronke, I, 218-20). To shift the ground of this discussion, I would suggest that Hilary in these poems is casting about unsteadily for a way to write a love poem to a boy. Though the medieval tradition of homosexual verse included appreciations of boys and complaints about them (which Marbod and Baudri successfully combine in their poems to boys), it did not offer many models of love poems addressed directly to them and did not have at its disposal the rich models and conventions of heterosexual love poetry.

Twelfth-century love poetry addressed to women, especially vernacular poetry, conventionally drew for both vocabulary and poses on two major sources, feudalism and religion. As knights swore fealty to their lord and expected protection in return, so the courtly lover expressed his subservience to his lady. Indeed, in troubadour verse he often called her "midons," my lord, rather than my lady. The poet looked to his lady for protection and favor. Love poetry could also imitate the language of religious worship, including the language of the Song of Songs, which was often used in poems to Mary. Relying on these sources and on traditional poems of courtesy addressed to women, Hilary addresses three of the women of his poems as "domina," my lady; in the conclusion of "To Rosea" he moves beyond the language of love service to the language of love worship, calling Rosea "divam," goddess.[13] With its references to temptations ("tentamina"), prayers ("precamina"), and a good virgin ("virgo decens," a title eminently applicable to Mary), this concluding stanza could easily be taken for the end of a religious poem.

When faced with writing a love poem to a boy, Hilary had no comparable conventions to fall back on. At one point in "To William" he makes a feeble stab at incorporating the language of subservience — "I thirst to know whether you have need of my service" ("sentire sicio/ si sit opus meo servitio") — but he does not develop this idea, nor does he use it in any of his other poems to boys. It would have been ludicrous for an older man — especially if that man was a boy's superior within a religious community — to call a boy "lord" or "master," or to claim to worship him. Moreover, devotional language in a homosexual poem could backfire, for it could too easily remind the reader or the boy of religion's official disapproval.

Without the guidance of a viable tradition, Hilary in his poems to boys restlessly shifts from metaphor to metaphor and from pose to pose. This shifting suggests that Hilary finds no single metaphor or pose adequate to represent the emotion or relation he intends. He proliferates poetic ideas in order to compensate for a missing center.

TWO TRADITIONS

The homosexual verse that survives from the Middle Ages constitutes a much narrower tradition than medieval heterosexual verse. Though homosexual verse comes in many genres — from dream vision to invective, from debate to elegy — many others are not represented. For example, there are no homosexual pastourelles; when knights or scholars venture out they never run into seductive or seducible shepherd boys, only shepherdesses. Similarly, there are no homosexual aubades; never do we see two men listening to the lark at dawn and taking reluctant leave of each other. More surprisingly, no homosexual poems open with that most familiar of medieval openings, the description of spring.[14] Nor do any homosexual poems survive that seem to be popular in origin or destination: we find no dance songs, no simple lyric effusions. And as we have seen above, no homosexual poems follow the patterns of courtly love or echo the language of religious devotion. These were reserved for heterosexual poetry or for poems addressed to women: the two lesbian love poems that survive from the Middle Ages use language recalling the Song of Songs (Dronke, II, 478-81).

What we find instead is a narrow, learned tradition of poems written in Latin. No twelfth-century vernacular verse I know of expresses the love-longing of a man for a boy or another man.[15] This suggests a specific source for medieval homosexual poetry, namely, religious communities. Most poets who wrote in medieval Latin, as opposed to those who wrote in the vernacular, had been educated and continued to live in communities of men and boys organized around a cathedral or abbey. We know for certain that Marbod and Baudri lived their lives in such communities; this may help to explain the differences between their descriptions of beautiful boys and girls.

For men in such communities, women always remained other. Though these men would have some contact with women, still women lived their lives outside the bounds of the community, and women's bodies remained hidden under clothes. Not surprisingly, then, Marbod and Baudri ignore women's bodies and focus beauty in female faces. These faces become bigger and better than life, swelling physically and exceeding ideals in nature. For Marbod and Baudri this superreality may have expressed women's otherness. And perhaps for the same reason, women not just in Marbod and Baudri but in medieval poetry generally tend to have paler personalities than their vernacular counterparts. Early vernacular poetry originates not from religious communities but from secular courts.

Boys, on the other hand, were always around. Living in the same community, they shared the medieval Latin poet's world. Their bodies could be seen, their personalities observed closely. The importance of boys' bodies and the livelier description of their personalities in Marbod and Baudri may simply reflect close day-to-day contact.

Attending the cathedral or monastery schools, boys also shared a medieval Latin poet's education, and medieval homosexual poetry reflects this shared learning. Hilary's poems are a prime example, for many of the ideas that fill his poems to boys are simply school stuff. About the time that Hilary was his student, Abelard wrote *Sic et Non*, which places contradictory statements by church fathers next to each other and leaves them unresolved. Hilary's discussion of Rumor in "To William" refers slyly to Abelard:

"Fama malum" dixit Virgilius;
bene, dixit nihil unquam melius.
"Fama bonum" dixit Hilarius;
verum, dixit nil unquam verius.

("Rumor is a bad thing," said Virgil;
He spoke well, never spoke better.
"Rumor is a good thing," said Hilary;
He spoke true, never spoke truer.)

In pitting his authority tongue-in-cheek against Virgil's, Hilary appeals
to learning he would share with a boy.

More significantly, in each of his poems to boys Hilary refers to
classical literature and mythology. Though his poems to women refer to
biblical figures (Eve and Lot's wife), the verses remain innocent of
classical mythology. In addressing boys, however, Hilary decorates his
poems with Virgil, Dido, Hippolytus, and most importantly Ganymede,
a figure who occurs in three of Hilary's four poems to boys. In classical
mythology Ganymede, a Trojan boy, so inspired Jupiter with his beauty
that Jupiter took on the form of an eagle and snatched him up to the
heavens. There Ganymede became Jupiter's cupbearer and paramour,
and took up permanent residence as Aquarius, one of the signs of the
zodiac. Throughout the Middle Ages homosexual verse kept returning to
this and to other classical myths of homosexual love. Orpheus — to
whom Baudri compares his proud young man above — is another example. After he lost his wife, Eurydice, a second time to the underworld,
Orpheus turned from women to the delights of tender boys. For this
he was eventually ripped to pieces by angry and frenzied Ciconian
women.[16]

Some heterosexual poems also display learning: Baudri's poem to
Constance, for example, dwells on Jupiter's dalliances with mortal
women. But learned poetry constitutes only a fraction of heterosexual
love poems, while it accounts for almost all of medieval homosexual
poetry. (For another example, Marbod's description of the beautiful boy
begins with a learned reference to Horace: *Odes*, IV, 10.)

The recurrent reference to classical literature in medieval homosexual
poetry represents more than just an appeal to a shared education; it
may also be interpreted as an attempt to place homosexual love in a
respectable context. The twelfth century studied classical literature with
greater interest and less mistrust than earlier centuries had, and through
that literature came to respect classical Roman culture. Engaged like
other poets in this great revival of classical learning, poets writing
homosexual verse learned to employ this respect in a particular way.
Some poets invoked classical mythology explicitly, if ironically, to jus-

tify homosexuality (Boswell, pp. 392-98; Delisle, pp. 199-200; Hildebert, no. 48, p. 38). Most poets, however, used the myths incidentally: as part of a simile, for example, or as a means of paying a compliment. But its regular recurrence clearly implies that this incidental use had importance. Homosexuality in classical literature, especially in the most famous example of the Ganymede myth, could validate a love given no official sanction by the medieval world. In the midst of his unsteady search for ways to compose love poems for boys, Hilary consistently felt the need to mention the myths and literature of a more sympathetic culture.

NOTES

[1]The standard account of the twelfth-century renaissance is Haskins; as he points out, "twelfth-century renaissance" is a convenient designation for a movement that took place roughly from 1050 to 1250. For her generous help with this article I would like to thank Marsha Siegel. I would also like to thank the National Endowment for the Humanities for a year of fellowship support, during part of which I wrote this article.

[2]Carolingian poets: Alcuin, Walafrid Strabo, Rabanus Maurus. North African poets: the anonymous poets of the *Anthologia Latina* and Luxorius. Ausonius' homosexual poetry includes: epistle 27, pp. 281-82; epigrams 59, p. 334, and 62, p. 335; and uncertain work 6, p. 417.

[3]The translations of this and all texts quoted in this article are my own. Other examples of casual indifference to the loved one's sex include the anonymous "Tela, Cupido, tene" (Dronke, II, 465) and "Dissuasio intempestavi amoris" (Werner, no. 201, pp. 89-90).

[4]Line four of this text does not occur in the *Patrologia*; I have supplied it from Werner, no. 8, p. 5.

[5]Marbod is more difficult to assess in this way, in part because there is no good edition of his work. More poems concerned with heterosexual love are currently attributed to him.

[6]In the last line I have emended *corpora* to *corpore*.

[7]In a seventh-century description of a boy, Aldhelm praises Aethilwald not for strength but for nimbleness (Dümmler, *Epistolae*, III, 246-47). Hilary the Englishman and the anonymous poet of "Etas consimilis" both single out for praise a boy's winning conversation (Hilary, no. 9, p. 20; Werner, no. 24, p. 19).

[8]A few examples of love poems between men suggest their variety: Alcuin, "Pectus amor nostram" (Dümmler, *Poetae*, I, no. 11, p. 236); Walafrid Strabo, "Ad Liutgerum clericum," "Item ad ipsum," and "Ad amicum" (Dümmler, *Poetae*, II, nos. 31-32, p. 385; no. 59, p. 403); Baudri, "Ad amicum post reditum" and "Ad amicum cui cartam mittebat" (Baudri, no. 165, pp. 160-61; and no. 170, p. 163); Serlo, "Qualia Serloni Serlonis" (Serlo, no. 8, p. 90); and anonymous, "Quocumque more motu" (Hilka and Schumann, no. 65, pp. 27-28).

[9]Geoffrey did write a description of an ideally beautiful boy but did not include it in his *Poetria nova*; the portrait is typically feminine (Faral, pp. 38-40).

[10]For example: Ennodius, epigrams 52 and 55, col. 344; Luxorius, no. 295 (Buecheler and Riese, vol. I, fasc. 1, p. 251); and Walter of Chatillon, no. 4, stanza 27, p. 70.

[11]We can leave aside as idiosyncratic the difference between their eyes. Starlike eyes like hers are common, while his black eyes are unusual and may lend his portrait an exotic beauty. But starlike eyes are not reserved to females; Baudri's beautiful young man has eyes like a double star.

[12]Geoffrey of Vinsauf and Matthew of Vendome both include women's bodies in their model descriptions of female beauty (Matthew, pp. 43-44; Geoffrey, pp. 36-37). Matthew also makes Helen of Troy's neck and shoulders whiter than snow, as Fortunatus, the major European poet of the sixth century, made women in descriptions outdo roses, violets, flames, snow, etc. (Dronke, I, 193-94). Matthew makes Helen's rounded abdomen swell out from a narrow chest and waist, and Geoffrey gives his other beautiful women rounded and full (though not swollen) lips. For other examples of descriptions that mention women's bodies, see Dronke, II, 374-76, 383-84, and 449-52.

¹³Hilary addresses the women in nos. 4 and 5 as "domina" (Hilary, pp. 11-14). In another poem, he describes the chaste relationship between Eve and Hervius, who also refers to Eve as "domina" (Hilary, no. 1, l. 101, p. 5). Dronke discusses the tradition of poems of courtesy in "Love, Praise and Friendship" (Dronke, I, 192-220). In the sixth century Fortunatus was already referring courteously to a female correspondent as "domina."

¹⁴The "Altercatio Ganymedis et Helene" (Lenzen, translated in Boswell, pp. 381-89) begins with a spring landscape, but it is a debate, not a love poem. The strong presence of nature in the poem serves in part as a setup for the poem's eventual condemnation of homosexuality. Spring openings are common throughout the *Carmina Burana*; one of its three poems touching on homosexuality begins with a mythological invocation of the year's seasons (Hilka and Schumann, no. 65, pp. 27-28; the other two poems are nos. 95, p. 123, and no. 127, p. 211).

¹⁵The only references to homosexuality I know of in twelfth-century vernacular poetry occur in Marie de France's *Lanval* (Marie de France, pp. 105-123) and Conon de Bethune's "L'autrier avint en chel autre pais" (Goldin, pp. 344-47). In both a lady uses an accusation of homosexuality to insult a knight. (Compare these to Hilka and Schumann, no. 127, p. 211, which implies the same dramatic situation and includes a vernacular refrain.)

¹⁶Ovid includes the stories of both Ganymede and Orpheus in *Metamorphoses*, Books X and XI. It is Orpheus himself who tells Ganymede's story there (X, 155-61) as well as two other homosexual myths often referred to in medieval verse, the stories of Hyacinth and Apollo (X, 162-219) and of the beautiful youth Cyparissus (X, 106-42).

BIBLIOGRAPHY

Allen, Philip Schuyler. "Medieval Latin Lyrics." 2 parts. *Modern Philology*, 5 (1908), 423-76; and 6 (1908), 3-43.

Ausonius. *Decimi Magni Ausonii Burdigalensis opuscula*. Ed. Rudolf Peiper. Leipzig: 1886.

Baudri of Bourgueil. *Les Oeuvres poétiques de Baudri de Bourgueil (1046-1130): Edition critique publiée d'apres le manuscrit du Vatican*. Ed. Phyliss Abrahams. Paris: Honoré Champion, 1926.

Boswell, John. *Christianity, Social Tolerance, and Homosexuality: Gay People in Western Europe from the Beginning of the Christian Era to the Fourteenth Century*. Chicago: Univ. of Chicago Press, 1980.

Buecheler, Franz, and Alexander Riese, eds. *Anthologia Latina*. 2 vols. Leipzig: Teubner, 1894-1921.

Delisle, Léopold. "Notice sur une 'Summa dictaminis' jadis conservée à Beauvais." *Notices et extraits des manuscrits de la Bibliothèque nationale et autres bibliothèques*, etc., 36 (1899), 200.

Dronke, Peter. *Medieval Latin and the Rise of European Love-Lyric*. 2 vols. Oxford: Clarendon, 1965-66.

Dümmler, Ernst, ed. *Epistolae*. 4 vols. Monumenta Germaniae Historiae. Berlin: Weidmann, 1892-1902.

——. *Poetae Latini aevi Carolini*. Vols. I and II. Monumenta Germaniae Historiae. Berlin: 1881-84.

——. "Briefe und Verse des neunten Jahrhunderts." *Neues Archiv der Gesellschaft für ältere deutsche Geschichtskunde*, 13 (1888), 358-60.

Ennodius. *Patrologiae cursus completus: Series Latina*. Ed. J.-P. Migne. 221 vols. Paris: 1844-64. Vol. LXIII.

Faral, Edmond. "Le Manuscrit 511 du 'Hunterian Museum' de Glasgow: Notes sur le mouvement poétique et l'histoire des études littéraire en France et en Angleterre entre les années 1150-1225." *Studi Medievali*, 15 (1936), 18-121.

Fuller, John Bernard, ed. *Hilarii versus et ludi*. New York: Holt, 1929.

Geoffrey of Vinsauf. *Poetria nova*. Trans. Margaret F. Nims. Toronto: Pontifical Institute of Medieval Studies, 1967.

Goldin, Frederick, trans. *Lyrics of the Troubadors and Trouveres: An Anthology and a History*. New York: Anchor-Doubleday, 1973.

Haskins, Charles Homer. *The Renaissance of the Twelfth Century*. Cambridge, Mass.: Harvard Univ. Press, 1928.

Hilary the Englishman. *Hilarii versus et ludi*. Ed. J.-J. Champollion-Figeac. Paris: 1838.

Hildebert of Lavardin. *Hildeberti Cenomannensis episcopi, carmina minora*. Ed. A. Brian Scott. Leipzig: Teubner, 1969.

Hilka, Alfons, and Otto Schumann, eds. *Carmina Burana*. Vol. I, fasc. 2, *Die Liebeslieder*. Heidelberg: Winter, 1941.

Lenzen, Rolf. "'Altercatio Ganimedis et Helene': Kritische Edition mit Kommentar." *Mittellateinisches Jahrbuch*, 7 (1972), 161-86.

Marbod of Rennes. *Patrologiae cursus completus: Series Latina*. Ed. J.-P. Migne. 221 vols. Paris: 1844-64. Vol. CLXXI.

Marie de France. *The Lais of Marie de France*. Trans. Robert Hanning and Joan Ferrante. New York: Dutton, 1978.

Matthew of Vendome. *The Art of Versification*. Trans. Aubrey E. Galyon. Ames: Iowa State Univ. Press, 1980.

Raby, F. J. E. *A History of Secular Latin Poetry in the Middle Ages*. 2 vols. Oxford: Clarendon, 1934.

Serlo of Wilton. *Serlon de Wilton: Poèmes latins*. Ed. Jan Oberg. Stockholm: Almquist and Wiksell, 1965.

Walter of Châtillon. *Moralisch-satirische Gedichte Walters von Châtillon*. Ed. Karl Strecker. Heidelberg: Winter, 1929.

Werner, Jakob. *Beitrage zur Kunde der lateinischen Literatur des Mittelalters: Handschrift C.58/ 275 der Stadtbibliothek Zurich (Z)*. Aarau: Sauerlander, 1905.

Index